BEFORE THE
PYRAMIDS

Christopher Knight is a businessman and marketing consultant who began his writing career after 20 years of research into the origins of Freemasonic rituals. His first book, *The Hiram Key* (co-authored with Robert Lomas and published in 1996) became an instant bestseller. It has since been translated into over 40 languages, selling more than a million copies worldwide. He is co-author, with Alan Butler, of the best-selling *Civilization One*, *Who Built the Moon?* and *The Hiram Key Revisited*.

Alan Butler is a professional writer who has always possessed an absolute fascination for history. Originally an engineer, he set out on a two-decade search that led to the unravelling of some of the most important details regarding prehistoric knowledge and achievement in Europe. Alan has been writing on the subject of astrology since his early twenties and can probably claim to be the most published writer on the subject in Britain. His historical studies extend to in-depth research into the Cistercian monastic movement and the order of the Knights Templar, about which he has also written extensively. In addition to his interests in astrology and history, Alan Butler is also a time-served dramatist who has written many plays. He scored a significant success with *Aiden Dooley's Homecoming*, written in 2003 for BBC radio.

By the same authors

Previous books by Christopher Knight

(co-authored with Robert Lomas)
The Hiram Key
The Second Messiah
Uriel's Machine
The Book of Hiram

Previous books by Alan Butler

The Bronze Age Computer Disc
The Warriors and the Bankers
The Templar Continuum
The Goddess, the Grail and the Lodge

By Christopher Knight and Alan Butler

Civilization One
Who Built the Moon?
Solomon's Power Brokers
(published in paperback as *The Hiram Key Revisited*)

BEFORE THE PYRAMIDS

CRACKING ARCHAEOLOGY'S GREATEST MYSTERY

CHRISTOPHER KNIGHT
AND ALAN BUTLER

WATKINS PUBLISHING

LONDON

First published in hardback in the UK and USA 2009 by
Watkins Publishing, Sixth Floor, Castle House,
75–76 Wells Street, London W1T 3QH

This edition published 2011

3 5 7 9 10 8 6 4

Designed and typeset by Paul Saunders

Printed in India by Imago

British Library Cataloguing-in-Publication Data Available

Library of Congress Cataloging-in-Publication Data Available

ISBN: 978-1-907486-66-1

www.watkinspublishing.co.uk

Distributed in the USA and Canada by Sterling Publishing Co., Inc.
387 Park Avenue South, New York, NY 10016-8810

For information about custom editions, special sales, premium and
corporate purchases, please contact Sterling Special Sales
Department at 800-805-5489 or specialsales@sterlingpub.com

CONTENTS

Appendices

ACKNOWLEDGEMENTS

First and foremost, of course, we wish to acknowledge the patience, tolerance and invaluable assistance of our wives Caroline and Kate.

We have many friends who have helped us across the years, academics, mathematicians, engineers, astronomers, biblical scholars and even some archaeologists. We thank you all but we would like to record our special thanks to the following people:

The late Professor Alexander Thom, without whose lifetime's work and rigorous surveying none of our own research or investigations would have been possible;

Edmund Sixsmith, a London-based civil engineer and long-time champion of Alexander Thom who has picked up the gauntlet for our cause to push for a proper academic debate on our reconstruction of a super-science from prehistory, which he has designated the 'Knight & Butler Symmetries';

James Russell, a civil engineer from Northern Ireland who has conducted a range of highly impressive experiments to demonstrate how Neolithic astronomers would have measured the dimensions of the Earth with great accuracy;

Professor Philip Davies, a biblical scholar who has provided expert opinion over the years and has helped in every way he can, including introducing us to other experts;

Dr Jack Miller, a Cambridge University geologist who first alerted us to the reality of Noah's Flood and to the fact that Rosslyn could never have been part of an intended collegiate church;

Professor Archie Roy, the astronomer who was first to confirm that our suggested pendulum method of timing stars explains the Megalithic Yard;

Robert Bauval, freethinking gentleman Egyptologist who first identified the correlation of Orion's Belt with the Giza pyramids and has been very supportive of our investigations;

Dr Thomas Brophy, an astrophysicist for sharing his discoveries of super-ancient astronomical observatories in the Sahara;

Michael Mann, our publisher for his ongoing support and continued wise guidance;

Penny Stopa, our ever patient publishing manager who managed to deal with a very late manuscript when new discoveries impinged on deadlines. Our thanks also go to Shelagh Boyd, out tireless editor, and Paul Saunders who 'set' above and beyond the call of duty.

LIST OF FIGURES

LIST OF COLOUR PLATES

INTRODUCTION

This is an unusual book. It has caught us, its co-authors, completely by surprise.

Our intention was to catalogue an account of our researches into measurement systems used in Neolithic Britain, but what we ended up with is a story of the transmission of hugely ancient knowledge and priceless artefacts, spanning several millennia and culminating with 20th-century power-play at the highest level. We began with an important archaeological breakthrough but ended with what our publishers believe is a full-blooded rival for any Dan Brown novel. However, the difference between our work and a novel is that everything contained in these pages is true – fully testable and checkable. And anyone with internet access will be able to put us to the test very quickly indeed.

For the last ten years we have been doing our best to reconstruct a stunningly accurate and elegant system of astronomy-based measurements used in Stone Age Britain. This research suddenly exploded when we found a direct connection between the astronomer-priests of Stone Age Britain and the pyramid builders of ancient Egypt from the third millennium BC. Then, due to a chance connection we came to lift the lid on a careful and secret plan to create a 'New Jerusalem' in the New World – using knowledge that may well have originated an incredible 18,000 years earlier. That new city was Washington DC.

We have pinpointed a small, deliberately carved stone in the centre of Washington DC that is a most important key – a marker in the ground that Thomas Jefferson declared to be point zero on the face of the globe and which Franklin D Roosevelt much later used as the datum point for the location of the Pentagon. We believe that there is a chamber beneath this stone that holds a great secret known only to an elite group that is always made up of exactly 33 men.

The findings in this book have ended up as nothing less than sensational. The evidence we put forward is easy to follow and to check out by anyone – without specialist knowledge. This is bad news for us in one respect, because the archaeological establishment may use the 'sensational' revelations in this book as an excuse to ignore our key findings and to declare them non-academic. If this is the case it is a shame, but we hope that the high-profile nature of the 'conspiracy' we have uncovered will force through a very public debate on the origins of civilization that is long overdue. We are fully aware that this book will be attacked – most likely by people who have not read it. The individual who does not like change will skim the pages and pull out unusual findings and scoff. We will ignore unsubstantiated comments but we will welcome constructive criticism and vigorous debate – as long as it is based on facts and not preconceived ideas or prejudice.

Because of the nature of our Washington findings we will be accused of being 'conspiracy theorists'. It has become fashionable in some quarters to believe that this label automatically invalidates all evidence. This is not the case. There are two kinds of people who deny that conspiracies exist – conspirators and the naive!

There is nothing remotely odd about conspiracy. It is merely two or more people acting together in an undeclared way to bring benefit to themselves – and perhaps others. There are criminal conspiracies, unsavoury conspiracies, benign conspiracies and, we believe, benevolent conspiracies. The key component is simply secrecy. Did Bernard Madoff act alone in his Ponzi scheme that lifted billions of dollars from the wallets of the wealthy? If he was not acting alone, then it was obviously a conspiracy of embezzlement. We feel sure Madoff would have been a keen denier of conspiracies.

Whilst no one can know for sure, is it not probable that most conspiracies go undiscovered? After all, that is the entire point.

We hope you enjoy this book and that you find the revelations it contains to be helpful and significant. Please spread the word so that there is as much public opinion as possible pushing for a broad-based, academic evaluation of our findings. If you would like to keep up with developments please visit our website at: www.knight-butler.com.

Chapter 1

•

THE GIZA ENIGMA

Into the Desert

We were in Egypt on a hunch.

One of us had visited the country dozens of times; the other had never been here before. We were both interested in the pyramids but they had never loomed large in our personal researches – until now.

Now there was a chance, a small chance, that the precious location we were sure had once existed might just have survived the ravages of sand-storm, baking sun and human abuse across the millennia. We had studied maps and photographs back in England but quickly realized that we needed to be on the spot as soon as possible. The problem was that, from the aerial shots we had studied, it looked as though ground clearance of some kind had started – all around our chosen target zone. After 4,500 years – and now we had to rush? It seemed crazy but two weeks later we were closing in.

Ahmed looked entirely relaxed as he skilfully slotted his taxi through yet another impossibly small gap – this time between a battered, rust-coloured truck on our left and a boy on a straw-laden donkey, who was happily traversing the roundabout the wrong way. It was Friday and nearly midnight yet the entire city was buzzing in a chaotic manner that made a rush hour in New York or London look positively sane. Every now and again we would come across an intersection with flat tarmac and some road markings, but they were of little interest to the thronging hordes of drivers who would instinctively form four haphazard columns where only two lanes were marked out beneath the sea of wheels.

Cairo is a crazy and exciting city. Its smells, sounds and vistas linger in the memory of visitors but, for natives, life is hard. Some 18 million souls occupy Africa's largest city where there is huge competition for work – and little or no aid available from the state. It is often said that the average Egyptian had a higher standard of living at the time of the Pharaohs than he or she does today; a fact probably not unconnected with the unimaginable population explosion that has occurred over recent times. Every mile or two, roadside hoardings announce the city's current birth rate. 'A baby is born every 24 seconds' reads the sign, and Ahmed informed us that it was 26 seconds last year and 30 seconds not long before that.

'The problem is Viagra,' Ahmed announced, as he looked for our re-action in the rear-view mirror. 'It's Cairo's favourite drug. Men can do "it" more now and that means more babies. The government are not happy – but we are!' He laughed as he pressed his palm onto the horn to let the donkey and cart in front know he was coming through. 'And I'm doubly happy because I have two wives – one here in Cairo and one back home in Luxor!'

We finally arrived at our hotel and after parting with a hefty tip (one, we were told, that would help support each wife), we headed for our rooms after arranging a time to be picked up in the morning to begin our search for a possible unknown archaeological site some 7 km out into the desert.

As we rose the next morning the view from the balcony was particu-larly spectacular. Across the still solidly packed road was the huge pyramid attributed to the ancient king, Khafre, standing proudly against Egypt's brilliant blue sky. And the tip of Menkaure's pyramid could just be seen behind it.

Ahmed was waiting in reception for his new English friends and as soon as we had shaken hands he began to outline his plan for giving us a first-class tour of the pyramids and the sphinx. His almost permanently smiling Nubian face fell for a moment and his brow furrowed quizzically as we explained that we would rather have a trip to an anonymous patch of desert.

We showed Ahmed the map of our intended destination and with a shrug of his shoulders he led us to his car. The Toyota weaved through a network of backstreets at an alarming pace, and then, suddenly, the suburbs of Cairo ended as abruptly as the sea hits the shore. In the blink of an eye the mile after mile of tumbling brick and concrete boxes, teaming chaotically with human and animal life, were suddenly behind us. Gone were the jams of horses, beaten-up trucks, suicidal pedestrians and 'demolition derby'-grade taxis. Suddenly everywhere was sand.

The reality of the underlying landscape, where only the hardiest of tiny grizzled bushes hold out, was intimidating. How, we wondered, did the world's most famous early culture come to settle and flourish so spectacularly in this barren land? Nile or no Nile, this place is totally unforgiving.

Ahmed kept his ageing but relatively roadworthy Toyota pointing south. His eyes seemed to be fixed to the rear-view mirror as he chatted away – espousing the virtues of various 'establishments' he could recommend – whilst reassuring us that he never, ever took a cut for himself. We are not normally nervous passengers but it can only have been a highly developed sixth sense that kept the vehicle on the rough tarmac strip that he well knew would eventually lead to his hometown of Luxor.

We put our faith in the fact that the man had survived some 40 years – so we relaxed a little and peered out of the windows, searching for some kind of landmark that could correspond to the dots on our printouts of aerial views of this unremittingly khaki landscape. We knew from our researches back in England that close to the point where the roads to Luxor and Alexandria diverge there might be 'something' of great interest to us. We passed a lonely mosque we could recognize and, some 100 m or so to the west of the main road, we knew we were close.

We asked Ahmed to pull off the highway at several points until we could be as certain as possible that we had arrived at the place we intended. It was a desolate spot with flat stretches of sand and a few low walls near to the road. We found evidence of recent underground concrete structures and, together with the periodic piles of rubble, it soon became all too clear that this part of our mission was not going to be immediately fruitful. Ahmed explained that this area was scheduled to be a huge new development in the expanding '6th October City' – named after the day in 1981 when President Anwar Sadat was assassinated while viewing a military parade. Even if there had been some fourth-dynasty remains on the site it is quite likely the pragmatic developers would have bulldozed them away – Egypt has quite enough ancient monuments to keep the tourists coming.

Despite our failure to find any indication of ancient workings, we were still excited at the very new approach to unravelling the secrets of the pyramids that we had almost accidentally discovered. As we stood on a mound of sand under the hot morning sun we turned towards the northern horizon to admire the most famous historical objects in the world – the three massive pyramids of the Giza Plateau. Those distant pinnacles were, we still felt, connected to the spot beneath our feet.

A Ploughed Circle

We had always known that finding anything ancient at this location in Egypt's desert was a very long shot indeed, just as the corresponding location, nearly 4,000 km away, that had brought us here, was itself no longer discernible at ground level.

It had been just 16 weeks since we stood in a freshly ploughed field on the huge Newby Hall estate in North Yorkshire, England with our civil engineer friend, Edmund Sixsmith and the estate manager Peter Greenwood. We had had no luck in gaining permission to visit the location until Edmund rode in to our lives on his folding Brompton bicycle. Edmund, who runs an engineering consultancy in London, contacted us after reading about our work on prehistoric British units of measurement whilst he had been travelling on a train in Sweden. After our first meeting on the North Wales island of Anglesey, he became a significant member of our small, extended team of people with practical rather than purely academic expertise in the field of making sense of ancient engineering.

In conversation we had told Edmund of our difficulty in gaining access to the Newby Hall Estate – and we were quite amazed at his response.

'No problem. I'm pretty sure I can sort that out for you. The estate owner, Richard Compton, is a good friend of mine.' This was an extra-ordinary but most welcome coincidence and, true to his word, Edmund duly arranged a meeting at the estate manager's office at the end of February in 2008.

Peter Greenwood could not have been more helpful. He had pulled out old maps of the relevant parts of the estate and copied them for us. After giving us a brief of everything he knew, we stepped into Peter's four-wheel-drive and began a tour of the locations that interested us.

The most important spot was a sloping field that had no crop growth at this early part of the year. Notwithstanding the clear view of the soil we could detect nothing of the structure we knew had been built here nearly 1,000 years before the Giza pyramids. However, we had aerial photographs with us, which gave a clear view of the shape of the original artefact, thanks to differences in the subsoil.

Peter had shown us old maps that revealed the 5,500-year-old struc-ture had been clearly visible until it was ploughed out sometime in the early 20th century. We had deduced its location and its importance from three other similar structures that were very much intact – just 10 km to the northwest. Fortunately there was sufficient evidence available to identify the size of the absent structure and pinpoint its precise centre. This was to prove to be incredibly important.

As we left the cold, windswept hilltop that morning we knew that we would have to travel to Egypt because something extraordinary was appearing out of the mists of time. A completely unexpected picture of the past had presented itself. Against all sense and apparent credibility, it seemed from everything we now knew possible – or to be honest – highly likely that Hem-iwnu, King Khufu's principal architect had stood in this same English field before he began his ambitious project to create something wonderful on the west bank of the Nile.

Ancient Wonders

As we passed between Khufu and Khafre's man-made mountains we felt that sense of total awe that can never quite be captured by photographs or communicated though cinematography. The scale and shear solid mass of these objects creates an impression such that your entire body can feel their gravitational field. Close your eyes and they are still there.

Even today, without their original brilliant white limestone coverings, the pyramids are soul-stirringly beautiful, sculpted by the brilliant glow of the Egyptian summer sun. These geometrically perfect structures now stand rather battered but proudly aloof on the raised outcrop known as the Mokkatam Formation, where in ancient times, the Nile had washed its eastern-facing cliff during the annual inundation. But today the rocks mark the limits of the crazy cacophony that is Cairo's urban sprawl.

To say that the three pyramids of Giza have been studied in minute detail would be an understatement. The largest of them, known alternatively as the 'Great Pyramid', the 'Pyramid of Khufu', or sometimes by the Greek name 'Pyramid of Cheops', is the only remaining and certainly the largest of the seven wonders of the ancient world. Even without its original gilded ben-ben or capstone it is 138.8 m in height with an estimated internal volume of 2.5 million m^3 – (equal to 1,000 Olympic swimming pools). Strangely, the average block of stone is 1 m^3. Facts and figures are impressive enough but not nearly so inspiring as standing at the base of Khufu's pyramid and staring up at the unbelievable dimensions of something so huge it is hard to comprehend how anyone could have conceived its creation, let alone brought such an idea to reality.

According to the ancient Greek historian Herodotus, the pyramid attributed to King Khufu took around 20 years to build from start to finish. Quite what sources Herodotus had for this claim is unsure, but despite the fact that he was writing two full millennia after the event, he does have a good track record of getting his facts broadly right. If it is truly the case that the Great Pyramid was constructed so quickly, the implications are staggering. It means that working seven days a week and throughout the year for two full decades, the craftsmen and labourers involved must have cut, squared off, dragged to the site and erected 342 stones every single day. The average stone weighs two and a half tonnes, though many are far heavier. If Herodotus is to be believed a stone block must have been added to the pyramid every two minutes or so!

Anyone who has stood on the Giza Plateau between 11 am and 3 pm on any day between May to September will appreciate how physically draining it is simply to walk around the area. It seems impossible to imagine anyone continuously cutting, dragging and raising huge stone blocks under the unremitting glare of the desert Sun. Herodotus may have been proven correct about many of his writings, but we doubt he was correct on this occasion and we remain convinced that the Khufu pyramid must have taken much longer than 20 years to complete.

The other two pyramids in the sequence of three are smaller. The second pyramid, standing a little to the southwest of the Great Pyramid, is attributed to Khufu's third son, Khafre. It is almost as large as the Great Pyramid and unlike the other two it still has its higher faces covered in the original white casing, although it is now pitted and dulled with sand. Further still to the southwest is the pyramid of Menkaure, which looks almost 'modest' when set against its much larger companions, though it is still 61 m in height and is mightily impressive in its own right.

It is strange to reflect that these three amazing structures, as familiar as they are to people in every corner of the world, are almost as mysterious now as they were to the 18th-century European explorers who first started a bout of 'pyramid' fever. Orthodox accounts suggest that the Great Pyramid of Khufu was the first of the three to be constructed, most likely around 2500 BC. Since deep within the pyramid there are three chambers, one of which contains what is taken to be a sarcophagus, it is generally accepted that the Great Pyramid was intended to be tomb – built specifically to house the body of King Khufu, the first of the great kings of fourth-dynasty Egypt. Khufu cannot be rightfully termed a Pharaoh because this was a title that came much later in Egyptian history.

Inside the Great Pyramid the three distinct chambers, somewhat poetically and bearing no relationship to their ancient purpose, are known as the King's Chamber, the Queen's Chamber and the Unfinished Chamber. These modern, invented titles help shore up the widely held but entirely erroneous view that Egyptologists understand the intended function of these voids inside the pyramids.

The 'Unfinished Chamber' is a particular mystery. It lies 30 m below the surface of the plateau where workers chipped away at the bedrock to cut out what was once thought to have been the original burial chamber for King Khufu. For years Egyptologists claimed the chamber is 'unfinished' because Khufu suddenly decided he wanted his burial chamber to be up in the main body of the pyramid rather than below ground. We find it hard to believe that the people who designed Khufu's pyramid made such a gigantic error, or that Khufu was making up the layout as he went along. 'I think I'll have my burial chamber down here. Err, no, on second thoughts maybe it would be nice to have it up here.' It just does not sound right. Khufu and his architect, Hemiwnu, were so precise in everything they did that we cannot easily accept this explanation.

The mystery of this subterranean vault remains, but at least the orthodox Egyptology establishment has given up trying to sustain the notion that it was some kind of planning error. The powers that be have surrendered on this point, not least because there is also the problem that a similar 'mistake' happened with Khafre's Pyramid, which also has an unfinished subterranean chamber – although not at such great depth.

We had discussed these chambers at length and both of us had a strong feeling that they must have been not only deliberate but also highly important for some reason. After all, they were the first workings to be carried out on the Giza Plateau. We were later to find out that our hunch was right but we could never have guessed just how important these chambers are when it comes to understanding the enormous scale of extreme antiquity.

No one can know for sure, but the Great Pyramid probably did originally contain interesting and valuable artefacts. It was plundered by thieves during the New Kingdom, over 3,000 years ago, leaving only one item in place. The robbers had no interest in trying to extract a large red granite sarcophagus that weighs over three tonnes. It is generally and logically assumed that this stone box once contained the mummified body of Khufu as there is also a sarcophagus in Khafre and Menkaure's pyramid; or at least there was one in Menkaure's pyramid, until it was looted by British archaeologists in the early 19th century and lost at sea on its way to a museum in England.

The spellbinding beauty and scale of these three pyramids, along with a raft of unanswered questions, has led to a large number of ideas regarding what they were intended to achieve. These range from the safe assumption that they were simply grand mausoleums for the three named kings, through to wild notions such as the suggestion they were built by aliens or that the structures themselves possess super-advanced technological capabilities of various kinds. There are still people who claim that the building technology employed sprang from nowhere and that we lack the technology to build such edifices even today.

Both of these claims are false. It would be quite possible, albeit with some difficulty and considerable expense, to build the pyramids today. And the notion that the expertise necessary to create these stone giants suddenly appeared is also clearly false. There is ample evidence of an experimental evolution from simple mud-brick tombs that lead over a period of time up to the Great Pyramid itself.

The earliest Egyptians had buried their dead directly into the baking-hot desert sand, where the high, dry temperature desiccates the bodies to effectively mummify them. As the civilization developed, mud-brick structures known as 'mastabas' began to appear. These buildings were trapezoid structures – rectangular in plan with inward sloping sides and a flat top. Over time it became the practice to build one slightly smaller mastaba on top of another, which led to the development of the step pyramid (*see* figure 1). There then followed a phase during which the architects improved the design of the step pyramid by adding triangular infills for the saw-tooth sides, leading to the sort of smooth pyramid with which most people are familiar. The later stages of this process actually came about surprisingly rapidly – given the normally ponderous nature of building evolution.

Prior to the modern age, innovation in any architectural styling or technology was a rare event, and one that was usually driven by need rather than a search for aesthetic excellence. The one great exception to this obser-vation was the cathedral-building revolution initiated by the Order of the Knights Templar from AD 1130 onwards, when both the technology and the beauty of architecture leapt to previously unseen levels – almost overnight.

The first known stepped pyramid was that of Djoser at Saqqara, a few kilometres south of Giza. A series of developmental techniques followed, which included the Pyramid of Meydum, which was still a step pyramid but the stages were becoming so frequent that is was losing its saw-tooth

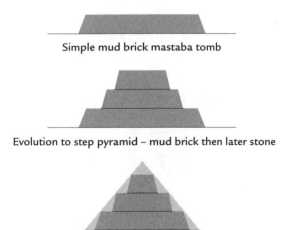

Simple mud brick mastaba tomb

Evolution to step pyramid – mud brick then later stone

Sides filled in to create true pyramid

Figure 1. Diagrams showing the evolution of the pyramids

profile. The so-called 'Bent Pyramid' at Dashour followed, in which the architects began planning structures with a super-ambitious angle of 60°. However, the realities of physics soon taught these experimental builders to moderate their ambitions and settle for sides that were slightly less steep.

A 'smooth-sided pyramid' appeared not long before the Giza complex was planned. It is known as the 'Red Pyramid' and was created at the instructions of King Snefru, who is believed to be the father of Khufu. The Red Pyramid has a slope of just over 43°, which is less that the later Great Pyramid, but it contained many of the architectural features associated with its grander and slightly later counterparts. It was built upon a foundation of stone blocks and contained interior tunnels and chambers of the sort found at Giza.

However, the Great Pyramid of Khufu and its two companion pyramids appear to be much more than just an improvement on their forebears. They have properties that link them to the stars.

Chapter 2

·

STAR WATCHERS

The Orion Correlation Theory

It is true that there is certainly a reasonably clear evolution of the pyramid builder's art, but the Giza pyramids are clearly superior both in their scale and build-quality – in addition they exhibit complex features that have no apparent antecedence.

One of the most hotly debated aspects of the Great Pyramid over recent years has been the series of narrow shafts cut into the blocks of rock. There are two in the King's Chamber, which run steeply upwards to emerge on the outside of the pyramid, not too far from its pinnacle. It was originally suggested that these were simply ventilation shafts but this idea has now been abandoned and it is generally accepted that the shafts had some ceremonial purpose. Experts have observed that the builders of the pyramid must have put a great deal of time and trouble into the integration of these beautifully accurate, narrow tunnels in the mass of stone. It would have been quite impossible to chisel them into the rock after the pyramid was complete because they are far too narrow. The only way they could have been created was 'layer by layer', as the pyramid began to grow. There is another pair of shafts in the so-called Queen's Chamber. These are similar to those in the King's Chamber but, curiously, they are blocked by squares of limestone deliberately set into the masonry at the time of the pyramid's construction.

Since the 1960s it has been argued that these shafts are aligned to specific stars – the polestar in the north and Orion's Belt in the south. Whilst this has been hotly debated, we are unaware of any alternative theory that makes as much sense. The reasons to suspect that it is correct are:

- The Egyptians are believed to have aligned the pyramids to the four cardinal points of the Earth using Thuban, then the polestar, to establish north.

- The stars close to the pole were important to the Egyptians because they never set.[1] They were therefore described in ancient texts as the 'imperishable' or 'undying' ones. The kings believed that they too would be 'imperishable' after death.

- The constellation of Orion has an important place in Egyptian mythology, being considered to be the soul of Osiris.[2] Traditionally Osiris is considered to be the Lord of the Two Lands: Lord of the Heavens and Lord of the Earth. He was also considered to be Lord of the Dead and in this capacity was always represented in mummy wrappings.

So, the star-alignment theory seems highly reasonable. What about the next theory that came along?

The path that had led us from the rolling green fields of northern Britain to the sandy wastes of Egypt was an entirely logical one based on the work of the well-known pyramid researcher, Robert Bauval – a man who had seen something quite special about the Giza pyramids.

Robert Bauval was born to Belgian parents and brought up in Egypt's second city of Alexandria, and has spent most of his life living and working in the Middle East. He was always keen on history and had not wasted his spare time amidst the remnants of Egypt's long and illustrious past. Bauval studied ancient documents, crawled around in old passages and climbed sandy hills in order to better appreciate the skills of his Bronze Age counterparts in construction. He became quite preoccupied with a book called *The Sirius Mystery*, written by the American polymath Robert Temple, that spoke of a very early lost civilization and an ancient understanding of astronomy and mathematics that had been previously unsuspected. Bauval also became interested in the 'Pyramid Texts' – a wealth of fables, folk tales and historical accounts that had been painted and carved onto the interior walls of a series of pyramids in Saqqara, close to Cairo.

Ultimately it wasn't any of the Giza pyramids in isolation that came to fascinate Bauval, but rather the Giza complex as a whole because, in what amounted to a flash of inspiration, he was the first individual to realize that there was something quite unique about the way the three pyramids at Giza had been arranged. As a result, Bauval set out to study the whole arrangement of the Giza Plateau in greater detail.

He came to believe that the three large pyramids on the Giza Plateau were not built in isolation, as were many temples and smaller pyramids surrounding the three significant structures. Walking down what was originally a ceremonial path from the pyramids to where the Nile waters once used to lap one encounters the Great Sphinx – surely one of the most enigmatic and unusual structures ever created. The Sphinx looked out due east across the Nile whilst a line drawn northeast from the Giza pyramids leads, some 8km away, to the site of the ancient city of Lunu, known in the Bible as On, or Heliopolis to the Greeks. This centre of solar worship is now completely lost beneath the urban sprawl of Cairo.

Bauval was troubled by the fact that the Giza pyramids are not quite in a straight line (*see* figure 2) and it was the discrepancy regarding the positioning of the third pyramid that caused him to sit up and make a mental connection. The three pyramids create a pattern that is uncannily like that formed by three of the most famous stars known to humanity throughout its long history – Orion's Belt.

Best viewed in Western Europe in the winter months, the constellation of Orion contains some of the most significant stars to be seen in our night skies. Amongst these is Sirius, the brightest object we can see apart from the Sun, Moon and some of the solar system's planets. Higher in the sky than Sirius, and rising well before it, are the three stars known as Orion's Belt.

These stars – Mintaka, Alnilam and Alnitak – are all bright and very conspicuous to anyone viewing the sky. They have been known to every

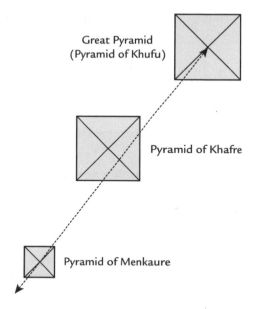

Great Pyramid
(Pyramid of Khufu)

Pyramid of Khafre

Pyramid of Menkaure

Figure 2. Giza pyramids showing offset

civilization, and by a wealth of names. Some peoples have called them
a string of pearls, three beautiful maidens or, in the case of Greek sky
watchers, the belt of the great hero and hunter Orion. But everyone who
looked at Orion's Belt could not fail to realize that they point towards the
rising of Sirius, which is the greatest star of them all and cannot be mistaken for any other. Follow the three stars of Orion's Belt down towards
the horizon and you are bound to come upon the silver-white orb of
Sirius, which has probably been venerated by humanity since our forebears first lifted their heads to admire the heavens.

There are many instances of groups of three stars forming a discern-
able shape in the night sky, which is not so surprising considering just
how many stars there are to be seen. But Orion's Belt is special, not only
in its clarity and brightness, but because of its distinctive shape. A glance
at figure 3 shows immediately that there is a slight 'dogleg' to the alignment of these three stars. It was this small deviation from a straight line

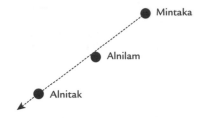

Figure 3. Stars of Orion's Belt showing offset

that alerted Robert Bauval to a possible association between the three pyramids on the Giza Plateau and the stars of Orion's Belt.

All of this took place some time ago. Bauval and his colleague Adrian Gilbert wrote *The Orion Mystery*, which was published in 1994, following ten years of research by Bauval. The sophisticated astronomical computer programs available to our own research were in their infancy when Bauval first outlined his theory regarding Orion's Belt. Nevertheless he took an image of the three stars and superimposed it onto an aerial view of the Giza pyramids. We have done the same thing many times and the result can be seen in figure 4.

The fit is amazingly good considering how small the stars of Orion's Belt actually are in the sky. We have to bear in mind that we are dealing here with naked-eye astronomy but nevertheless the distance apart of the three stars, and the dogleg they form, are more than adequately represented by the three pyramids of the Giza Plateau. Could it be, Bauval quite reasonably asked himself, that the ancient Egyptians had deliberately created the Giza complex to represent a part of the sky that was so familiar to them?

In order to substantiate what became a realistic theory Bauval called upon his knowledge of Egyptology and in particular the Pyramid Texts.[3] He pointed out how this particular part of the sky had been of great importance to the pyramid builders. The Egyptian kings had believed that after death they were translated to the stars. The fact is mentioned repeatedly in the famed Egyptian *Book of the Dead*, a series of funerary texts assembled during the New Kingdom – a period that includes the time when Moses was a general in the Egyptian army. Whilst this

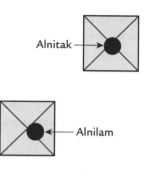

Alnitak

Alnilam

Mintaka

Figure 4. Orion's Belt superimposed onto the Giza pyramids

was around a millennium after the building of the pyramids, it seems almost certain that the Egyptian *Book of the Dead* itself related back to those ancient Pyramid Texts to be found at Saqqara. The Pyramid Texts represent a series of 'prayers' or 'rituals' that were considered necessary for the dead king or courtier to enjoy an afterlife.

Bauval came to realize that the constellation of Orion, and in particular the three stars of Orion's Belt, had been considered especially important since it was to this part of the sky that one of the most famous Egyptian gods, Osiris, had gone after his own death. Osiris was almost certainly venerated long before dynastic Egypt began to develop. To the ancient Egyptians Osiris was humanity's best ally. Through a long and complex pre-mythology this important deity gradually came to be considered the most significant god of 'life', as opposed to other deities such as Anubis, whose credentials associated them more with 'death' – a subject that appears to have obsessed the ancient Egyptians.

Osiris was more than a god of life – he was 'the' god of rebirth. Stories relating to Osiris during his own life reflect his association with rebirth. In the most famous of these he was murdered by the evil god Set but was brought back to life by his faithful and loving wife Isis. After this he took his place in heaven but it was always considered that, in some magical way, successive Pharaohs actually became 'Osiris on Earth' during their lives and for the duration of their reign. After death the correct funereal rites ensured that these same Pharaohs would unite with Osiris in heaven. And the place where the Pharaohs would enjoy their afterlife, subsumed by the figure of Osiris, was in that exact place in the sky where Orion's Belt could be seen.

Bauval came to believe that it wasn't merely Orion's Belt that had been replicated on the sands of Egypt. He arrived at the conclusion that other pyramids represented different stars in the constellation of Orion. Such a notion was beyond the scope of our current researches, however, because we had come to Egypt with the three major pyramids of the Giza Plateau in mind.

Despite its obvious merits, Bauval's theory has not been widely accepted in mainstream Egyptology. Like most academic disciplines Egyptology has its canon to protect, and radically new ideas are rarely acknowledged, much less objectively evaluated – especially when they come from a non-academic.

One of reasons often given for not taking Bauval's claims seriously is the argument that the ancient Egyptians did not develop any sophisticated astronomical awareness until much later in their development. Experts have never previously found anything that leads them to the conclusion that the pyramid builders knew much about the stars at all. One leading figure spoke for many Egyptologists when he said of the calendar system of 360 days:

> ...the simplicity of the Egyptian calendar is a sign of its primitivity; it is the remainder of the prehistoric crudeness, preserved without change by the Egyptian... it seems to me, that every theory of the origin of the Egyptian calendar which assumes an astronomical foundation is doomed to failure.[4]

There is absolutely no doubt that this observation made by Otto Neugebauer is a well-founded conclusion based on many years of high-quality research. But in Neugebauer's day there was no 'Orion correlation theory' to muddy the waters.

We looked to see if there was any evidence of greater sophistication of astronomy in the ancient Egyptians' ability to measure smaller units of time rather than just days of the year. The evidence is that the ancient Egyptians measured the passage of time by means of star clocks, which divided the transiting heavens into groups of stars that marked out hours – known as decans. The title of *imy wnwt* or 'hour-watcher' was in use right up to the Ptolemaic period when Egypt was ruled by the family of a Macedonian general from the army of Alexander the Great in the 3rd century BC.

However, this timekeeping by the stars looks as though it was, at later dates, little more than a memory of technique that had been introduced and forgotten a long time in the past. One Egyptologist makes the point well when he argues that knowledge of timekeeping seems to have occurred during a relatively brief period of the country's history:

> ...while we have lists of decans on various astronomical ceilings or other monuments to the end of Egyptian history, we have nothing at all approaching a star clock in form after the time of Merneptah (1223–1211 BC) and that that was a purely funerary relic is indicated by the fact that its arrangement of stars is 600 years earlier into the twelfth dynasty.[5]

This indicates a regression in the ability to understand and monitor passing time. Apparently, knowledge of methods of timekeeping had been lost around one and a half millennia before the time of Queen Cleopatra.

The whole feeling we take from looking at timekeeping in ancient Egypt is that it was not an indigenous skill. It appears to have been an overlay on their worldview – from some minority group or, more likely, from an external influence. Accurate timekeeping is an essential element of successful and detailed astronomy.

As a discipline, modern archaeology has become extremely good at producing information and building frameworks of understanding regarding past cultures. Some of the techniques available today are simply astonishing – such as the ability to trace the lifetime movements of individuals from fragmentary bodily remains through analysis of their mineral intake during the time they lived, sometimes many thousands of years ago. Where the discipline is, in our opinion, sometimes wanting is in the ability to consider a bigger picture and to deal rigorously with apparent paradox. Whilst this may sound disrespectful, it is not intended to be. Undoubtedly it is easy to spot weaknesses when one does not have to sign up to the convention of procedure that has to be the adopted to provide a framework of ground rules that govern required behaviour.

But, as the saying goes, all progress is due to the unreasonable person. Quite simply, it is sensible and reasonable to cooperate with the status quo – but any leap forward in understanding is likely to come from the individual who has the audacity to say, 'we could look at this very differently.'

If there is good evidence that fourth-dynasty Egyptians were not good astronomers, does it mean that any potential new evidence conflicting with that conclusion must automatically be assumed to be false? Why not suspend judgement and seek out scenarios that could allow both conclusions to coexist? Maybe there was a small group of architect-priests who *were* expert in understanding the stars and who were also good at measuring the passage of time but who had no opportunity of influencing the established calendar system. Or could a group of previously unidentified outsiders have been brought in to provide astronomical expertise? Certainly, the principle of Occam's Razor – which logically objects to the invention of unnecessary components in the search for a solution to any question – would preclude such speculation. But what if there are known entities that could influence the situation concerned – if only they were considered?

Unfortunately the modern convention (and it is no more that an arbitrary adoption) that insists on a silo structure of historical analysis rejects cross-cultural investigation unless there is obvious and repeated artefact-based evidence to demonstrate a connection. As a consequence, sensible questions sometimes go unasked, let alone answered. Valuable evidence is consigned to the waste bin because standing assumptions are considered too important to be challenged. This cosy complacency explains why so many breakthroughs in academia come from people outside the discipline concerned or from mavericks within the subject area who are brave enough to challenge their more conservative peers.

A perfect example of an outsider breaking the mould, but being ignored by the academic establishment, is the late Alexander Thom. He was a distinguished professor of engineering at Oxford University who, over 50 years of detailed surveying, discovered that the megalithic builders of the British Isles had been using a very finely defined set of standard units of measurement. This breakthrough in our understanding of the Neolithic period is central to our own research and we will return to Thom's work in the next chapter, but suffice to say at this point his findings were almost universally rejected by mainstream archaeology.

An example of a 'maverick' – whose discoveries are also important to our own investigations, is the late Livio Stecchini. As a professor of metrology (the science of measurement), he argued that the metric system of measurement, as devised by the French in the late 18th century, had been used in an almost identical form 4,500 years earlier in the land of Sumer. Despite his previously high standing in the academic community he was largely ostracized by his peers.

Robert Bauval belongs (like ourselves) to a third category of people who are largely ignored by the establishment, namely non-academics. The definition of an academic is someone who has been trained in a given discipline and is subsequently employed by a university to teach and possibly conduct research in that subject. They are expected to work procedurally, to apply scientific testing to their logic and to comply with conventional protocol. This includes the process of peer review prior to the possible publication of new information in academic journals.

Bauval is an engineer with a Master's degree in marketing. This demonstrates that he knows how to process information and comply with the conventions of a postgraduate education. But to the world of academia, he is not a member and therefore is not a peer – so he cannot be reviewed and therefore his work cannot be directly published by any of the archaeological journals.

So, if we put the 'establishment' view that the ancient Egyptians were not very skilled at astronomy to one side we can, for the moment, accept the evidence of the stellar-aligned pyramid shafts and the possibility of the Giza trio being a deliberate model of the stars of Orion's Belt. The next question to ask is: where could the star-based ideas and beliefs behind the culture that built the pyramids have come from?

We have to admit a bias in asking this question because our interest in the pyramids was initiated by a finding that would answer this question. At this stage of our researches we strongly suspected a connection between Neolithic Britain and ancient Egypt – but, assuming that we were right, we did not know whether the Egyptians influenced the Britons or vice versa. We needed to find out more about the origins of the Egyptian culture. Whilst we had a hypothesis to investigate we remained entirely open to what we might find, and open to changing our minds – as we have had to do on many occasions.

The First Time

To gain an insight into the thinking behind the creation of structures as special as the Giza pyramids it is essential to understand the theological and mythological heritage of a civilization. As they say, 'there is little new under the Sun.' New religions are hardly ever invented – rather they are improvements on older cults or an amalgam of the best bits of the rituals and beliefs from various sources.

It is from the ancient Egyptians and the Sumerians that the later gods of the Greeks, Romans and the Jews ultimately sprang. Later, Christianity and Islam arrived as reworked versions of older ideas. Abraham, the pivotal figure from the earliest annals of the Old Testament, was from the Sumerian city of Ur and went into Egypt talking about his 'God of our Fathers' – meaning that the deity was the god of that specific city. Meanwhile Judaism claims to date back to Abraham and his son Isaac, and the Old Testament carries other Sumerian legends such as Noah's Flood and the story of Enoch.

When the story of Jesus Christ was found to be valuable to the Roman state it was changed to include the key aspects of Mithraism, a cult of Persian origin, which was already very popular in Rome and the wider empire. St Paul had been brought up as a follower of Mithra and the idea of the death and resurrection of a man-deity made immediate sense to him, whereas the Jews of the Jerusalem Church must have been horrified by this alien concept being grafted onto their heritage. For them the long-anticipated Messiah was a king to lead them into battle against oppressors – not some physical aspect of their God, Yahweh, who would take responsibility for their individual wrongdoings.[6] The powerful icon of the dying and rising god stems back to ancient Egypt and, no doubt, long before that. And the main festivals of Christianity, including Christmas and Easter, were thousands of years old when Jesus Christ was born. Ancient astronomy lies behind these modern religious celebrations – Christmas being the winter solstice, when the rising Sun reaches its most southerly point on the horizon and Easter, the springtime of rebirth, is calculated by the Western Church as being the first Sunday after the first full moon following the vernal equinox.

So what influences did the ancient Egyptians have to form their early beliefs? This is difficult because writing was only invented around the time that the Egypt we call ancient Egypt was created by the unification of Upper (southern) and Lower (northern) Egypt, which is thought to have taken place around 3100 BC during dynasty 'Zero'. One of the earliest hieroglyphic inscriptions is the Narmer Palette, which dates from about that time. It is thought by some to depict the unification of the two lands by King Narmer. On one side of the palette the king is depicted with the white crown of Upper Egypt and the other side depicts him wearing the red crown of Lower Egypt.

The indications are that the time before history began in Egypt, agriculture had developed around the Nile by the so-called 'Badarian' people. They were essentially semi-nomads who appear to have had a belief in the afterlife as they buried their dead in small cemeteries on the outskirts of their temporary settlements. Bodies were interred in the foetal position and they were always laid facing west, towards the setting Sun.

Archaeologists have been able to track subtle changes in the habits and lifestyles of the Badarian people which started to take place around 4500 BC. The culture in Upper Egypt from this period is referred to as Naqada I, after the town of Naqada on the west bank of the Nile in the region of Qena. The Naqada people would prove to be the most significant culture to emerge in Upper Egypt. Instead of simply accepting the bounty of the annual Nile flood the Naqada embraced it, building irrigation ditches and canals and creating a form of agriculture that was far more sophisticated that that practised during the Badarian period. The nomadic lifestyle ceased and true towns began to emerge, which opened the door for trade and a diversification of skills.

Despite the apparent evolution from nomads to farmers and then to city builders over a period of 1,500 years, ancient Egyptian texts recall a lost period in deeper history when there had been an advanced civilization which, for some reason, regressed. They called this lost golden age Zep Tepi, meaning 'The First Time'. The Egyptians associated the first appearance of the phoenix, the mythical bird that regenerated from its own ashes, with this distant epoch. R T Rundle Clark, former professor of Egyptology at Manchester University, commented on the meaning of this First Time:

> Anything whose existence or authority had to be justified or explained must be referred to the 'First Time'. This was true for natural phenomena, rituals, royal insignia, the plans of temples, magical or medical formulae, the hieroglyphic system of writing, the calendar – the whole paraphernalia of the civilization ... All that was good or efficacious was established on the principles laid down in the 'First Time' – which was, therefore, a golden age of absolute perfection ...[7]

Why did the Egyptians have to invent Zep Tepi? Maybe it is simply a romantic attempt to explain how they came to exist – or possibly it really is a cultural memory of some previous period of advanced development that crumbled for some reason. We would later come across new evidence that points, very powerfully, to the second of these options.

But what about the possibility of input of astronomical knowledge from a source other than the Egyptians' own abilities? A nation that lacks technical ability can always buy in special skills. According to tradition, Solomon, the second Jewish king of Jerusalem, had to bring in Phoenician expertise to build his famous temple. He paid Hiram, King of Tyre to provide an architect who could design this edifice as a functioning astronomical observatory that connected Earth with heaven.[8] Could the ancient Egyptians have done something similar 1,500 years before Solomon's time? And, if so, where could they have gone to get the skills required?

The inspiration for our journey to Egypt had begun nearly 4,000 km away, in the quiet fields of northern England. We definitely had an answer that begged a question.

Chapter 3

·

THE SILENT STONES SPEAK

An Engineer Makes a Breakthrough

From the gaunt and impressive standing-stone circles of the island of Orkney in the far north of Scotland, right down to the giant avenues of stones in their frozen march across the fields of Brittany in France, Alexander Thom (1894–1985) spent each and every summer for almost five decades carefully measuring and making notes. Together with family members and a small but staunch group of interested friends and associates, he gradually built up a greater database, regarding megalithic achievement in building, than anyone before or since.

It is thanks to the tenacity of this quite extraordinary individual that we have been privileged to embark on an adventure that has taken up well over a decade of our lives. It remains one of our primary objectives to encourage supposed experts in ancient British archaeology to accept, as we are convinced they must do one day, that Thom's findings regarding megalithic measurements are absolutely correct. The evidence we have amassed over recent years makes it certain that Thom was right all along and only ignorance of the available facts is holding back the development of a new paradigm of understanding regarding Western Europe in the Neolithic period.

Thom identified the use of a standard unit he called a 'Megalithic Yard' (MY), which he specified as being equal to 2.722 ft +/- 0.002 ft (0.82966 m +/- 0.061 m). He claimed that there were also other related

28

units used repeatedly, including half and double Megalithic Yards and a 2.5 MY length he dubbed a Megalithic Rod (MR). On a smaller scale he found that the megalith builders had used a fortieth part of a Megalithic Yard, which he called a 'Megalithic Inch' (MI) because it was 0.8166 of a modern inch (2.074 cm). The system worked like this:

    1   MI = 2.074 cm
   20   MI = ? MY
   40   MI = 1 MY
  100   MI = 1 MR

Thom was a first-class engineer and he was therefore perfectly qualified to analyse the structures created by other engineers – albeit 5,000 years before his own time. He would survey a megalithic stone circle or lines of stones and estimate, from the general layout, what the builders had set out to achieve. So good was his intuition in this matter that he could often deduce a missing standing stone in a plan – and predict the socket hole that would be found when the ground was examined.

The lifetime work of Alexander Thom and his rediscovery of the Megalithic Yard resulted in a stunning conclusion that created an immediate paradox – how could an otherwise primitive people build with such fine accuracy? Why did they do it and how did they do it? Thom made no attempt to answer these questions. He reported on his engineering analysis and left the anthropological aspects for others to explain. He did comment that he could not understand how these builders transmitted the Megalithic Yards so perfectly over tens of thousands of square miles and across several millennia and he acknowledged that wooden measuring sticks could not have produced the unerring level of consistency he had found.

Thom's mathematical ability was called into question by archaeologists who could not reconcile such amazing levels of measurement perfection from a culture they considered to be primitive. We read as much as we could of the criticisms of Thom's findings and found that, to a large extent, people would refer to his errors by quoting each other, without much in the way of substance at the root of the repeated claims. Today there are people who set themselves up as expert on megalithic sites and who refute Thom without apparently having even a basic grasp of the statistical analysis used to verify Thom's findings.

Ten years has passed since we first set out to try and find if Thom was a genius or simply a deluded eccentric who wasted his life's work. As non-mathematicians ourselves we could not hope to gain any new insight from delving deeper into Thom's published data, so we set out with a much simpler and more direct hypothesis. Our premise was that if the Neolithic people of the British Isles had established a universal unit of measure it is likely to have been derived from nature rather than a complete abstraction.

After a great deal of delving and thought we eventually came to realize that there is only one way that any unit of measure can be repeatedly and reliably derived from the natural world. This is through measurement of the passage of time as expressed by the Earth spinning on its axis, and perceivable by the apparent movement of stars in the night sky. Appendix 4 explains the process in detail for those who want to delve deeper, but the principle relies on using a pendulum to measure the passage of a star or planet across a predefined gap.

We think it is fair to suggest that the first machine ever invented by man was the plumb-bob/pendulum. A small ball of clay on the end of a piece of twine or long strand of straight hair is a wonderful device that interacts with the Earth in a very predictable way. Held stationary, it will always point downwards to the centre of the planet, which allows the user to check verticals during construction of any sort. Verticals are also necessary for good observational astronomy. When the device is swung gently to and fro in the hand it becomes a timekeeper, like a modern metronome (which is only an inverted pendulum).

But the real beauty about pendulums is that the frequency with which they swing is only determined by their length, so if you count a set number of beats for a given period of time (such as the period it takes a star to traverse a known gap), you will always end up with the same pendulum length.

We found that a half Megalithic Yard pendulum was the origin of the whole measurement system rediscovered by Thom.

By the time we published *Civilization One* in 2004 we knew that it wasn't only the megalithic measurements Thom had rediscovered that were unexpected realities from the past. We had also come to realize that the Megalithic Yard, Rod and Inch were merely components of an integrated measuring and geometry system the like of which the world has not seen since – even including measuring systems we use today.

In particular we came to recognize the existence of a system of time measurement and geometry that had relied on circles of 366°, as opposed to the 360° convention we use today. We showed that the adoption of this system was entirely logical because there actually *are* 366° in an Earth circle.

The Wisdom of the Ancients

Let us explain briefly. The Earth goes around the Sun once per year, which is a circle of around 940 million km. Even if prehistoric sky-watchers did not know about the movement of the Earth around the Sun, they would quickly realize that patterns formed by the Sun and stars on the horizon are repeated after two consecutive winter solstices (a year). The same individuals would also note that the stars repeat their performance on a daily basis due to the Earth's spin on its axis (a sidereal day).

Incidentally, it is highly likely that they would also realize that sunrises across the year move exactly like a pendulum. At the spring equinox (currently around 21 March) the Sun will rise due east and then rise a little further north each day until the summer solstice (21 June) at which point it stops and reverses its direction back to the autumn equinox and on to the winter solstice, by which time it will rise well into the south. The Sun's behaviour across a year, as viewed from the Earth, creates exactly the same frequency model as a pendulum. It displays a faster rate of change in the centre and slows gradually to the solstice extremes, where it stops and reverses direction.

So, Neolithic sky-watchers would clearly have understood that there were two constantly repeating patterns taking place – the day and the year. It is almost impossible that they would have failed to realize that the daily pattern fitted into the yearly pattern 366 times. As far as they were concerned the year was a great circle of 366 days in duration and so the origin of the degree of arc as 1/366th of a circle. By contrast the modern convention of 360° in a circle is as primitive as the ancient Egyptian year of 360 days – it simply isn't correct. The two errors are entirely historically related, and though we now do at least use a year of 365 days, we never corrected the mistake regarding the number of degrees in a circle.

The 366-day year differs from the modern year of 365 days in three out of four years, as it represents the 'true' state of affairs regarding the Earth's passage around the Sun, as measured against the background stars. In any case, those who first created the megalithic measuring system dealt exclusively in integers (whole numbers), and for good reason since a circle containing 365.25° would be quite unworkable. The later 360° circle had been adopted by the Sumerians as well as the Egyptians, who both celebrated a ritual year of 360 days, which required significant alterations and compensations in order to constantly bring it back to the true state of affairs regarding the Earth's passage around the Sun. This system of geometry was eventually adopted by other ancient cultures, not least that of the Greeks, and so became the norm across the world.

The ancient system of geometry had greatness running right through it. It divided the Earth's polar circumference into 366° and then subdivided each degree into 60 minutes of arc, with 6 seconds to each minute. And, amazingly, each second of arc is exactly 366 MY in length. How neat! We call this unit of 366 MY a Megalithic Second of arc (Msec).

The Msec appears to have been adopted by the Minoan culture that existed on Crete around 2000 BC because they used a 366° circle and a standard unit of length equivalent to 30.36 cm,[1] which is exactly a 1,000th part of this geodetic subdivision of the planet. The Minoan foot is just a whisker shorter than a modern foot of 30.48 cm – which means that 1,000 imperial feet is itself very close to 1 Msec. But we realized quite early that the modern imperial system, with its feet, pounds and pints, developed from the old integrated megalithic system. This can be demonstrated because a cube with sides that are 1/10th of a Megalithic Yard (4 MI) holds exactly one pint, and weighs one pound when filled with cereal grain.

There are many unexpected correlations between elements that stem back to an ancient integrated system. For example, Thomas Jefferson discovered to his amazement that, for no apparent reason, a cubic foot of pure water weighs precisely 1,000 oz. When he considered this oddity alongside other unexpected connections between measurements in different aspects of the British measuring system Jefferson stated in a report of 4 July 1790:

> What circumstances of the times, or purpose of barter or commerce, called for this combination of weights and measures, with the subjects to be exchanged or purchased, are not now to be ascertained. But (they) ... must have been the result of design and scientific calculation, and not a mere coincidence of hazard ... from very high antiquity.

So, the man who would become the third president of the United States of America correctly spotted that modern British units of measure had come from a common source in the extreme distant past!

It is worth comparing the beautifully integer Megalithic Second of arc with the modern metric system, which is also based on the polar circumference of our planet. Whilst the Neolithic system had a coherent 366 MY to 1 Msec, the current second of arc is a meaningless and arbitrary 30.87 m in length. We have gradually lost the harmony and beauty established by these Stone Age astronomers.

What is more, the power of the megalithic system of measurements extends beyond the Earth. When one applies the megalithic system to the Moon, it can be seen that when the Moon is split, using the same length of Megalithic Yard present on Earth (*see* Appendix 7) there are exactly 100 MY to a Lunar Megalithic Second of arc. As we will discuss later, Jim Russell, an engineer who shares our curiosity and has rebuilt megalithic astronomical apparatus with modern materials, found that the ancient techniques allowed the users to achieve unexpected results. Rather bewildered he asked us in an email:

> I have realized the vertical rail could be used to determine the diameter of the Moon, once the Earth circumference is known. Is there any evidence the ancients knew the Moon's diameter?

The full scope of our discoveries, once we had established the original existence of the megalithic system of geometry, took an entire book to explain and the magnitude of this brilliant concept, from before history began, is still revealing itself at an incredible pace.

We know very well that the fully integrated megalithic system of measurements deals wonderfully with time, linear distance, mass and volume. In terms of the Megalithic Yard, this unit appears to have been created partly because it is perfectly integer to both the Earth and the Moon – to an accuracy that is essentially flawless. The full measuring system was also tied directly to the mass of the Earth. Many modern units of measurement, such as the British pound and pint, developed directly from the megalithic system and are still in use today.

We originally thought that the creation of the metric system of measurement in the 18th century had sounded the eventual death knell of megalithic achievements but as we shall see, even that assumption turned out to be incorrect. In reality there are no mainstream measuring systems in common use today that fail to owe a debt to the original, integrated megalithic system.

We have created a series of appendices at the back of this book so that those with sufficient interest can look at a fuller description of all our findings, since it is our intention to keep as many numbers out of the body of this book as possible. Nevertheless, we do not expect anyone to take our word alone for all we have suggested and every proof of our findings is available to those who wish to check them.

What we had found demonstrated that a pre-literate culture, with little in the way of technological sophistication, possessed a way of looking at the world and beyond it, that makes our present methods of measuring our environment appear clumsy by comparison.

Nobody has ever told us where our logic, evidence or mathematics is wrong, and those people deemed to be experts simply refused even to look at our findings whilst the majority remained totally silent about them. This is not too surprising because for any well-known archaeologist or historian to break with orthodox teaching and to accept the totality of our discoveries without being absolutely certain we are not deluded, could mean professional suicide. This is especially true since much of what we published worked well mathematically and astronomically but could not be proved by way of any physical evidence.

For example, if we were to suggest that ancient man had been in possession of coin-operated slot machines that could dispense espresso or cappuccino coffee on demand, we would be expected to back our claim with datable evidence. We would require the components of such a device to appear in some archaeological dig, not to mention hard evidence that both coffee and coins were in use at the time. The only machine we were suggesting, namely a simple pendulum, could not survive the ravages of time intact. If it was made of twine and clay it would simply disintegrate in the ground, whereas if it was a pierced stone it might be interpreted as a weight for fishing or a loom. Wooden poles used for star and planet sightings could also be expected to rot quickly and, even if they did survive by some miracle, they could just as easily have been the components of some building or boundary fence. The desert climate of ancient Egypt desiccates and preserves organic material – in the damp conditions of the British Isles such materials normally return to earth within a handful of years.

There is certainly plenty of evidence that the Megalithic Yard and Rod were realities, since Thom found them present in just about every stone circle, fan or avenue he measured. However this sort of evidence is easy to dismiss. Thom's Megalithic Yard has been described as an 'abstraction', a 'mistake' or the result of plain bad surveying. It was further suggested that once Thom had focused his mind on the existence of the Megalithic Yard he subconsciously searched for it in the decades of surveying that followed. This, though never expressed as such, is an accusation of 'cheating' on Thom's part that we think unjustified and quite out of character with the scrupulous nature of the man. But it does remain a fact that at the time we published *Civilization One* we were heavy on theories – all of which worked perfectly, but light on testable, tangible evidence.

That is no longer the case.

We had suggested the use of the number 366 as being central to the whole megalithic system of measurement, but try as we may we could not find a stone circle in which the number 366 appeared in terms of Megalithic Yards or Rods. We had gone even further, predicting that our ancient ancestors were probably fascinated by circles in which whole numbers of units for both the diameter and the circumference of the circle were possible. In particular we had pointed out that any circle with a diameter of 233 units would have a circumference of 732 of the same units: (732 being twice 366), but once again this was a theory, and without any substantial and tangible proof it could be readily dismissed as some kind of numerology.

It seemed for a while that all our efforts to champion the megalithic system would come to nothing as far as orthodoxy was concerned. True there was a small nucleus of people around the world who were fascinated by our discoveries and who were ready to give us all the assistance they could, but these were not people who were archaeologically influential. But the interest of both mathematicians and engineers has been much easier to find. This is probably because both mathematicians and engineers are fundamentally scientific. The social or historical reasons for two and two making four don't matter too much to a mathematics teacher – what counts is being able to do the sum. Similarly, to an engineer, evidence shows that a proposed bridge or building will be able to cope with the forces it is likely to encounter. Those interested in mathematics have taken our information on board because it pleased them to exercise their minds, and we can report that, no matter what scrutiny has been brought to bear on any of our findings, we have not been questioned on either our methods or our results.

So we took our case to people who had no axe to grind; individuals who could understand the significance of what we had found and give some sensible assessment of its potential merits. Those people were school teachers – most specifically science teachers.

The British Association of Teachers of Science ran a review of our book *Civilization One* on their website and invited members to read it for themselves. The result was clear:

> There is a very well argued description of the process by which the passage of Venus across the sky, passing between two markers at easily standardized distance apart sets a unit of time during which a pendulum is regulated until it swings 366 times. The length of the

pendulum string at that point is exactly one half of a Megalithic Yard. It is indisputable, I think, that Venus was a very important sky object to all early civilizations and its use in this way is certainly plausible. They begin by deriving the fact that 366 MY is precisely equivalent to one second of arc of the Earth's circumference. The number 366 is equivalent to exactly 1,000 Minoan feet. I have summarized very briefly the beginnings of the authors' thinking but it is this that set them off on the train of investigation which reveals itself so dramatically and, I have to say, convincingly as this easily read book progresses. This book sets out a plausible case for the remarkable connections between systems of measurement – linear, volume and mass – from the dawn of time through to the imperial pint, the avoirdupois and troy systems, the metric system and even the esoteric measurements used today in the United States. Having read this book twice, I am convinced there is something about it – there is definitely a case to answer, so to speak.

So mathematically literate teachers think our evidence stacks up and there is a case to answer.

Meanwhile, engineers who have looked at our work have pronounced our experiments with pendulums and braced wooden frames to be entirely acceptable – irrespective of whether they are historically 'likely' or not. The engineer asks 'could it have been done?' and he or she doesn't worry in the slightest that our discoveries and theories might be treading on any professional toes.

An Engineer Joins the Team

Such an individual is Edmund Sixsmith, a civil engineer with degrees from two of the world's greatest seats of learning – Cambridge University and the Massachusetts Institute of Technology. Edmund first contacted us in August of 2007, during the period we were busy researching this book. To say that Edmund is a 'character' is an understatement. At the time he made contact with us Edmund had completed an article on the work of Professor Alexander Thom that he intended to submit to the *Journal of the Institution of Civil Engineers*. He wanted our permission to use extracts from our previous books.

Edmund has an excellent mind and is quick on the uptake, but he is certainly not gullible in any way. During the time we have known him he has proved to be one of our best supporters, but also our sternest critic if he thinks that we are not being consistent about accuracy and significant figures.

It was high summer and Edmund was spending time with his family on the island of Anglesey, off the north coast of Wales, and we agreed to meet him there so that we could acquaint him better with some of our more recent and, at that time, unpublished findings. We met Edmund at one of Anglesey's more famous burial mounds and were slightly amused when he turned up, pedalling furiously across the very uneven ground on a folding Brompton bicycle. We were less amused, and quite frankly astounded, to see the resemblance between Edmund and an historical character whom we had come to admire hugely during the writing of *Civilization One*. Edmund is the absolute image of Thomas Jefferson, signer of the Declaration of Independence and the third President of the United States of America.

The meeting with Edmund was both useful and enjoyable. He has proved to be a staunch ally but a continued critic on occasions. However, it wasn't so much this meeting that made that August break so significant but rather what happened after Alan left Anglesey.

Some days earlier Alan had seen a television documentary presented by British architectural historian, Dan Cruickshank. The programme in question was an episode of the series *Britain's Best Buildings*. This fascinating series found Cruickshank visiting London's Tower Bridge, Durham Cathedral and the Palace of Westminster, to mention but a few. However, the episode that was important to our researches had found Cruickshank in the city of Bath. Bath is not too far from Bristol in the southwest of England and is famous for being a Roman town, as well as its wonderful buildings, many of which were built in the Regency period (18th century). Because of its naturally hot mineral springs, the place first appealed to the aristocrats and the growing middle class of Regency England. Many people bought houses in the town and would come there for the 'season' when they were not at their country estates or in London.

In a sense most of Bath could be termed a 'new town' because the greater part was planned at more or less the same time in the 18th century and some of the most famous sites were designed and built by the same man, a remarkable architect by the name of John Wood. In the documentary, Cruickshank spent a great deal of time extolling the beauty and symmetry of a large circle of houses that John Wood had created. This is known as the King's Circus and is as magnificent today as it was when it was first built.

What was immediately interesting were the dimensions Cruickshank identified in relation to the King's Circus. He stated that John Wood had been obsessed with ancient standing-stone circles and that the Circus owed its dimensions to a megalithic stone circle close to Bath. The circle in question is called Stanton Drew. The diameter of the King's Circus, from building front to building front across the circle, is 318 ft. This measurement was remarkable because it produced a circle with a circumference of 366 MY to an accuracy of 99.7per cent – a tiny variation that was probably not meaningful in the assessment of measurement of these buildings.

What this meant was, to a very high degree of accuracy, that John Wood had (knowingly or otherwise) designed the King's Circus to have a circumference of 366 MY. Of course one might suggest that the whole thing was a coincidence were it not for the fact that John Wood was a professed Druid and was extremely familiar with a number of stone circles in his own part of England. Further investigation showed that John Wood had personally measured Stonehenge, and this turned out to be much more important than Stanton Drew.

Interest in the megalithic monuments was starting to take off in the 18th century. Archaeology was in its infancy and many people at the time thought that Stonehenge might have been built by the Romans. Wood thought it owed more to the Druids, a mystical religious component of Celtic British culture at the time of the Roman invasion in AD 43. Despite the fact that Druidism was more or less wiped out in both France and Britain by the Roman legions, it still retained a mystical fascination for rich 18th-century antiquarians. An order of recreated Druids (The Ancient Order of Druids) was formed in London in 1781, just a few decades after the death of architect John Wood in 1754, but we know from Wood's own writings that an Order of Druids already existed at the time he was building the King's Circus in Bath. This 18th-century Druidism was closely linked to Freemasonry.

On Midsummer's Day in 1717 the Freemasonic Grand Lodge of London had been formed by a group of lodges meeting in the city's public houses – and the same week, in the same inns, they founded the Modern Order of Druids.

Of course any notion that the original Druids had anything to do with Stonehenge or indeed any of the megalithic sites, in any direct sense, is extremely unlikely. Over 1,000 years had passed between the building of the stone circles and the time of the Druids but the connection seemed tenable to the 18th-century historians and information about the Druids was available from Roman sources, such as the writings of Julius Caesar.

Alan and his wife Kate went to Stanton Drew and obtained some reasonably accurate measurements for the site, but nowhere could they find a circle at Stanton Drew with a circumference approaching 366 MY. The mission to this site had drawn a blank, but Stonehenge was a different matter – and now we were alerted to the possibility that our prediction of a 233/732 ratio might have indeed been employed as a near perfect pi calculator to deliver a circle of 366 equal parts.

In our attempts to find a stone circle conforming to the 366 pattern which we anticipated must surely have existed, we had looked at examples across the length and breadth of Britain. However, we had not looked at earlier Neolithic sites that did not contain any stones. Although Stonehenge would become the most famous stone circle in the world, it certainly did not start out that way, and within its earliest ground plan we hit upon everything we had been searching years to find – and, as it turned out, much more besides.

During the years of our common research it had not occurred to us to measure surviving sites that Thom had ignored. Thom had been initially looking for astronomical observatories. He assumed that the stones, sometimes moved many kilometres across the landscape, had been set into their eventual positions so that they performed some specific function. For example, when seen from the centre of a circle a particular stone might line up with a cleft in a distant hill where the Sun could be expected to break the horizon at the time of the summer solstice.

As a result, all of Thom's measurements dealt with the positions of stones, together with the circles and alignments of which they were a part. But it had not been within Alexander Thom's remit to measure any circle that had 'no' stones. Why should he have done so? Such a structure could not betray its astronomical significance and in the mind of Thom it probably didn't even have one.

It is a fact that across Britain there as many circles without stones as there are circles with them – in fact there are almost certainly many more such examples. A particular group of these have come to be known as 'henges'. This is actually a particularly inappropriate name because the word 'henge' comes from an Anglo-Saxon word that meant 'hanging' or which could alternatively describe a 'gibbet' where the hanging of miscreants took place. For example, the world's most famous stone circle, that of Stonehenge, actually means 'hanging stones'.

Good name or not, the word henge has come to be associated with usually circular mounds and ditches that are to be found almost everywhere in Great Britain. They range in size tremendously and doubtless the vast majority of them are lost beneath trees, farmland and buildings. Fortunately some do survive, and a few of these represent such magnificent examples of Stone Age engineering that it is a near miracle they are not much better known.

When we looked at recreations of Stonehenge during its various phases (between at least 3100 BC and 1500 BC) we could have kicked ourselves for not having noticed something that should have stood out like a sore thumb. As its name implies, Stonehenge was originally just a henge – a simple circular ditch and bank within which all the later stones were erected. When one isolates the henge from the later additions something becomes clear. It had a circumference of 366 MY! It had been right under our noses for years and we had failed to see it. This was one of those 'Eureka' moments that make our investigations so fascinating and occasionally exciting. In a moment it set us looking in a new and very productive direction.

It now became obvious that John Wood the architect had not based the dimensions of the King's Circus in Bath on just any circle and certainly not that of Stanton Drew, but rather that of the henge at Stonehenge, a site that he not only knew well but which he had personally measured in some detail. Whether he had simply 'copied' the measurements of Stonehenge or if he actually knew something about the Megalithic Yard was a moot point at the time but it would become far more important later.

The information about Stonehenge was very welcome, but one henge that conformed to the expected patterns we had predicted years before was not enough. We had to make our argument so watertight that nobody could argue.

Chapter 4

•

THE CIRCLES OF THE SKY

The Thornborough Henges

With the idea of henges firmly in his mind, Chris took a look at a major Neolithic site on Google Earth; the free-to-use internet program that provides seamless aerial photographs of the planet's surface – and in considerable detail in well-inhabited areas. The site he had chosen to study was a group of three well-preserved henges on the outskirts of the hamlet of Thornborough, near to the North Yorkshire town of Masham. We had both visited the site previously but had made no attempt to measure its dimensions. These three giant circles were made around 5,500 years ago by mounding up earth to a height of 6 or 7 m with openings roughly northwest and southeast. The three circles are joined by a causeway some 65 m (214 ft wide) that are over 1 mile in length. Whilst the banks around the circles have obviously broken down somewhat over the passing millennia, they remain in remarkably good condition and are still distinctly circular in appearance, although the sheer scale of the site makes it hard to discern the curve at ground level.

Now, Chris zoomed into the central henge and opened up the Google Earth measuring tool in this fantastic internet facility; he carefully gauged the inner centre-mound and external diameter of each ring by taking averages across several directions. The northern henge is now covered in trees and is less easy to measure accurately, but previous surveying has established that all the henges are the same size. Knowing that these henges had been once covered in white gypsum to produce glowing, jewel-like rings, Chris was particularly interested in their outer dimension. He put the resulting distance of 193 m into his calculator and divided by 0.82966 to convert it into Megalithic Yards and stared at the outcome – 233 MY.

This seemed too good to be true and Chris checked all measurements again, and yet again, to ensure this was a correct result. The conclusion was clear – whether by coincidence or design, all three of these henges were examples of the 233/732 circle we had predicted some three years earlier. An external diameter of 233 MY meant that the outer extremity was precisely twice 366 MY in length!

In our opinion, henges were created to observe star movements by providing an artificial horizon – a horizon that was level and at a known distance. And here was a powerful indication that the builders had used Thom's Megalithic Yard to construct henges that divided the horizon up into 366 equal parts – each 2 MY across.

This would have allowed an astronomer standing in the centre of one of any of these circles to view exactly one 366th section of the sky if they erected two posts 2 MY apart on the outer edge of the circle. Each gap then gives the viewer a guaranteed 1 Megalithic Degree horizontal section of the sky. Such posts would have needed to be tall to appear above the bank, but the builders could also segment the posts in an upward direction to provide perfect gaps of 1 Megalithic Degree.

These massive henges must have been the world's first high-performance astronomical observatories.

Further investigations of the dimensions at that stage were equally breathtaking, to say the least. From centre to centre of the northern henge to the central henge is 366 Megalithic Rods and the distance from the centre of the middle henge to the centre of the southern henge is 360 Megalithic Rods. We already knew that 366 and 360 are two numbers that work together within the system of megalithic geometry that we had identified several years earlier. There was no longer any doubt that Alexander Thom's Megalithic Yard and Rod are real. They are alive and well in North Yorkshire, ready to be inspected by any archaeologist whose head is not stuck in a bucket.

Chris noted one further dimension that stood out – but this had to be a coincidence ... didn't it? The three henges were offset slightly in a dogleg so the centre-to-centre distance between the centres of the northern and southern henges was just 1,500 m. Had the three henges been in a 'perfect' row this distance would have been 1,525 m.

Scientific Instruments

The type of henges found close to the present village of Thornborough are known as class IIA henges. This means that they have two opposed entrances within a single bank inside of which is a ditch (*see* figure 5). Each henge is so large it would be possible to fit the much more famous Stonehenge circle into each of them 20 times over.

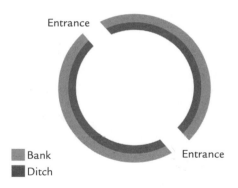

Figure 5. Type IIA henge

It was once thought that all circular earthworks on the British landscape that had banks and ditches were defensive structures, but such a notion was eventually dismissed when it was realized that the majority of true henges have the ditch, from which the banks were raised, on the inside of the circle. This would make absolutely no sense defensively because if one wished to keep people out of such an earthwork the ditch would clearly be on the outside of the bank. Such an arrangement would allow defenders to stand on the top of the bank hurling missiles and presumably insults on the attackers as they attempted to cross the ditch. With the ditch on the inside the attackers would have the advantage of elevation and the fortification would be useless.

Current archaeological thinking is that henges were places of worship for some unknown deity. In our opinion such a wild guess is as pointless as suggesting that they were some kind of sports ground for proto-cricket or tossing the caber. Had these massive henges been simply places of worship they could each have comfortably held a congregation of over 100,000 people – probably the entire population of northern England at the time!

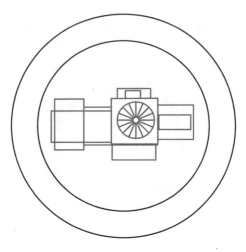

Thornborough central henge with St Paul's Cathedral, London, superimposed upon it, in order to give some impression of the physical dimensions of these structures.

Figure 6. Thornborough central henge

Although the Thornborough henges are not well known, even in Britain, they have been studied to some extent by archaeologists. It is known from objects discovered in the ditches and within the circles themselves that they date back to circa 3,500 BC, a period that is significantly older than any known stone circle. Of the three henges, the northernmost example is in the best condition – but that is because it is now heavily wooded and seems to have been this way for a very long period of time. The presence of the trees and shrubbery has prevented some of the erosion that has taken place in the case of the middle and southern henges. Unfortunately such dense undergrowth makes accurate measuring of the northernmost henge difficult. Meanwhile the middle henge is in fair condition, with some of its banks still reaching to 3 m or more, whilst the southernmost henge is much more weathered and is now not nearly as impressive as its companions.

According to archaeological data there had been a previous central henge with a diameter of 240 m – which gives a circumference of 366 Megalithic Rods. At some point soon after its creation this was removed in favour of the present henge with a circumference of 732 MY. (Remember, there are 2.5 Megalithic Yards to a Megalithic Rod.)

Here were three gigantic exercises in earthmoving that had been planned and dug before any stone circle was created in the British Isles. They had eluded Alexander Thom's relentless gaze because they contained no stones. To him they would probably mean little or nothing, but to us they were the first tangible proof that what we had been suggesting for nearly a decade was the absolute truth. We had spent years looking at the measurements of every stone circle we could find in order to see our theories regarding the number 366 borne out on the ground, and as it turned out the truth of the matter had been on our own doorstep all along.

With a renewed zeal we began to cast around Britain to see if any of the other known giant henges were also of Megalithic proportions. We found one almost immediately that was. It was in Northern Ireland and was known as the Giant's Ring. Unfortunately this particular henge might not stand as proof of our theories because archaeologists suggested it had been substantially altered across the many thousands of years of its existence. We knew there were a number of type IIA henges not far from Thornborough itself; though these interested us greatly and would come to be very important to us, many of them were badly eroded, so that although it was highly likely they had been the same size of the Thornborough henges we could not be specific.

It wasn't long before we discovered another type IIA giant henge, this time at some considerable distance from Yorkshire. It was located in a place called Dorchester-on-Thames in Oxfordshire – or at least it had been. We were stunned to discover that it had been destroyed some decades ago in the relentless extraction of gravel that was taking place in the area. Fortunately for us it had survived long enough to be fairly accurately measured and there isn't any doubt that it was exactly the same size as the henges at Thornborough.

Ultimately we turned our attention to that most famous of megalithic monuments – Stonehenge. True, Stonehenge is now famous for being a complex series of stone circles, but the site has a long history and before any stone had been raised there it had originally been nothing more than a henge. It differed from the henges at Thornborough and Dorchester in that it had its ditch on the outside of the bank and it was much smaller. But what made it so significant (and we could have kicked ourselves for not realizing the fact before) is that it had a circumference of 366 MY.

Suddenly, after being in the realms of theories and speculation for so long, we now had a wealth of hard-and-fast archaeological evidence that could not be dismissed. What made the whole situation even more exciting was that it was obvious that the builders of the Thornborough complex had first created one henge built on Megalithic proportions, only to replace it with another henge that also reflected Megalithic measures. In addition, because the slightly later henge had a circumference of 732 MY, it had a diameter of 233 MY. In our book *Civilization One* we had predicted that our megalithic ancestors would almost certainly have been drawn to such a size of circle because to them it must have seemed magical because it is very rare to find circles that have an even number of units for their diameters and also an even number of the same units for their circumference. The number 233 happens to be one of those infrequently occurring numbers that when put through the mill of pi comes out at the other end as an almost perfect 732. (In fact it comes out at 731.99.)

On a number of occasions we stood on the bank tops of the central henge at Thornborough, or within the trees and thickets of the northern henge, where the banks are still at their original height and in better condition. We constantly marvelled at the careful planning and then the scale of the work that went into creating these three gigantic masterpieces. This may not have included quarrying and moving large stones, as had been the case for the later circles, but the demands of the project had been just as great, and in fact much greater. Many thousands of tonnes of earth and gravel were dug from the landscape alongside the river Ure to create the henges, and what made the whole business even more incredible is that those who created them had changed their mind about the dimensions early on, and so had therefore gone through the whole procedure not once, but twice. What is more, archaeologists were sure that the banks of all the henges at Thornborough had once been covered with white gypsum, a stone that must have been visible from miles off when the Sun shone upon it.

The whole task would have been arduous enough using modern machinery but the people in question had no mechanical excavators, not even any metal for picks and shovels. Their picks were deer antlers and their shovels were the shoulder blades of cattle. Every part of the task they had chosen to undertake would have been tremendously complicated and time-consuming and it is generally accepted by archaeologists that the population of Britain at the time (3500 BC) was extremely small.

We know precious little about the lives of the late Stone Age people of Western Europe. Certainly by the time Thornborough was completed the population was composed, in the main, of farmers. Much of the dense forest that had once covered nearly all of Britain had, by this period, been felled. The climate was probably warmer then than it is now, and it may not have been all that difficult for people to cultivate the crops they needed to sustain themselves and their families, though even farming would have been extremely time-consuming. The late Stone Age farmers had only the most rudimentary of ploughs and, even if they enjoyed better summers and warmer winters that we presently do, they still had to cope with the vicissitudes of an island climate of the sort Britain has always enjoyed.

These people also kept livestock. This would include cattle and sheep, and they would have supplemented their home-produced meat with the odd wild animal, such as boar; with fish from the river and with wild birds and their eggs.

Overcrowding of the landscape doesn't seem to have been the problem in late Stone Age Britain that it would become by the Bronze Age. As a result, life was probably relatively peaceful, though here we are in the realms of conjecture because so little is known about a people who have left almost no tangible evidence of the times in which they lived. Almost everything they used was organic in nature, such as wood, plant fibres or leather, and in the damp climate of Britain, with its acid soils, little that is so perishable survives the ravages of time. Stone artefacts do exist, such as exquisitely crafted hand axes and flint implements of one sort or another, but they can throw little light on the thoughts, aspirations or religious imperatives of people so long ago.

Only a few scant burials and the ephemeral echoes of post holes where huts once stood offer evidence of the ordinary lives of people who, when we look at their achievements in the form of huge structures such as the henges, must have been complex and very capable. If the later Britain of the Iron Age can be used as a model for late Stone Age life, family groups probably formed a part of clans, which were ultimately components of a large tribal system. However it has to be admitted that this is speculation because although we have fairly good evidence for the Iron Age, thanks to the Roman invasions of Britain, we have no such testimonies for a period as early as 5,500 years ago.

One thing is certain; the people of Britain during this early period may not have been on the same level as we are in a technological sense, but they were certainly no less bright. What is more, their achievements on the landscape, especially at sites such as Thornborough, which was probably by no means unique, show that they had good organizational skills and sufficient free time to create structures that must have taken many years to complete.

We now had the evidence we so badly needed and we knew it would be difficult from this point on to dismiss Alexander Thom's rediscovery of megalithic measures out of hand. From our own point of view the giant henges of Yorkshire and other parts of the British Isles were so significant to our research that we simply had to understand how they had been created. We also needed to know why such a fantastic exercise in community effort obviously seemed necessary to an apparently simple farming community.

Our next task was to examine the henges more closely to find out why they are laid out as they are (including the dogleg), and try and understand what those using these sites could have achieved from using their remarkable observatories.

Chapter 5

·

GIANT HENGES AND THEIR USES

Degrees of Excellence

It would be fair to suggest that archaeologists have always found themselves in something of a quandary when it comes to explaining the purpose of the ancient henges dotted about the British landscape. There may once have been many hundreds or thousands of these structures and, if those that remain are anything to go by, they differed greatly in scale.

A small henge, of which there are still many examples, could quite reasonably be suggested as a simple 'meeting place' for a local community. Such a notion could easily make sense, and thus the henge might be seen as a very early form of the later 'thing' or 'ting'. This was the name given to an open-air meeting place used by the Scandinavian and Germanic peoples who came to occupy Britain at a much later date. It was in such locations that local laws were made, where justice was meted out and disputes were settled.

In the case of the Thornborough henges such a usage, as any primary purpose, can be ruled out immediately. The three Thornborough henges are so large that any local or even regional meeting that took place within any one of them would seem like the proverbial pea on a drum. It is worth pointing out once again that the measurement across each of the Thornborough henges is 233 MY, which is 193 m. Anyone who, like us, has stood at the centre of such a henge, immediately becomes aware that such an area can easily swallow a cathedral-sized building, which would make it far too big for any conceivable gathering of people.

It has also been suggested that the henges at Thornborough might have had a defensive role to play, but such a suggestion is, in our estimation, just as absurd as the concept of a meeting place. As we have already noted, the ditches at Thornborough were 'inside' the banks. Only a fool would build a castle in which the moat existed inside the castle walls. Even if this were not the case, defending such large structures with the manpower that was available to any community in the late Stone Age would have been impossible.

Maybe, some experts have asserted, the henges were places where domestic animals could be corralled and kept safe from wild animals and would-be rustlers at night? Once again such a suggestion cannot apply to Thornborough, mostly on the grounds of the physical dimensions of the henges. Nobody would go to all the effort expended at Thornborough to protect a few sheep or cattle when a much smaller enclosure would have served the purpose far better. It is highly likely that animals were allowed into the henges – if only to keep the vegetation within them short, but this was clearly not their primary function.

What we are left with is the understandable fallback position of something that simply cannot be explained in terms of a practical use – namely a place of religion and ritual.

In this suggestion we may be approaching something like the truth. The three henges are connected, and probably always were, by a wide 'avenue'. Such avenues are known to have existed elsewhere, for example at Stonehenge, and are thought to have been used at certain times of the year as processional routes from one part of a sacred landscape to another. Britain is also covered with long, usually straight, earthworks from early prehistory, known as 'cursuses'.

If the giant henges at Thornborough and elsewhere seem to have proportions that are far larger than would be necessary for any human purpose, perhaps that is because they were never meant to be 'human sized' but rather 'god sized'. It is also possible that they were so large on the landscape that it was thought by their creators that they were certain to be 'seen' by the gods, who were undoubtedly looking down on humanity from above. This theory is supported by the fact that the banks around the henges at Thornborough were once covered with a mineral called gypsum. This would have shone out brightly in sunlight or moonlight, though from the ground it would hardly have been discernible – especially as there is no high ground in the locality from which to view it. This massive undertaking in 'lighting up' the henges can surely only have been for the sake of the gods?

Of all the suggestions put forward by archaeologists to try and explain the existence and purpose of the Thornborough henges, only the ritual one makes any sense, though even this seemed to us to fall short of a total explanation for so much work.

So we asked ourselves, what were these henges for?

Given that they were planned using the Megalithic Yard and Rod, which are derived from timing the stars, it strongly suggested that astronomy must be of central importance. As we have said, the distance between the centres of the two outer henges is a curiously accurate 1,500 m, which we thought must be a coincidence. However, we were convinced that these structures were built for astronomical purposes, using astronomical techniques. So we wondered whether there was an astronomical factor in the layout – in terms of latitude and longitude.

The intelligence of the Neolithic people was no different than that of human beings today. Curious and thoughtful people could not help but notice how the heavens look different as one moves about from one geographical location to another. Any careful observer will quickly realize that the stars behave differently even over relatively small distances. As a person moves north or south, the point at which stars rise above the horizon changes. The further north one travels on the surface of Earth, the higher a given star will rise into the sky from the perspective of the observer. In addition, as a person moves east or west, the time of day of any stars rising changes. With accurate time-keeping (using a pendulum) it is possible to measure distance on the Earth's surface (*see* figure 7). For a full explanation of how pendulums were used to measure a multitude of different astronomical happenings *see* Appendix 4.

If a Neolithic sky-watcher understood the culmination rule, he could erect a pole at two different places and gauge the difference in terms of

Figure 7. A simple pendulum

Megalithic Degrees or seconds of arc. An archaeologist would quickly point out that because they 'could' have done something does not prove that they 'did', unless there are datable artefacts to support a claim. As these people did not have metals we are unlikely to find any tool that represents a modern sextant, but there are many ways to measure relative angles.

But, even without unearthing a prehistoric sextant we can be sure that these henge builders could measure latitude from the stars.

When we checked the difference in latitude between the centres of the outer henges we found there is exactly 4 Msec of arc (41 × 366 MY) between them.

This was astonishing! The accuracy of measurement is simply incredible, given that the Megalithic Second of arc is the smallest unit of geometric division apart from the Megalithic Yard itself, but the facts speak for themselves. Highly competent astronomers built these Neolithic structures. We were at a loss to understand how they could have measured such fine differences in latitude – but it seemed that somehow they did.

Next we pulled back to take in the bigger picture. Given the science that we could now see underpins the entire site of these gigantic structures we needed to consider why the people creating them had constructed a slightly bent alignment and built them with openings to each henge along an avenue pointing approximately northwest to southeast.

The first thing that is obvious is that the site is remarkably flat with only a very gentle slope from north to south. There are no large hills in the vicinity and so the view to all sides of the henges is unobstructed. There are hills in the distance, especially to the east, but when the banks were fully in place these would have been obscured. All heavenly bodies seen from the centre of any of the henges would rise from and fall back to the top of the banks, and there are no reference points on the horizon as are found at many stone circles. This is because from inside the henges there are no natural horizons to be seen, except through the deliberately engineered openings.

The location of the Thornborough henges is unusual in a British upland context because there are no hills of note for a staggering 127. 9 km (79.5 miles) to the southeast; the first being the 77 m-high hill upon which Lincoln Cathedral now stands. Strangely, the angle of the central and southern henges, their openings and the avenue, all point like a gun sight in the direction of the Lincoln mound. We could not think of any other location in the British Isles that delivers up such a long stretch of almost flat land. This seemed unlikely to be coincidence.

But what function could this virtual sightline serve? The curvature of the Earth makes it impossible to see such a distance but is there something significant about the location of Lincoln Cathedral? We were well aware that churches were often built on the ancient 'holy' sites from prehistory. Indeed, the tallest megalithic standing stone in Britain, with a height of 8 m and a circumference of 5 m, stands next to an old church in the village of Rudston, close to where Alan lives. The church and its graveyard were built inside Neolithic earthworks.

The distance between the centre of the southern Thornborough henge and the highest point at Lincoln is 127.13 km, which does not convert to

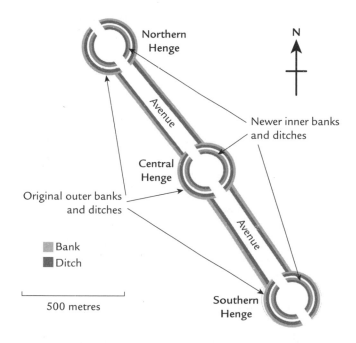

Figure 8. Thornborough henges circa 3500 BC

any apparently meaningful distance in megalithic units. It was obvious that these Neolithic people could never have measured such a distance across the ground, using ropes for example, because every rise and fall would completely distort the result – even if they found a way to measure across rivers they would end up with a meaningless figure. But it occurred to Chris that they could use astronomy very accurately to measure relative latitude – the distance between two points on the Earth's surface in terms of the north to south divide.

Using Google Earth, Chris carefully measured from the centre of the middle Thornborough henge to a point on the same latitude as the Lincoln mound, following the longitude of the henge centre to establish the north–south distance. The result was almost beyond belief.

The two places are exactly 1 Megalithic Degree of latitude apart – which means that they mark out 1/366th of the polar circumference of the Earth.

Simply stunning! This level of information changes everything we thought we knew about Thornborough – and about the extent of Neolithic scientific ability.

Out of curiosity Chris next projected the line in the opposite direction from the central henge through the northern henge, but here it crosses large hills and mountains. Nevertheless he continued the line across the Scottish mountains until it hit the Atlantic – very close to the Isle of Lewis.

Knowing that the beautifully preserved Megalithic stone circle of Callanish was on this northern island Chris measured the distance from the circle back down to Thornborough. The line from the Callanish circle to the centre of Thornborough is a rather meaningless 546,488 m, but when converted to Megalithic units it looks very interesting:

546,488 m = 658,689 MY

When divided by 366×360, to express the distance in Megalithic Degrees, the result is 5 Megalithic Degrees. A coincidence? We choose to make a decision based upon the evidence rather than on any preconceived ideas about intelligence or technical abilities of the inhabitants of the British Isles 5,500 years ago.

This prompted a question of whether or not the location of the Thornborough henges is geographically significant in any really fundamental way. A quick check revealed that these henges stand on a very significant latitude. To a very high degree of accuracy they are placed at a point that is 1/10th of the planet's circumference from the North Pole!

A Special Location

The group behind these henges must have made measurements up and down the length of the British Isles – and maybe further – before they discovered that the area now called Thornborough is very special indeed.

In addition to the henges and their flat sightlines we went on to discover yet more reasons why this location would have been meaningful for the architects concerned.

For the Neolithic peoples, Sirius, as the brightest star in the night sky, was almost certainly considered to be the chief object of the fixed heavens. It just so happens that Sirius was part of a very unusual relationship when viewed from the latitude of Thornborough. At the point in history that the Thornborough henges were built (circa 3500 BC), Sirius rose and set at the same point on the horizon as the Sun at the winter solstice (then 18 January) – this was almost exactly SE and SW. Such a happening must have created the impression that Sirius was linked in some way with the Sun when observed from Thornborough. At this location the Stone Age astronomers could witness the star apparently stopping the Sun's progress across the horizon from north to south. (At midwinter when viewed from the northern hemisphere the Sun rises as far south as it ever does. The days are short, the weather cold and nature effectively dead. If the Sun cannot be prevented from travelling even further south then surely death and destruction must be the result.) From Thornborough it appeared that the great star Sirius halted the Sun's southern progress and persuaded it to begin moving northwards again, towards summer and a time of plenty. To Stone Age farmers this must have seemed crucially important.

They would have realized that Sirius (like all stars) passed over their heads once per day and a total of 366 times per year. One can imagine that this would have prompted them to divide the circle of the day into 366 parts – which in another sense can be seen as 366 divisions (or degrees) of the sky. They could achieve this by creating a henge and dividing the circle of the banks into 366 parts. They would designate the divisions or degrees with thin poles pushed into the bank tops to mark out the width of one degree. With these in place the astronomer-priests could observe the movement of the stars across the horizon. To measure rising stars, such as Sirius, they would have made a frame – one-degree square as seen from the centre of the henge – and they would then have tilted it so that Sirius rose vertically in relation to the frame. In the case of Sirius this experiment was most probably done at the autumn equinox when Sirius was easiest to see.

Whilst we have been very critical of the general direction that archae-ology has taken over recent years, there is no doubt that a tremendous amount of good work has been done at a technical level – and occasion-ally on an inspirational level as well. One archaeologist has made a rather guarded suggestion that the existence of the Thornborough henges may have had something to do with astronomy. Dr Jan Harding from Newcastle University has put forward the idea that the dogleg layout of the henges may be present because the builders wanted to construct the henges in a formation that copied the three stars we know as Orion's Belt. And furthermore perhaps the nearby River Ouse was likened to the Milky Way.

When we first read this we thought it was a bit of a wild guess – poss-ibly secretly inspired by Robert Bauval's similar claim for the Giza pyramids. Whilst Bauval had a number of cultural as well as artefact-based reasons for his Orion claim in Egypt, there seemed to be nothing more than a similarity of shape at Thornborough. However, a check of the relative positions of the stars and the henges provided a near perfect fit (*see* figure 9).

Having found a raft of reasons to link these henges with the stars, we began to feel a great deal more sympathy with Harding's suggestion and we started to investigate possible usage of the site in connection to Orion's Belt and Sirius – to which this star group points.

The bank tops of the Thornborough henges formed an unchanging artificial horizon. When any planet or star appeared over a bank top it did so at exactly the same altitude as any other planet or star. This is not the normal state of affairs in an undulating landscape. (*See* figure 10.) As long as the bank tops are even, and also take account of the very slight slope upon which the henges were built, the scene is set for the most perfect form of naked-eye astronomical observatory possible.

One of the most important prerequisites for a successful series of experiments is to make sure that the circumstances under which they are carried out remain the same. This requirement was catered for perfectly by the giant henges of Thornborough and Dorchester-on-Thames. It is also clear that for experimental astronomy the use of stones, such as those to be found at Stonehenge and other circles, would be inefficient and

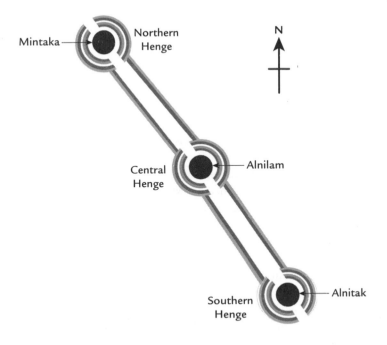

Figure 9. Thornborough henges with Orion's Belt superimposed

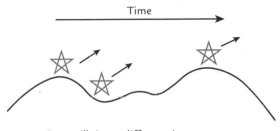

Stars will rise at different times across
an undulating horizon, making useful
experiments difficult or impossible.

Figure 10. Stars rising on an undulating horizon

totally inappropriate. Markers could be used at the super-henges and undoubtedly were, but these would have been wooden poles, dug into the soil just beyond the bank tops wherever they proved to be necessary. These could be 'tweaked' or removed altogether if necessary and placed somewhere completely different. It would have been relatively easy to move such poles around to wherever they were needed. Instructions from the centre of the henge, which was the 'eyepiece' of the naked-eye telescope, would allow helpers beyond the banks to do what was necessary to ensure that marker poles occupied 'exactly' the right spot.

Day after day, night after night, probably for centuries, specifically trained people would refine their knowledge of astronomy, maintain the ritual and agricultural calendars, and fix the date of special celebrations or events from their observations within the henges. So, what sort of observations could be undertaken utilizing the henges? The answer is – a multitude.

Observers within the henges could track the position of the rising Sun throughout the year, marking its northerly and southerly movement with the seasons. They could 'fix' the points of the Sun's extreme positions in the midsummer and midwinter by use of marker poles. We know from lunar calendars carved onto antlers and bones from a very early period that humanity has always been fascinated by the strange and difficult-to-assess behaviour of the Moon. The Moon could have been studied for decades from the henges. Observers would eventually realize that its movements, in a monthly sense, mirror those of the Sun in its yearly behaviour. They would also pick up on more complicated lunar rhythms, such as the 'Saros cycle'. The Saros cycle can be judged from lunar movement across a long period of time and is a combination of different types of lunar month that can be used to predict the occurrence of solar and lunar eclipses.

The observatories at Thornborough and at other henges could also be used to track the rising and setting points of both planets and stars. In the case of planets a better understanding of their sometimes tortuous movements would be gained, and absolute values for their periods could be established. Because planets are nearby objects that orbit the Sun, on more or less the same plane as the Earth, they appear to have highly complex movements. The stars are many light years, sometimes millions, further away than any planet and so they rise and set in the same place on the horizon for long periods of time – but not indefinitely.

There is a phenomenon all astronomers understand that is known as the precession of the equinoxes, and anyone using the giant henges as observatories across a long period of time could not have failed to notice its effect. Precession comes about as a result of secondary movements of the Earth. In addition to turning on its axis, and orbiting the Sun, the Earth has other, long-term movements. One of these is a tendency to behave somewhat like a child's spinning top, which in addition to spinning, also 'wobbles' on its axis (*see* figure 11). One whole wobble takes a very long period of time in human terms (approximately 26,000 years). From the point of view of an earthbound observer the effect would be that, very gradually, stars would change their rising and setting points on the horizon. Even a couple of human generations would see stars altering their rising and setting points by a full degree, and so long-term observation would betray the existence of precession to the astronomer henge builders.

This last example offers a perfect explanation for the henges being so large. We would judge the gradual movement of a rising star on the

The Earth does not simply spin on its axis (A).
It also spins about its poles like a top (B).

Figure 11. Earth precession of the equinoxes

horizon these days with advanced optical instruments. Telescopes make very small things look very big and, if they are fitted with crosshairs and measuring dials, they can be used to measure very small increments. The naked eye of a human being is far less sophisticated in terms of its ability to discriminate a small gap at a great distance. The best way to compensate for this inadequacy is to somehow 'make' the gap in question bigger. How can this be achieved? The answer is by looking out at the largest circle possible. In the case of naked-eye astronomy the true horizon is best, but it undulates and it is also sometimes difficult to see stars rising on the horizon because of atmospheric anomalies.

A very small henge might work reasonably well for some observational purposes but there would be a greater opportunity for error. If you wanted a really good scientifically accurate observatory you would want it to be very large, but not so big that you could not shout instructions from the centre. A perfect size would be the Thornborough trio. A series of straight poles driven into the earth just beyond the bank top would appear to be the finest of lines when seen from the centre of the henge. At night such a pole would not be seen at all, but what 'would' be seen would be the instant appearance of a star or planet that had just passed behind a first pole, which could then be timed until it appeared from behind a second pole placed 2 MY away in line with the star's trajectory. Using a pendulum for timing the star produces split-second results.

Most archaeologists, and even some experts in the field of astroarchaeology, which is the study of ancient astronomy, would accept that there are great limitations to what could be expected of naked-eye astronomy. In a sense this is true because of the nature of human vision when compared with accurate telescopes. But we have already shown in our book *Civilization One* that there is another factor involved that is often either forgotten or not fully understood. This is an ability to measure the passage of time accurately, without which any form of astronomy is bound to be extremely limited in its possibilities. The best telescope in the world would be virtually useless in an astronomical sense if it were not allied to an accurate clock.

The three super-henges at Thornborough did not stand alone in the Stone Age landscape of North Yorkshire. Other super-henges have been noted around them. Some of these have only been detected since the advent of aircraft because they have been so degraded by weathering and ploughing that they now represent little more than 'parch marks' in the landscape. There are in fact no less than six large henges altogether in this part of the world, and their presence in so small an area tends to add to the feeling that this area of Britain was considered in some way very special by those who laboured to dig the ditches and throw up the banks.

Dr Jan Harding is in no doubt that a religious imperative underlies the astronomical possibilities of the henges. We can accept that this may be true in part, but it must not obscure the excellence of the science involved. The study of astronomy, which is a purely scientific endeavour, is considered to be a recent innovation. Human beings all over the globe have been looking at the heavens for countless generations, but only around the 18th century did some investigators begin to abandon the notion of heavenly movements being associated with religion and fate. Before that time, and even today, for millions of people around the world, the patterns of stars to be seen in the sky and the complicated interplay formed by the Sun, Moon and the planets could be viewed as portents of future events. This is the study of astrology, and though modern astronomers get extremely agitated when the word astrology is mentioned, it is interesting to note that one of their greatest heroes, Sir Isaac Newton, spent far more of his life studying astrology than he did astronomy or physics.

To our ancient ancestors the sky, and especially the night sky, must have been a thing of wonder and, as we will discuss later, dread. Its significance is lost to us these days for a number of reasons but the greatest amongst these is light pollution. Most people in industrialized nations now live in an urban setting, surrounded by artificial lights of all kinds. This makes viewing the stars much more difficult. If any readers want to gain some appreciation of the way our ancient ancestors saw the night sky they will need to take themselves to some very isolated spot on a clear, crisp night, preferably when there is no Moon. The broad sweep of the Milky Way across the heavens, the panoply of stars and the apparent patterns created by the brightest and most magnificent of them all, form an awe-inspiring sight, even to those of us brought up to understand what planets and stars actually are. However, one star is brighter than all the others. This star is Sirius and it appears to have been of the most crucial importance to our species, both astronomically and astrologically, since the dawn of human awareness.

The presence of Sirius, as seen from Thornborough, might perhaps have represented one of the most compelling reasons for creating these massive structures.

The presence of Sirius each day at the southeastern portal of the henges gave us some of our most important clues as we went on to discover that the apparent association between the three henges of Thornborough and Orion's Belt was definitely no coincidence.

Chapter 6

·

SEARCHING FOR SIRIUS

Locating Sirius

There are literally millions of stars to be seen in the night sky, and tens of thousands that could be called bright and distinctive. No wonder then that our ancestors found it so easy to create imaginary pictures, the better to remember different parts of the sky. By the simple law of averages there are hundreds of instances in which three stars seem to stand in a row, as seen from a human perspective. We were well aware of this fact as we first read of usually conservative archaeologists making the suggestion that the three super-henges at Thornborough could be meant to represent the three stars of Orion's Belt, because even if the henges were meant to be stars at all, why this particular trio?

The stars that make up Orion's Belt are Delta Orionis, Zeta Orionis and Epsilon Orionis – better known as Mintaka, Alnitak and Alnilam. They are all extremely bright and are grouped away from other bright stars, which makes their line pattern all the more obvious. To the Greeks they represented the belt or girdle of the giant hunter Orion, whose constellation is one of the largest to be seen in the night sky. In the northern hemisphere it is best seen in the winter months.

As the Earth wobbles on its axis (precession) and as the galaxy slowly turns about its centre, the view of the stars as seen from the Earth gradually changes. These alterations are so small that they have barely impinged on humanity's view of the sky across millennia but, even despite this, Orion's Belt is one of the longest-lived parts of any constellation. It has been visible in its present pattern for the last 1.5 million years and is likely to remain that way for another 2 million years. All ancient cultures must have known Orion's Belt and many used it as a navigational aid.

What was it that convinced those who had looked closely at the Thornborough henges that they might have been intended to represent the three stars of Orion's Belt? As it turned out there were a number of reasons, not least of which was the unique shape of the pattern they form on the landscape.

Figure 9 (*see* page 61) shows the three Thornborough henges as they appear from the air. We had measured them very carefully, both from an aerial view using satellite technology, and on the ground with long measuring tapes. All our measurements were taken to and from the henge centres. We knew that the distance between the northern henge (henge A) and the centre henge (henge B) was slightly different to the distance between the centre henge (henge B) and the southern henge (henge C). The first distance was 366 Megalithic Rods and the second was 360 Megalithic Rods (a difference of something under 2 per cent). When we very carefully measured the distance between the three stars of Orion's Belt it seemed as though the relative gaps between Mintaka and Alnitak and Alnitak and Alnilam had about the same ratio as the distances between the henges.

We then used a photograph of Orion's Belt, much enlarged, which we placed proportionally over the aerial view of the henges. We did nothing to distort the image, merely manipulating its overall size until the three stars stood over the henges. The result can be seen in figure 9 (*see* page 61). Somewhat to our surprise, not only were the gaps between the stars almost identical to the gaps between the henges in a proportional sense, but the dogleg also seemed almost perfect.

As we were concluding the manuscript for this book we were discussing the problem of the apparent accuracy of the henges as a copy of Orion's Belt and the improbability of these ancient people being able to achieve such engineering precision. It was agreed that Alan should break off our writing schedule to give it one last check. His email to Chris the next day conveys his excitement:

I've just done something I've never done before. I took the actual stars of Orion's Belt (well at least a picture of them) and I blew it up massively in order to get the exact relative distances between them. I then drew lines on the art program from the middle of star A to the middle of star B, and from the middle of star B to the middle of Star C. I then blew up these lines proportionally until the longest of them (AB) measured 366 cm on the drawing program. When I did this I could see that the shorter of the lines (BC) was just a tiny bit under 360 cm.

I now carried out the same experiment with the henges, from a Google Earth image. This time I took the image into the drawing program and built circles around each of the henges so that I could tell 'exactly' where the centre was in each case (so there was no guess-work at all involved). I drew lines as I had done with the stars and then increased the lines proportionally until the longer line AB was 366 cm long on the drawing program. I then noted that the shorter line BC was exactly (not nearly, not very nearly but quite exactly) a tiny bit under 360 cm. Result. The Thornborough henges are not a good copy of Orion's Belt, they are not even a very good copy of Orion's Belt. They are an exact, absolutely, absolutely, absolutely exact copy of Orion's Belt.

I would say that this result is impossible, but I've done the whole thing three separate times and it works out the same every time.

There can be no doubt that these Stone Age astronomers where incredibly skilled – and no doubt that these henges are indeed a copy of Orion's Belt.

We have long been convinced about the Orion's Belt theory but we still wanted to know if there was more evidence to be found. This was forthcoming as a result of our previous experience in recreating the night sky as it had appeared thousands of years ago.

Using very accurate and powerful astronomical computer programs we are able to achieve something that only a few decades ago would have been either impossible or else extremely time consuming. In a moment we can look at exactly what our ancient ancestors saw when they viewed the night sky on any date, at any period right back to 4000 BC. It did not take us long to arrive at two major conclusions regarding the way the henges at Thornborough had been placed on the landscape.

The henges run from roughly northwest to southeast, and have their entrances aligned with the line of the henges themselves. In other words, it would have been possible to walk from the centre of henge A to the centre of henge C without having to climb over a bank top. As we have said, the alignment of the B and C henges pointed directly to the mount on which Lincoln Cathedral now stands, but there was more to this particular direction. The point where the Sun rose at its most southerly extreme, on the day of the winter solstice, in 3500 BC was also where Sirius rose ahead of it. As Sirius reached around 4° it stood over the centre of the avenue between the henges, like a guiding light – and a few hours later the Sun did the same thing.

If Orion's Belt is a famous group of stars, Sirius is even more famous. This is partly because it is the brightest star in our skies and has been so for as long as human beings have walked the Earth. The importance of Sirius in a mythological sense cannot be underestimated and it appears in the folktales, and even the religion, of almost all ancient civilizations. It was of the greatest relevance to the ancient Egyptians and to the people of Mesopotamia, and was doubtless just as important to the henge builders of ancient Britain.

If we look at figure 12 we can see how, in the night sky, a direct line taken across Orion's Belt to the south will lead to Sirius – indeed, Sirius has often been located using this technique – together with other parts of the night sky that were, historically, considered important for ritual reasons or for navigation.

So far so good, but the presence of both the midwinter Sun and rising Sirius immediately led us to realize something that had been puzzling for years; how did our ancient ancestors reconcile the differences between days marked out by the Sun and days as perceived by the stars – because they are distinctly different.

For most of us today, time is a simple matter of consulting a wristwatch or our diaries. The new day begins at midnight and the next year is simply when the clocks strike 12 at midnight on 31 December. In reality these are arbitrary approximations – albeit very useful ones.

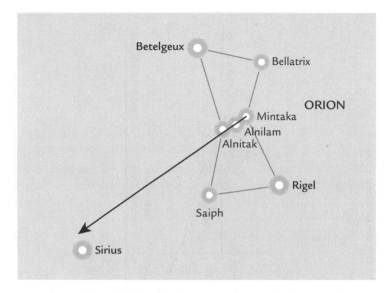

Figure 12. Orion's Belt lining up towards Sirius

Time recording is based on astronomical observation of the movements of the Earth, and is torturously complicated. Days actually vary in length slightly, but a mean solar day is taken as having 24 hours of 60 minutes, split again into 60 seconds – giving a total of 86,400 seconds to the day. However, if we watch any star such as Sirius, it will return to the same point in the sky in 86,164 seconds (236 less than the solar day). This is called a sidereal day. It occurs because the stars are actually stationary and their apparent movement is due to the Earth's rotation on its axis. The solar day is longer because it also takes into account the planet's movement around the Sun, which makes one turn of the Earth seem to take longer.

In one orbit of the Sun (a year), all those 236-seconds difference between the sidereal and mean solar days add up to exactly one extra day. So there are 365 sunrises in a year but 366 star rises.

It is clear that the Neolithic astronomers of Britain fully understood this difference. If we take the gap in any one of the Thornborough henges

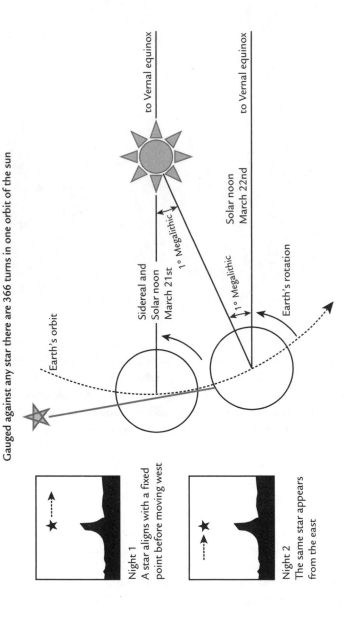

Gauged against any star there are 366 turns in one orbit of the sun

to Vernal equinox

to Vernal equinox

Solar noon
March 22nd

1° Megalithic

1° Megalithic

Sidereal and
Solar noon
March 21st

Earth's rotation

Earth's orbit

Night 1
A star aligns with a fixed
point before moving west

Night 2
The same star appears
from the east

Figure 13. The spin of the Earth

in the southeast and view it, day-by-day across a year, from the centre of the henge, this is what we would notice. For the Sun to rise to the same point over the gap in the henge on two successive occasions would take 365 days. Meanwhile the star Sirius would have risen 366 times before returning to the same point.

This apparently mysterious state of affairs would, no doubt, have fascinated these early astronomers and, in any case, their virtual obsession for the number 366 had shown us long ago that they were quite conversant with a year made up of sidereal days – which has no modern name but which we call a 'star year'. The importance of this realization cannot be understated, and once again the super-henges had served to confirm our predictions regarding the methods and knowledge of the ancient British astronomers.

A Sirius Henge

However, the presence of Sirius appearing in the southeastern gap at the winter solstice seemed to confirm that the three henges might well have been constructed as a faithful reproduction of Orion's Belt. After all, Orion's Belt in the sky points directly to Sirius and the three giant henges served the same purpose for earth-bound observers – which it had clearly been intended to do.

A rather tenuous possibility occurred to us almost immediately we had discovered the Sirius alignment with the henges. If those creating the super-henges had seen fit to reproduce Orion's Belt on the Earth, might they not have also recreated Sirius as well? We knew there were other super-henges in the locality, some of which we had already identified and measured, but was there one in the place where Sirius should be (relative to the Thornborough henges) if it had been translated to the ground?

With a little effort we answered the question to both our surprise and our delight. There was indeed a henge to be found directly in line with the southeastern entrances of the Thornborough henges. We had missed this particular henge before because it has been almost totally destroyed by many centuries of ploughing, though it can still be seen as parch marks in the soil when conditions are right. It seems to have once been a henge on the same proportions of those at Thornborough and it is near a place called 'Cana Barn'.

We measured the distance between the southern 'Orion's Belt' henge and the Cana Barn henge to see if there was an interesting integer in Megalithic Seconds of arc. We were temporally mystified to discover that the distance from the centre of Thornborough henge C to the centre of the Cana Barn henge was almost exactly 10,000 m – as close as it was possible to measure this gap was 10 km. At first we dismissed this as being a rather incredible coincidence, until we remembered that there was 1,500 m between the centres of the two outer Thornborough henges.

It was highly unlikely that two key dimensions could be in metres by random chance – yet how could these Stone Age henge builders have possibly used metres to lay out their henges?

It was very strange, but far from impossible because metres are far more ancient that most people believe.

Careful measurement of the distance between the third star in Orion's Belt (Alnilam) and Sirius, as they appear in the sky, gave us the probable distance on the ground between Thornborough henge C and a hypothetical Sirius henge. As best as we could estimate a scale on the ground, the distance between Thornborough C and a Sirius henge should have been a little over 11 km. The actual distance between Thornborough C and Cana Barn henge being 10,000 m suggested to us that its positioning was of ritual importance.

We also noticed on the sky maps that, although the stars of Orion's Belt point more or less in the direction of Sirius, the 'arrow' is not exactly in line. When we transposed both Orion's Belt and Sirius onto an aerial map of Thornborough and Cana Barn, we realized that, although the distance between Thornborough C and Cana Barn was not exactly proportionate with the stars, the offset alignment of the Cana Barn henge was in tune with the star pattern. In other words, there seemed no real doubt that Cana Barn super-henge was part of the same complex as Thornborough, and had been a definite – and quite startling – attempt to place Sirius on the landscape.

As we have already recounted, thanks to the intervention of Edmund Sixsmith we were able to visit the site of the Cana Barn henge. And it was here that our thoughts drifted towards the Giza Plateau. Could the ancient Egyptians have copied this Orion's Belt layout when they built the pyramids some 800 years after Thornborough? And could the Giza pyramids have a counterpart to Cana Barn henge?

Neolithic Science and Technology

Although archaeologists have suggested that the Thornborough henges could well be a representation of Orion's Belt, what they have not done is to make any suggestion as to how the arrangement came to be so incredibly accurate. In the night sky the three stars cover a distance roughly equivalent to a human fist held at arm's length. The slight difference in distance between Mintaka and Alnitak, as opposed to the gap between Alnitak and Alnilam is barely visible with the naked eye and, even if it were perceptible, how on earth could anyone using naked-eye astronomy get these relative gaps correct when recreating the stars on the ground at such a grand scale?

It appears that archaeologists have not considered *how* anyone with Stone Age technology could have mapped out such a huge, yet accurate, representation of Orion's Belt on the ground. Perhaps they imagine that the builders made an artist's impression of the star pattern and then scaled it up. Perhaps the astronomers looked up at the sky and then held up a big piece of slate with a scribe putting chalk marks to represent the stars.

The relative position of the outer two stars would be easy to mark out – because they could not be wrong. It is only the positioning of the middle star that matters, with its offset to one side and the slight off-centre gap between the outer stars. One can image the scene as the man with the chalk followed orders to place the third dot. 'Left a bit, down a bit. No not that much. Now right a little – yes that's it … I think.'

Having created a scale drawing that satisfied the astronomers as a good representation of the stars, they would then have to scale it up. Assuming they had a large piece of slate that allowed them to draw the outer two stars say, 1 m apart, they would have to scale it up 1,500 times to get the distance we find at Thornborough. Given that a metre representation would have to be split 504.132 mm and 495.868 mm to copy the stars –

it would be utterly impossible to get anything near an accurate result across 1.5 km of land.

However, we do know the method they used.

Using sight alone this simply is not tenable, and if anyone stops to think about the situation for a while they are surely going to arrive at the conclusion that either the Stone Age astronomers had access to accurate optical measuring devices, or that they used some other technology to achieve such stunning accuracy. The first of these suggestions is certainly not within the realms of what we know of the period, and it turns out that the answer to this puzzle once again confirms our previous suggestions about the use of pendulums.

As we have already said, these devices are the oldest machines known to mankind. We have experimented with many potential techniques, and we believe that these henges were specifically designed to incorporate as much 'magic' as possible – which meant building in all kinds of layers of astronomical values.

They must have taken a variety of data into account before they started. It is known that there were originally earthworks called cursuses (*see* page 79) on the site before they built the first henges that slightly pre-date the ones we see today. The cursuses were probably used to conduct the measuring of the heavens required for the task. As we have said, the outer star can be in any position they wanted and only the middle henge mattered. They therefore needed to understand the relative distance between the stars.

There were two separate ways this could have been achieved, and it is likely that those planning Thornborough used both methods to check and double-check their results. The first method would have found them not at Thornborough but at its companion henge in the south at Dorchester-on-Thames. Since the henge there is a single structure, it is likely that it was built before the more grandiose Thornborough array. Around 3500 BC we envisage that an astronomer-priest, holding a pendulum with a length of a half Megalithic Yard stood at the centre of the henge, looking to the east and waiting for Orion's Belt to start its climb over the bank top. When the first star appeared above the bank, at 3° to 4° altitude relative to the true horizon behind the banks, he or she would start the pendulum swinging. By the time the third star appeared the pendulum would have beat 1,452 times. Translating the pendulum string length to actual linear measurements would have produced 1,452 half Megalithic Yards, which when halved makes 726 full Megalithic Yards. So those carrying out the experiment must have suspected that according to the will of the gods the two outer henges had to be 726 'somethings' apart.[1]

There is a second and even more surprising method, and in this case the absolute position of the middle henge relative to its companion henges is included. To achieve this we believe they erected a long vertical pole on flat ground with an unobstructed horizon and then stood at a point a little way to the north of where the stars of Orion's Belt could be obscured by the pole when the stars were at their culmination (highest point) in the south.

The stars at this point are at the top of their arc and therefore briefly moving almost perfectly horizontally to the ground. They then waited for the instant that the first star of the trio to appear from behind the pole – and began the pendulum swinging. They counted the beats until the moment the second star emerged and then the third star appeared. The time taken for each swing would have been around 1.002 modern seconds, and the pendulum length would therefore have been as close to a modern metre as makes no difference

We did the experiment using astronomical software, which is obviously calibrated in minutes and seconds. Mintaka to Alnitak took 366 seconds and Alnitak to Alnilam took 360 seconds.

This result was immediately compelling.

We had no need to translate the findings into Megalithic Yard pendulum swings because the numbers were already perfect. We already knew that there are 366 Megalithic Rods between the first and second henge, and 360 Megalithic Rods between the second and third henge. Somehow the henge builders had translated a second of time in the sky to a Megalithic Rod on the ground. What is more 366 + 360 = 732, so the first method that had indicated 732 'somethings' between henge A and henge C was also correct.

We immediately suspected that we had found an explanation for the apparent use of the metre, as the second and the metre are two halves of the same thing. And they were both in use 4,500 years ago – so it is far from impossible that they might go back another 1,000 years to the building of Thornborough.

A Super-science from Deep Prehistory

The Sumerian civilization developed in the region around the Tigris and Euphrates rivers in what is now Iraq. Prehistoric peoples known as the Ubaidians had originally settled in the region, establishing settlements that gradually developed into the ancient city-states of Adab, Eridu, Isin, Kish, Kullab, Lagash, Larsa, Nippur, and Ur. As the region prospered, Semites from the Syrian and Arabian deserts moved in, both as peaceful immigrants and as raiders. Then, around 3250 BC, a new group called Sumerians arrived and began to intermarry with the native population. These small, dark-haired newcomers were intellectually and technologically highly sophisticated, and they spoke an agglutinative language that is unrelated to any other known language. No one knows where they came from.

As the Sumerians gained control, the country grew rich and powerful. They invented glass-working, the wheel, and writing; their language eventually became the language of the intellectual, just as Greek and Latin did at later dates. They also are credited with devising the second of time.

We have shown in our book *Civilization One* that the Sumerians had also been pendulum users. However, the Sumerians did not use the 366° geometry we find in Western Europe. Rather, they are credited with having invented the 360° with which we are familiar today. Because they were apparently divorced from the 366° system, neither did they use the Megalithic Yard or Rod. Instead they opted for a linear length that was equal to a pendulum beat for a tiny part of the day they did recognize – namely the second of time.

Using exactly the same astronomy-based method of observing the turning of the Earth, the Sumerians were able to keep the length of their 1-second pendulum accurate across their entire history. In their case, the length of such a pendulum was, to all intents and purposes, a metre long, being 99.88 cm – a unit they called the 'double-kush'.[2]

This unit was confirmed by the late Livio Stecchini, a distinguished professor of metrology, who has also argued that the double-kush had been used by the Sumerians to produce units of capacity and weight that were almost identical to the litre and kilogram. In his work 'A History of Measures', Stecchini concluded that all ancient measures are, by definition, related. He used numerical analysis of data to confirm the idea to his own satisfaction but his ideas are rejected by most academics today on the basis that his proof is not of the kind they prefer or even understand. Like Alexander Thom, Livio Stecchini had a first-class brain and he has made a major contribution to a better understanding of the past.

Although history credits the Sumerians with the creation of 360° system and with an advanced counting system, we have long doubted that they had actually been responsible for its origination.

The evidence of the apparent use of the metre and the second at Thornborough has strengthened our previous impression – namely, that these units predate the Sumerians. But we soon realized that there was a strong in-dication that the metre predated even the building of the henges at Thornborough.

Henges were a new innovation in around 3500 BC, and the structures that predated them were rather mysterious earthworks known as 'cursuses'. The term is believed to have been coined by William Stukely (1687–1765) and was based on the Latin for 'course' because Stukely, and others at the time, thought these earthworks had been Roman athletic courses. We now know that the cursuses of Britain predate the Romans by several thousands of years, and though the idea of them being anything to do with athletics is now redundant, the name stuck.

Most cursuses are parallel banks and ditches, forming generally, but not always, straight tracks. The smallest of the cursuses are only around 50 m in length but the largest ones, so far identified, stretch to 10 km. The width of each cursus also varies from a few metres up to 100 m. Archaeologists are aware that the cursuses were not simply roads or tracks because they have deliberately closed ends. Some of them may well have been used as a means of getting from one place to another, but they clearly also had some more important and most likely 'ritual' purpose. Nobody knows what cursuses were for.

Chris was reading an article about the Greater Stonehenge cursus, which planted an idea. It reported how a team from the University of Manchester, led by archaeologist Professor Julian Thomas, has dated the cursus as being contemporary with Thornborough and some 500 years older than the Stonehenge circle itself. They were able to pinpoint its age after discovering an antler pick used to dig the cursus. When the pick was carbon dated, the results pointed to an age between 3600 and 3300 BC – which caused something of a sensation among archaeologists.

Professor Thomas was reported as saying: 'The Stonehenge cursus is a 100-metre wide, mile-long area which runs about 500 metres north of Stonehenge.' Now, it could easily be that Professor Thomas was rounding up the dimensions for sake of easy communications or, just conceivably, he might be accurately reporting dimensions. Obviously he would not make anything of the round numbers in metres because he 'knows' that the Neolithic builders had no units of measure and, anyway, the metric system was invented by the French in the late 18th century, so any correspondence must be a meaningless coincidence.

But we have different information and, just maybe, there could be more to it than simple chance.

Chris went to his shelf of books on Neolithic archaeology and lifted down *Inscribed Across the Landscape – The Cursus Enigma* by Roy Loveday. This is an excellent book from a man who has spent several decades studying these curious earthworks. Skimming quickly through the pages he came to a couple of graphs that told an amazing story.

The first one showed the size variation of cursuses up to 800 m in length. The graph showed a hugely disproportionate number of cursuses with integer lengths in metres. The ones that were 100, 200, 300, 400 and 750-m lengths accounted for the majority of them. Of course Loveday could be rounding these up, but he had not done so for all of them. However, the next graph was even more telling.

This graph showed the distribution of both henges and cursuses by average monument width. Again, the cursuses show an overwhelmingly integer distribution of 20, 30, 40, 50, 60, 70 and 100-m widths. But, importantly, the henges do not follow any pattern in terms of metres. Of the 23 cursuses, 20 display these integer widths.

Roy Loveday would have no reason to round his dimensions up or down just for the cursuses and not for the henges. It looks as though the metre, or more precisely, the seconds-pendulum length of 99.55 cm was used as the standard measure before the henge builders began using the Megalithic Yard. Some of the cursuses are 6,000 years old, so the second and the metre are almost certainly extremely ancient indeed.

Where could the second/metre have come from? We had an impression that we were looking at something that was probably already ancient when these cursuses were constructed. It felt as though this was a reconstruction, not an origin. For a start, we know that light travels at 600,000,000 half-kush per second in a vacuum, and that the oldest known method of counting is the Sumerian system of using 60 and 10. So it seems highly likely, if somewhat surprising, that the originator of the metre and second knew about the speed of light.[3] This seemed crazy but we do not allow our preconceived ideas to block facts or blunt investigation. Later, we were to come across a scientist who has a potential answer to this vexing question. A completely stunning solution!

Yet we also knew that the apparently later megalithic system was also the result of a fantastic level of scientific awareness that is inconsistent with the apparent abilities of the Neolithic people of the British Isles. It was clearly based on knowledge of many special relationships involving the physical nature of the Earth – and even the Moon and the Sun. In addition, the 366 system indicates an awareness of other marvellous harmonies in both light and music.[4] And it even suggests a stunning scale of temperature where the freezing point of water is zero degrees, boiling point is 366 degrees and absolute zero (the lowest temperature in the universe) is exactly minus 1,000 degrees. All too neat to be an incredible series of coincidences.

We realized that we had accidentally tripped over something utterly remarkable – something that was far more important than the niceties of Neolithic archaeology. Our civil engineer friend, Edmund Sixsmith, has drawn together all of the powerful workings and correspondences that we have found within the 366 system. He calls them the 'Knight and Butler Symmetries'. But we have been far from the first to find evidence that contradicts the traditional view of the past. The 'chaos to order' theory that believes that the evolution of societies has been a fairly smooth upward curve from ignorance to excellence, is ridiculous and obviously wrong. The distant past is obviously far more complex than archaeology claims.

Thomas Jefferson carefully studied all known British measurements in the 18th century and concluded that they were the result of scientific knowledge from somewhere in deep antiquity. Like his colleague, Benjamin Franklin, Jefferson was a polymath, with a truly first-class brain, who took a macro view of his subject. Alexander Thom and Livio Stecchini were metrologists of the 20th century who were not frightened to investigate the facts on a macro level and cold-bloodedly report inconvenient facts.

Thanks to the aid of modern technology we have been able to put the fabulous work of these men into a context – and provide many new facts that amount to the evidence that standard archaeology claims is not there.

It is time for a rethink. Facts can only be ignored for so long.

Chapter 7

·

OVERTURNING OLD IDEAS

A Wall of Silence

We have been openly critical of archaeologists and the way that archae-ology is run – but we do have considerable respect for the good work that is done by so many people. At various stages of our separate and mutual researches we have made contact with many world-class scholars in the fields as varied as biblical studies, geology and astronomy. Most have been highly cooperative and some have become great personal friends. Archae-ology has proved much harder to penetrate.

We are aware that the whole topic of 'mysteries of the past' has always attracted some odd people and there are some rather weird theories flying around. Academics cannot take the time to assess every new idea that is put before them – but some theories can quickly be seen to have more merit than others. Neither of us set out to form a new paradigm of ancient history but we were taken to it by evidence that presented itself.

When were working on our first joint book we contacted the world's first professor of archaeoastronomy, now professor emeritus at the Uni-versity of Leicester. We received a reply that he had read and enjoyed one of Chris' previous books, *Uriel's Machine* which, with significant contri-butions from Alan, first introduced the idea of the pendulum origin of the Megalithic Yard. This was a great start but unfortunately that was the end of the short relationship. All future attempts at correspondence with this particular expert have failed to solicit any kind of response. We even wrote to him pointing out that his important position surely made it a duty to respond at some level – even if it was to disagree.

We wrote to Aubrey Burl, a much-published digger of megalithic sites who, before retiring, had been a principal lecturer in archaeology at Hull College of Higher Education in the East Riding of Yorkshire. We received a polite reply, which stated that he had never 'seen a Megalithic Yard' as if it were a simple matter of taking out a tape measure.

Having had a very positive response from a range of mathematicians, a leading astronomer and a number of engineers after *Civilization One* was published, we wondered about approaching someone who had a generic interest in science and was used to reviewing new and challenging ideas. As previously mentioned, we asked the British Association of Teachers of Mathematics to look at the evidence we had uncovered and received a very positive response. We then decided to contact Michael Shermer, the American who founded the Skeptic's Society, and is Editor in Chief of its magazine, *Skeptic*. Here was a man and an organization that specialized in challenging new ideas.

We sent a brief outline to Shermer and asked if he would like a copy of the book. The response came back quickly enough but it was rather strange. He sounded like a bored aristocrat, mentioning that he was rather enjoying sipping his fine tea on the lawn. The next thing we knew was a review of our book in *Skeptic* magazine.

Shermer had passed the copy of *Civilization One* to a junior freelance writer called Jason Colavito, a young man who, we believe, had become a born-again Christian before rather rapidly losing his newfound faith – causing him to be deeply resentful of all new ideas. The review was nothing short of witless and rather hysterical. He described the book and the ideas in it as follows:

> Superficial and often unreadable because of a dense number of math-ematical equations, the book commits the lust sin of popular literature: it is no fun to read. Crammed into just over 250 pages are so many unbelievable assertions and unproven speculations that it would take a book-sized rebuttal to do adequate justice to this triumph of numerology over science.

In other words, he had not been able to follow the basic sums (no equations except for technical appendices) and had found the subject matter too hard to get his head around. There were neither assertions nor unproven speculations in our book, as we had been especially careful to provide very solid evidence for everything we said. It was a pity that Colavito did not provide one single example of where we made unwarranted claims or where we had made an error.

Sad really – we are hungry for objective criticism and reasoned debate, but reviews of this variety achieve nothing but a diminished reputation for a publication that allows such poor journalism to exist within its pages.

In the summer of 2008 Chris was in northern Scotland in the company of Malcolm Sinclair, the Chief of the clan Sinclair and the Earl of Caithness. Malcolm has many henges and megalithic structures on his estates and he was very interested to hear about the work we were involved with. He suggested that we should make contact with Richard Bradley, a professor of ancient archaeology at Reading University, as he himself has a number of new ideas concerning henges. We duly prepared a briefing paper and sent it to Richard Bradley.

The reply was polite but less than encouraging. Professor Bradley pointed out some mistakes that Alexander Thom had made due to his inexact understanding of archaeology, but also gave the engineer some credit for opening up the subject. Bradley did not agree that Thom had been entirely ignored, saying that few archaeologists would now dismiss the idea of ancient metrology entirely. He confirmed that some re-analysis of the megalithic sites he had surveyed had vindicated a number of Thom's claims.

But he did feel unqualified to comment on the calculations that are the basis of our argument, saying:

> But you must appreciate that my grasp of the maths is rather tenuous, so I cannot comment on that aspect of your work.

We are very grateful for the response from Professor Bradley, and his admission that he is not especially numerical is fair enough – but if mathematics is a part of understanding the past, is it not time to extend the range of tools available to the discipline? Our challenge to find someone with the blend of skills necessary continues.

Highly Civil Engineers

Because our civil-engineer friend, Edmund Sixsmith, believes that the work of Alexander Thom has been unwisely ignored – and he considers that the 'Knight and Butler Symmetries' deserve recognition and serious examination, he has invested a goodly amount of time in trying to correspond with the anti-Thom experts and seeking well-placed allies to take them on.

He wrote to archaeoastronomer Clive Ruggles saying:

> I am writing a brief 'biographical sketch' article for the Royal Statistical Society magazine, which they plan to publish shortly, and I thought I should consult you in its preparation.
>
> The article aims to be factual and non-controversial. In about 1,500 words it will summarize the story of Thom's megalithic work, his 'findings' and the response they generated.

He received no response. A follow-up call to Ruggles' secretary confirmed that he had received the letter. We believe him to be a charming and extremely bright man and do not expect him to reply to unsolicited letters from the public, but Edmund felt this was a disappointing performance in the circumstances. It is clear that the professor would like everyone to regard the case as being closed.

Edmund found Aubrey Burl an excellent letter-writer and unfailingly courteous. One day he had a telephone conversation to follow up some queries about past Megalithic Yard research work. Burl was forthcoming about the work and believes that while regional yardsticks were used (a Perth Yard, a Boyne Yard, etc.) there was no single precise unit. He admired Thom's prodigious output of surveys but disagrees with his conclusions. Edmund was curious to find out how Burl dealt with statistics. Had he acquired statistical expertise himself? Or had he engaged a statistician to assist him in the work, and if so who? The answer was –

neither. Aubrey Burl had led the team and relied on his own measurement, arithmetic, logic and intellectual abilities.

The academic Thom debate seems to have ended in 1999 when Clive Ruggles banged the final nail in the coffin of the Megalithic Yard as an accurate unit. He concluded his judgement by saying 'for a thorough statistic critique the best source, once again, is Heggie'.[1]

Edmund's new step was to approach Douglas Heggie, who is professor of mathematical astronomy at Edinburgh University. This proved to be much more fruitful. Asked, by email, where he stood on the Megalithic Yard, the distinguished professor replied that his main approach had been to question the supposed accuracy of the Megalithic Yard rather than the concept itself, which he said survives in some rather elusive form. However, Professor Heggie was open about the fact that he did not consider himself to be expert in statistical analysis.

Edmund responded by saying that he had taken it that Heggie was the key expert and that he was a little surprised to hear his modesty about his statistical expertise. Heggie confirmed that there was nothing particularly expert about his discussion of the Megalithic Yard. What he had sought to do in his book, *Megalithic Science*, was to marshal the kinds of suspicions that any scientist would consider when faced with apparently strong statistical evidence for a new hypothesis.

Douglas Heggie has been totally honest and, of course, has acted entirely properly. But this does splendidly illustrate the way that the processes used within academia can create a situation where everyone cites everyone else in criticizing an unwanted theory. Follow the audit trail back far enough and there is some good quality debate but nothing that could be said to prove Thom wrong.

This is the root of the problem.

Aubrey Burl had once declined even to look at our findings on the basis that 'because we had started with an error (the Megalithic Yard) all our further work was nothing more than a compounded error'. If, as they say, all progress is due to the unreasonable man, then we could also observe that all progress can be halted by the man who believes that he knows too much to need mere evidence.

We cannot stress how incredibly difficult it is to gain an intellectual foothold with new ideas, even when they do not challenge any generally accepted facts. But what we have challenged – head on – is the veracity of certain embedded ideas of what the Neolithic peoples of northwestern Europe could and could not have achieved. To suggest that they understood complex matters such as the spherical nature and dimensions of the Earth, Moon and Sun is written off as wrong, without the tedious necessity of considering new evidence – especially when that evidence requires some new skills for many archaeologists.

Edmund is not easily put off his mission and he continued to try and find a way to bring our discovery of a beautifully integrated system of measurement from deep prehistory to the attention of an intelligent, numerate audience. As a next stage he sent a letter to *New Scientist* magazine. This excellent weekly publication had run a cover feature in its 31 January 2009 issue under the title 'Six mysteries of the solar system'. This prompted Edmund to write them a letter entitled 'Earth Symmetries and Mysterious Mnemonics'. The letter, shown below, introduced the magical 366 system in a way that let the concept stand by virtue of its own remarkable qualities.

Dear Sir,

Every schoolboy knows that the Earth goes round the Sun at 1/10,000 the speed of light.

There are six less-well-known mnemonics concerning Earth, Moon and Sun. The mnemonics depend on two integers M and N, and a unit of length L.

Earth's polar circumference is M^2N units
The Moon's polar circumference is 100 MN units
The Sun's circumference is 40,000 MN units

You could work out M very quickly. It is 366. (The ratio of the size of the Earth to the Moon is 366:100. Given that the Earth makes that number of sidereal spins in a year (to the nearest integer) you might think that is a nice number. Or days in a leap year.

N times the unit of length is not a very pretty number but if we – quite arbitrarily – take N as 360 it gives the unit of length as 2.722 ft.

Obviously 360 is a very friendly number formed by the first three primes $2 \times 2 \times 2 \times 3 \times 3 \times 5$

So far so good, but nothing very remarkable given the ratio of Earth, Moon and Sun is 366:100:40,000

One thing that is rather nice is that the unit of 2.722 ft is not just any old number. If you stick 2.722 ft into Google it will tell you it is a unit called the Megalithic Yard. It was 'discovered' 40 years ago by Prof. Alexander Thom. He was unaware that the Earth and Moon could be divided up so neatly (into 'pigs' like an orange) using his unit.

We have a set of mnemonics for someone who is capable of re-membering the number 2.722 feet, but this is nothing very scientific or spectacular.

The next three mnemonics are however a bit of a surprise to some people.

Every 10,000 days the Moon turns M times in relation to the stars.

If a temperature scale is defined with water's freezing point as zero and boiling point as M°, absolute zero is minus 1,000°.

The mass of the Earth is MN X 10^{20} imperial pounds.

Mighty odd.

Using data overleaf you can check these on a calculator. These three are each accurate to within much better than one part in a thousand.

It is all a bit weird.

New Scientist gets a thousand letters a week from all over the world, and publishes fewer than ten and they did not publish this one – it seems probable that no one got around to reading it carefully as it looks very odd at first.

However, Edmund had more success with *Significance* magazine, which is published on behalf the *Journal of the Royal Statistical Society.* Its circulation of 6,000 reaches those people in Britain who are most inter-ested in statistics and the analysis and interpretation of data. It seemed a good prospect for Edmund's campaign.

The editor of *Significance* sees a lot of fringe material and was initially sceptical. But when given a calculator and guided through the improbable properties of the Megalithic Yard, he said that he would 'have to think about it in his bath'. He did so, and a week later he agreed to publish something. At the time of writing he is trying to work out with Edmund how best to arrange and present the story of Thom and his Megalithic Yard and the neatly nailed-down coffin in which they rest.

What better group of readers to judge whether the Knight and Butler Symmetries deserve recognition? The Symmetries may not be explicable, they may be weird, but statisticians are well placed to judge if they are a series of freakish coincidences or an inconvenient fact. Call us optimists, but we think that Thom's work will eventually be rehabilitated – and our own work absorbed into accepted knowledge.

A Second Engineer

Chris, who is a regular reader of *New Scientist*, came across a particularly interesting letter to the publication reproduced in June 2008. The letter penned by James Russell of County Antrim in Northern Ireland referred to an article the previous month:

> You quote Colin Renfrew's 'sapient paradox' that while the human brain has changed little genetically in 60,000 years, behaviour changed suddenly 10,000 years ago. Renfrew will no doubt be basing his view of human behaviour on an archaeological doctrine that if no evidence exists on land, then none exists.
>
> I put it to him that it is no coincidence that 10,000 years ago is also when the last ice age ended and sea level underwent its last major change. Any evidence of structures, however substantial, built in northern Europe before then would have been scraped into the sea by the ice; and any less than 60 metres above the then sea level would now be under water. Had there been an interglacial Stonehenge, there would be no evidence of it now.
>
> An archaeologist in 10,000 years' time, examining a map of the UK above the present 60-metre contour, would conclude that we

had no major towns, no nuclear or thermal power stations, no long-span bridges, no parliament, no politicians … in fact, that we were hill farmers with a sideline in electricity from windmills. The paradox disappears if human behaviour did develop gradually over 60,000 years, but all evidence of this development is now erased.

Here was a kindred spirit. Here was someone who was using his common sense and was not afraid to challenge even archaeologists of quality and standing such as Colin Renfrew. Chris attempted to find out more about James Russell and see if he could make contact with him.

Chris found a man by the right name in the right location and sent an email to see if he was the author of the *New Scientist* letter. A reply came back straight away:

Dear Chris,

You've got the right James Russell, I am a civil engineer working in the piling business, so the Earth and its strata are of interest to me. I see the materials laid down over thousands of years every day and have to decide on its qualities as foundation material.

The letter in *New Scientist* was edited due to space limitations on their letters page, and may have come across more blunt than was intended. The missing paragraphs explained the logic of my argument.

'During the last ice age (10,000 yrs B.P.) human activity would have been on lands much nearer the equator. The British Isles and northern Europe were under ice and the sea level was 200 ft lower than today. Temperature falls by 3 degrees every 1,000 ft elevation, rainfall erodes mountains and rivers carry nutrients to river valleys and coastal areas. In coastal areas, river valleys and flood plains, crops thrive due to fertility, moisture and heat, wildlife prospers. Humans would have led easy lives near sea level, with good supplies of plant and animal food.

'Had civilizations developed during this glacial period they could not have been on what is now the British Isles due to the ice, they are bound to have been nearer the equator, and, as a consequence of the above argument, near the then sea level. Even today our major cities, most of our infrastructure and the lifeblood of our civilization – our electricity generating plants, are situated near sea level…' Hence the reference in the letter to the power plants and infrastructure.

The point of my letter was that Colin Renfrew had made the perfectly reasonable logical deduction that there is always a steady development process, and that this could also apply to the functioning of the human brain, and consequently the development of civilizations. My impression of the article was, he appeared to argue that the sudden appearance of cities and complex civilizations should have been preceded by examples of progressive development, which have not been found. He then proceeded to rubbish his own correct intuitive idea, by saying that there were no artefacts to support his hypothesis. My suggestion was, to consider that due to climate change the artefacts, perhaps as big as cities, could well be under the sea.

I am off to work now, but I leave you with the thought that archaeologists will find very few artefacts dating back more than 10,000 years until they put on their scuba gear. Even then, those artefacts will have been disturbed by wave action as the sea rose, or by trawler fishing, or buried by deposits on the ocean floor.

It turned out that Jim Russell is a chartered civil engineer who understands issues about the nature of the Earth's surface, having patents for piling equipment. Chris responded by explaining our area of interest, and adding that we have always found engineers to be intelligent (in the rich sense of the word) and open-minded. The email we received in reply was extremely encouraging:

Your observation that a civil engineer would be open to evidence and discussion I consider to be bang on target. Engineers in general are educated to observe the situation, process the information and propose the best idea, generally without a predetermined bias toward a solution.

I developed and patented a piling and a pile-testing system which the established contractors said would never work, and have had 25 very successful years doing subcontracts and testing piles for those same people.

I am certainly willing to converse on your subject. Perhaps a fresh mind with a different background may make an observation or suggest a different approach to your work which would be beneficial.

This was welcome news and the next part of Jim's email demonstrated that he was a free spirit, unbent by the niceties of scientific convention. He was asking all kinds of 'unreasonable' questions:

I watched part of a programme on the Greenland ice sheet cores a few nights ago, that, and the deep sea mud cores seem to be the only deposits which would span ice ages uninterrupted. Techniques for air analysis are remarkable. Would there be any telltale changes in air quality from human activity? In the mud samples is there any indication in the pollen count from agriculture or plant breeding or unexplained intercontinental transfer of human food crops? Has anybody looked?

All areas of the continental shelves below today's sea levels would have been in the tidal zone for some time as the sea gradually rose, and subject to wave destruction. Present-day sea defences built with modern materials are often destroyed in a few years by wave action. What chance is there of very ancient structures surviving? There may be a few places in the world where tectonic plate movements submerged civilizations in a short enough timeframe for the wave action not to have been totally destructive. A journalist by the name of Graham Hancock has been working in this area, and has some interesting observations. Once again, as he is not establishment his ideas are overlooked, I believe they need serious consideration.

Chris replied that Graham Hancock was a friend whose ideas were becoming more important to us as time went on. Having dinner with Graham many years ago Chris (as a scuba-diving instructor himself) had offered to train Graham prior to his underwater investigations of possible ruins off the coast of Japan and in the Indian Ocean. We will return to the subject of Graham Hancock's theories a little later in this book. We sent Jim a briefing of our key findings regarding the Megalithic Yard, pendulums and Neolithic astronomy. He replied that he had never heard of the Megalithic Yard, but it was clear that his engineer's brain was having no difficulty in understanding the issues involved.

> With any length of pendulum and any unit of measurement, a few bits of wood, a few lengths of string, a bit of patience and fairly good eyesight, a megalithic engineer could easily have approximated the circumference of the Earth. If I can demonstrate that it works, it moves your proposal of their knowledge of Earth circumference from 'impossible' to 'possible', it will then be up to you to take it through 'probable' and on to 'definite'.
>
> If I wanted to study the movement of the planets and stars without modern instruments I would need a fixed point from which to make measurements. I would need middle-distant reference points to check the star and planet movements against an artificial horizon. Ideally I would be within shouting distance of my assistant placing the reference points 360 (or 366) degrees around my reference point (right a bit, left a bit, SPOT ON).
>
> The points would be on a similar scale to the object star so I could detect tiny variations, maybe illuminated by candles placed in marks.
>
> Ideally my eye would be at the same level as the circle of reference points on the Artificial Horizon (A.H.) ...

Jim's intellectual identification of the need for an artificial horizon was very important indeed – because we had not told him about henges. And we have long argued that most, if not all henges were created as artificial horizons! Just like Alexander Thom, here we had an engineer who had sufficient empathy with this Neolithic problem to reconstruct the same solution some 5,500 years later. He even went on to describe the size and usage of the henge in human terms:

> It would function by me sitting at the centre and observing the stars and planets as they appeared above in the east and set below my A.H. in the west. I could mark the A.H. and record and variations. I could count the swings of my pendulum between the rising and

setting of known fixed stars and the wandering ones, and eventually plot and understand their movements across the sky.

Next Jim began to 'predict' the move from henges with wooden poles to stone or megalithic structures – exactly as it happened in prehistory.

A wooden structure might 'do me my day' but if observations were to continue beyond one or two lifetimes the wooden structure would move through shrinkage and rot and become useless as a reference point.

My descendants would have to think again, massive stone would be the only material to scaffold an A H which would look over the vegetation and be stable enough to observe down through the generations. My descendants would be confident many generations of observers could stand or sit at the centre with the fixed point really rigid on a stone tripod and the A.H. would be as rigid as possible. My wooden (easy to mark) A.H. could sit on the stone scaffold; if it rotted they could make a small copy segment and replace the A.H. reference ring only.

Jim has proved to be a very valuable asset to our enquiries because he has lots of knowledge about engineering but no preconceived ideas about archaeology. Most archaeologists are the product of university departments that take their students in straight from school, and then proceed to test them on their ability to absorb the standard world-view of the past. If you want a good degree it is essential to be able to recite accepted idea. Even postgraduate studies expect close conformity to standard protocols and incremental advancements based on accepted wisdom. The next email from Jim highlighted his fresh, logical thinking:

I cannot believe how close to a perfect basis for a sky-monitoring instrument Stonehenge would be. Any (TV) programmes I have seen involving it look at it from ground level as a place of worship. If I were living on UK mainland in the Neolithic period, and requiring an observatory, it would be located in the south to cover as much of the sky as possible. I would see that with a little timber modification I could superimpose a timber artificial horizon on the perimeter stones and indulge myself in a little stellar and lunar observation. The payoff would be, with eclipse prediction knowledge and the implied power over nature, I would wield enough power over the masses worshipping my chosen god down below to keep improving my scientific instrument and keep me in a style to which I would have become accustomed. (Using religion as a tool of submission is primitive compared to AK47s, famine and chemical weapons used in our modern developed civilization!)

Stonehenge fits my engineering requirements, but there may be other requirements such as visibility of the horizon, or local weather conditions 4,000 years ago, which may make the proposal inappropriate. Every option should be examined with an open mind.

Much of the thought process develops by association and discussion; if my suggestion is false, the idea may inspire someone else to offer a better one.

Perhaps I am covering old ground here, but I have never seen this solution to the function of the building before. Is this old material or is it something new?

This was music to our ears!

Of course, Jim is just another deluded engineer like Thom, as far as some archaeologists are concerned. But we believe that this 'back to basics' is appropriate for prehistoric periods such as the British Neolithic.

Jim then began to refine his thinking, as the complexities and possibilities occurred to him:

My ancient engineer would have realized after a couple of nights that the celestial sphere axis is spinning around the North Star, and that axis is tilted with respect to the horizon. A vertical pole in the north side would sweep the northern sky and allow measurements in that sector. My ancient henge could be modified in timber to achieve this.

Next Jim's thought processes caused him to ask a significant question:

Does ancient astronomy always seem to be based on Earth horizon events, or could it have been leaning towards what NASA spends millions on today; early warning of Earth impacts from anywhere in the sky? If an ancient civilization had been traumatized by an Earth impact when they had seen a short-term warning in the sky, it could have encouraged the building of an observatory.

Like us, Jim found it hard to believe that people have not understood the basic working of the Sun, Moon and Earth for a very long time indeed. The light pollution we have in our modern built environment prevents most of us from even noticing the sky at night, whereas Neolithic man would have been much more in tune with, and much more observant of, the natural environment than we are today.

Watching the way the Moon is illuminated, sometimes before the Sun goes down, makes it difficult not to see the Moon as a sphere lit up by the Sun. We have long suspected that the period when people thought the Earth was flat was a short-term regression when dumbed-down religion became more politically powerful than science. (Unfortunately we are seeing a mini-resurgence of superstition trying to overtake scientific reason in some quarters, particularly in parts of the United States.)

Jim came to the same conclusion, giving an example of how the effects might have been noticed with everyday objects such as a round ball of clay – such as we believe was used for pendulum weights.

He suggested that if Neolithic astronomers had placed such a ball of clay between their index finger and thumb, and then revolved it around at arm's length, as though to inspect its accuracy, they would have noticed certain things. During the day they would only see the ball, but at night with a single source of light, such as a campfire, they would see a miniature model of the Earth, Moon and Sun system, and the phases of the Moon in the shadows on the surface of the ball.

Spinning it around in the right plane they could even see the ball eclipse in the shadow of the head, and even the campfire eclipse behind the ball. This would also work if they had walked around an object like a fruit hanging on a tree. Is it too far-fetched, Jim asks, to imagine a Neolithic man 4,000 years ago with a clay ball or fruit in his hand doing exactly this, and noticing the similarity between the shadow on the stone and the shadows on the Moon, and the eclipses?

Jim was going through rather similar stages of thought as we had covered in our own questioning – but with an engineer's insight. He raised the possible use of water in henges, which is an idea that has fascinated Chris for some time for two reasons: First, because it provides a quick and foolproof way of identifying a perfect level (just as a spirit level does today); and secondly, because it provides a perfect mirror to reflect the stars, which would aid alignments over a short distance. But Jim, who knew nothing of the possible use of water in henges, went further. He emailed saying:

> Use of the natural profiles of the horizon places severe limitations on the accuracy of observations of horizon events. Vegetation growth on far-off horizons, or between the observer and the horizon, leads to inaccuracies. The significance of the use of water as a datum for establishment of a truly level plane of observation seems to have been overlooked in archaeology. In its simplest form, consider an observer (with good eyesight) on a platform in the middle of a small lake, with a pole at eyelevel. Consider a series of poles set in a circle, with horizontals set between the pole tops, say, 6 metres away (further means more accuracy) and exactly the same distance above the water. Lining up, by eye, the centre pole and the top of the outer poles produces a horizontal-plane-of-sight instrument, comparable in accuracy with optical levels used on building sites today. Sightings could be made far beyond the perimeter of the circle, even to the stars. The same instrument made from water and wood, used after dark, could monitor 'artificial horizon' events with great accuracy by marking the perimeter rail. Replace the lake with an artificial lake in a trench on dry land, stick a few poles in the trench, and you have the makings of a henge. The centre pole could be set later by sighting across the perimeter without water anywhere near the middle.

However, Jim was not quite right, insofar that a small number of archaeologists have identified water as being present in some, if not most, henges. But because they have not thought of henges as astronomical instruments they have missed the importance of this feature entirely.

Jan Harding, the henge expert from Newcastle University who has done so much good work at Thornborough, has said:

> Henges are generally located in low-lying positions, on the floor of natural bowls or valleys, and many are sited in close proximity to water ... There are also instances where henge ditches may have contained water for long periods over the year.[2]

Colin Richards of the University of Manchester, who specializes in Neolithic archaeology, architecture and monumentality, and ethno-archaeology, has suggested that archaeologists have misconceived the visual appearance of henge monuments – most particularly the probability that the enclosure ditches involved with henges were created as receptacles for water.[3]

But both Harding and Richards attribute the water to the religious or spiritual needs of the henge builders – some part of the notion that these were very unsophisticated people who built superb structures to carry out religious practices of some unspecified variety. Richards says that he wishes to focus attention on the importance of the 'social constitution of nature and landscape'.

The problem is that there are no written records to confirm what these structures were used for, and it is like trying to complete a complex jigsaw puzzle with a handful of pieces.

A Comet Warning Station

Having identified a need for still, standing water, Jim's journey of discovery moved on to another aspect of henges that had long interested us. He said:

> Taking flying lessons years ago, I remember the subject of 'lookout for traffic' on collision course was important. I remember being told that if approaching traffic appears to stay in the same spot in the windscreen, then that traffic will come through the windscreen at that spot! If it apparently moves away from that spot then you are not on collision course.

Could the same be said for an approaching comet? Would it be the case that an object passing across the sky is definitely not on collision course, but one getting bigger and staying in the same spot, relative to other stars, is on collision course? If so, it would be a very simple test requiring only an artificial horizon to mark the spot and a pendulum to measure the time from the rising of a known fixed star.

This is a key point from a geologically orientated engineer. As already mentioned, in 1997 Chris had been led to investigate a cometary impact that may have caused a global flood, by evidence supplied to him by leading Cambridge geologist Jack Miller. This had resulted in the publication of *Uriel's Machine* in 1999, which argued that a massive tsunami caused by a seven-part comet impact had indeed devastated the planet around 9,000 years ago.[4] Memory of this event is recorded in virtually every culture of the world and an increasing number of geologists are now of a similar opinion.

In his book, Chris recreated a machine described in the Book of Enoch, arguably the oldest written story in the world. A figure described as an 'angel' (not necessarily an otherworldly description at that time) and by the name of Uriel – meaning 'flame of God' in early Hebrew – dictates instructions to Enoch for the building of a machine. When reconstructed this machine turns out to be a circle of wooden posts carefully aligned using the sine wave of a pendulum to mark the horizon movements of the Sun. One of the principal benefits of this device is its ability to indicate whether or not a distant comet is on a trajectory that will lead to an impact with the Earth. If it sustains such a trajectory, the user knows to set off to the Alps, the Rocky Mountains, or any other substantially high ground if they do not want to be wiped off the face of the planet by a giant tsunami.

Jim Russell had again intuitively identified a genuine usage for ancient astronomy. Chris sent him a copy of *Uriel's Machine* and, after carefully reading it, Jim said that Chris' deciphering of the Book of Enoch was a logical interpretation of what had been to him a total mystery.

Using Henges

Jim Russell is a busy man, but he has created a considerable amount of time to conduct a range of practical experiments to establish just how much could be achieved with Neolithic technology if one had some basic astronomical awareness. Appendix 6 was written by Jim as an account of his approach and the results of his astonishing experiments.

Jim has suggested two methods to estimate the Earth's circumference – a horizontal method and a vertical method. He points out that the horizontal method should be much more accurate than the vertical method as the sighting distances can be further apart. But, the horizontal method can only be carried out with clear skies at dawn at equinox, whereas the vertical method can be done on any suitable day in the year. Both methods work with either the stars or the Sun to calculate the Earth's circumference at the observation latitude.

The apparatus Jim has constructed, as proof of concept, is very large but still relatively small scale compared to that which would have existed in Neolithic times. The apparatus 5,500 years ago could have been many times larger and hence more accurate.

On 21 March 2009, as proof of concept, Jim took the 'away' vertical sight rail 30 miles from home on a lorry, set up in 30 minutes, took the readings in 3 minutes and brought the sight rail back to the yard the same evening. The result of this short experiment was a value for Earth circumference of 25,802 miles. Jim realized that the error of about 3 per cent in this result was due to the effect of the wind on the unprotected plumb line on the wooden pole. Perfect weather (good visibility and no wind whatsoever) is critical to the experiments. With minor equipment modifications, Jim is confident that larger vertical equipment or the horizontal method would better the ±50 miles accuracy. In the conclusion of his report Jim observes that, considering that six months ago no one had even proposed a Neolithic method of determining Earth circumference, his experiment must be considered a remarkable success.

Jim considers he has demonstrated that Neolithic astronomers could have experimentally determined the diameter of the Earth, and could have produced more accurate results than he has, using full-scale equipment.

Some may say that, just because Neolithic peoples could have done this does not mean that they did. Some would deny the relevance of the experiments because there are no remains of any such equipment. But whilst wood rots, the outcomes of these measurements do not. As Jim Russell has said: 'The only evidence of the use of either method would be the results.' And the results are there in abundance for those willing to open their eyes.

Chapter 8

·

SQUARING THE CIRCLE

Chain of Fire

It is many years since we discovered that Alexander Thom's Megalithic Yard was at the heart of a stunningly comprehensive 366-degree system, quickly recreatable by anyone through the use of a pendulum. Over time we have found more and more extraordinary attributes for a unit of measure that Thom found, but did not understand. The chances that this was a unit derived through error or inaccuracy, are effectively zero. Any statistical technique applied to the stream of features displayed by this oddball unit of 2.722 ft or 82.966 cm, would make it downright perverse to assert that they were not connected.

In short, Thom's Megalithic Yard is real.

One of the first, and most intriguing features of the Megalithic Yard is its geodetic properties – the fact that a second of polar arc in the 366-system is exactly 366 MY long on the ground. An immediate consequence of discovering this fact was an acceptance that Neolithic astronomer-surveyors must have understood the circumference of the Earth to an exactitude that is still unsurpassed. The experimental work conducted by engineer Jim Russell has shown how they could have achieved that feat and the existence of major artefacts demonstrates that they did indeed do it. For Thornborough to have been placed at 1/10th of the planet's circumference from the North Pole is an unlikely accident, but when one realizes that the north and south henges are latitudinally exactly four seconds of arc (4 × 366 MY), centre to centre, coincidence surely disappears as a rational option for any scientifically minded person.[1]

In circa 3500 BC, when Thornborough was built, Sirius rose at the same point as the Sun at the winter solstice – but only at that precise latitude. The astronomer-priests that planned Thornborough also had the benefit of a star (Alphard) rising exactly in the east and setting in the west. Alphard would only have achieved this wonderfully helpful trick perfectly for 100 years or so – and no visible star does this today. It must have greatly aided the henge builders' understanding of astronomy for, whilst Alphard was the only star to rise and set at the same point at every latitude in the British Isles, they would have noticed how the highest part of its path across the sky changed over even quite small distances. The further south they went the higher its culmination, and northwards it got lower.

We have identified that the henge builders knew how to measure latitude (position north and south between the poles) by observing the differences in angle of any star at its culmination. However, establishing longitude is a great deal more complex – the main reason being that there are no obvious starting and finishing points. Whilst the north and south of the Earth obviously culminate at the poles – the points of the axis – the east–west direction is endless.

This absence of a natural break point has been solved artificially by creating a primary meridian at Greenwich (near London) and an International Date Line on the opposite side of the world. These are, of course, just a convention created by the rulers of the once mighty British Empire. Other countries, including France and the United States of America, have attempted but failed to establish their own meridians.

So how could the Neolithic people understand the relative position of different sites in terms of longitude (east-westness)? The answer came from Jim Russell when he put himself in their shoes. When considering how they understood the Earth's circumference he proposed that they could have used signal fires to measure the difference in rising times of stars as they came over the eastern horizon. This made Chris think about the possible Lincoln connection – the high ground some 127 km away that the Thornborough avenues point towards like a rifle sight. He called Alan to discuss an interesting theory:

'I think we might have a solution to how the henge builders could measure relative longitude as well latitude and it's all to do with Lincoln and Thornborough. We know the two locations are exactly one Megalithic Degree of latitude apart and Jim Russell has come up with a technique that could answer how they measured the relative longitude. He has suggested that straight east–west points could have rapid communication to time a star's different rising time – but I have noticed how this should work at any angle.

'Remember Alphard,' said Chris 'Back then it rose and set east–west at every point that these people could view it – no matter what their latitude or longitude.'

'But only for a hundred years or so,' Alan replied.

'Quite long enough to lay out a grid system across these islands if they had wanted to,' replied Chris. 'Imagine the scenario. The master astronomer from Thornborough sends out a team to the Lincoln hill, which they knew was exactly 1 degree south. They then build a pile of dry timber ready for a bonfire at Thornborough and at Lincoln – and at say 5-km intervals in between. Each timber pile is screened with two sets of sewn animal skins – one covering the view to the north and the other to the south.'

Alan was busy drawing the proposed set-up on his pad. Meanwhile, Chris continued.

'The Lincoln team are armed with a pendulum to measure time – either in Megalithic Seconds or, more likely, modern seconds. Whilst the team at Lincoln are 127 km away as the crow flies, they are further east by about 66 km in terms of longitude from Thornborough. That means they will see Alphard first by several minutes.'

'Yes,' Alan replied. 'Just give me a moment …'

The Skype call went quiet briefly whilst Alan performed a quick calculation on his astronomical software. 'Nearly there!' he said and then there was another pause. 'Chris,' said Alan after a moment, 'it's exactly 4 minutes – and I mean 4 minutes, not 3 minutes 59 seconds or 4 minutes 1 second – exactly 4 minutes!'

An almost frantic conversation followed as we discussed the implications. The significance of 4 minutes was not lost on either of us. In a mean solar day, 4 minutes is the amount of time it takes the Earth to turn on its axis by 1 modern degree of arc.

The southern Thornborough henge and the Lincoln mount are precisely one Megalithic Degree apart north to south, and one modern degree east to west!

For years we had held on to a common hunch that the Megalithic 366-degree system of geometry and the 360-degree geometry we use today had once been used in tandem – and here was a confirmation of the fact. It looked almost certain that the Megalithic 366 system had been used to measure longitude and the 360 system to measure latitude.

We were stunned. Not many readers will immediately grasp the sheer magnitude of this result. This finding has massive implications and it delivers a *coup de grace* to the archaeological establishment who are doing their best to ignore the existence of Neolithic metrology. For the Thornborough henges to point at the Lincoln mount across the flattest 127 km in the UK and then to find that the two are exactly 1 Megalithic Degree (366 × 60 × 6 MY) apart by latitude and 1 modern degree apart by longitude is beyond any conceivable chance of coincidence.

We had long discussed the thought that the Megalithic Yard and its associated 366-degree system represented the night (stellar based), and the metre/second and 360-degree system was of the day (solar based). Here was a first indication, a powerful indication that we were right.

Everywhere we look we are blessed (or maybe sometimes cursed) by major new discoveries, all of which deserve someone embarking on a doctorate to concentrate on them specifically. In a conversation lasting, so far, less than a couple of minutes, we had identified another.

Of course only Alphard would provide the henge builders with the ultimate tool they needed because of its east/west behaviour for that short period of time.

This important discovery had, quite naturally, hijacked the conversation, but after an hour or so Chris returned to his original thoughts about how these amazing Neolithic astronomers had achieved such accuracy. 'How they did all this is really clever,' said Chris. 'Using a fire arrangement, such as Jim has suggested, the process almost certainly worked like this: Shortly before Alphard was due to rise, everyone in the chain stokes up their masked fires. Being further east, the team at Lincoln see Alphard rise first and they then immediately drop their screen facing north – and at the same they time start a pendulum swinging and count the beats. As the next team along the line see the light of the Lincoln fire they drop their northern screen, and so on along the chain until the relayed signal reaches Thornborough. The Thornborough team immediately drop the screen facing back towards Lincoln.'

Alan could see what was coming. 'Wow – I see where you're heading.'

'Yes, as Jim has suggested – the message goes back along the line as each station drops their opposite screen for a few seconds. Once the signal is received at Lincoln they note how many beats have passed at that point. But they still keep the pendulum going.' Alan's drawing was getting quite busy on his notepad.

Chris continued. 'The split-second that the Thornborough team see Alphard rise they send a second flash from their beacon fire. When this is relayed to Lincoln the team there stop counting. Now for the really clever bit that Jim came up with. The two teams are 127 km away from each other – how quickly do you think they could compare notes on their timings of Alphard rising, and how accurate in terms of pendulum beats do you think they could be in measuring the difference?'

Alan paused before answering. 'I was going to say that the Lincoln team would have to send a person back to Thornborough with their information but they must have been able to use the fire signals in some way to communicate. And somehow, as we have just found out, they were spot-on accurate.'

'You're right. They were accurate to within a single beat and the entire communication took seconds not hours or even days.'

'What?' said Alan. 'That speed is incredible!'

'It certainly is. I doubt we could improve on it today using mobile phones. The trick was that they had designed into their experiment a brilliant correction method to compensate for the inevitable time delay in signalling. When the first signal came back from Thornborough to confirm receipt of the original signal from Lincoln, the team noted how long it took – say 22 beats, i.e. 22 seconds. They then halved that to 11 seconds as the known time it took for the message to transmit one-way between the two locations.'

'So, hold on there a moment,' said Alan, as he made some further calculations. 'When the team at Lincoln see the second signal flash …' He paused briefly '… they would have counted 251 beats since they first saw Alphard then deduct the 11 beats taken by the signal fires and they know they are 240 seconds east of Thornborough. And because they knew that Alphard is visible in winter for half of the Earth's turn they could quickly calculate the precise distance east.'

'We cannot know for sure that they actually did it this way,' Chris admitted. 'But given that there now can be no doubt that they did measure the Earth and understood the concepts of latitude and longitude, they must have used a technique like this.'

'One other thought,' said Alan. 'The team at Lincoln could also have informed the Thornborough lot about the result of the experiment pretty quickly by using the fire transmission method – long fire exposures to indicate minutes and short flashes for the seconds. But we now know that they only needed four long flashes – if they used minutes of time like we do today, which seems highly likely. It looks like the Sumerians must have learned of these units from the people of Britain.'

What we could see was a culture that understood a great deal about how the heavens worked – the stars, the Moon, the Sun, the Earth and probably the planets. Most importantly, they clearly understood how to map the heavens down onto the Earth – with stunning accuracy. They had produced a perfect and gigantic copy of the stars of Orion's Belt and their apparent version of Sirius 10,000 m away. And that had apparently been planned at another henge hundreds of kilometres away in Oxfordshire.

Who were these people? All of the evidence points to an integrated powerbase; an astronomer-priesthood who planned structures across thousands of square miles and many centuries. The standard archaeological establishment idea that henges were locally conceived places of worship to unknown deities is dead in the water. These people were, first and foremost, astronomers; their understanding of the heavens may well have had a theological component, but giant circles on the face of the Earth were scientific instruments, not proto-churches!

We wonder what archaeologists of the distant future will make of the huge underground structures at CERN, which is the world's largest particle physics laboratory. The Large Hadron Collider is a 27 km-circumference circular tunnel buried 100 m beneath the Franco-Swiss border. Stripped of its hardware the empty structure could be anything – so it must be a tomb or a place of worship for underworld deities?

In actual fact this rather plain circular structure is a super-scientific instrument serviced by 2,600 locally-based people for the benefit of 7,931 scientists from 580 universities across 80 countries. Amongst the many achievements made at this circular hole is an invention made by Sir Tim Burners-Lee – the internet. And current research is designed to facilitate time travel; albeit only for subatomic particles.

The CERN analogy with Thornborough and other henges across Britain may not be as far-fetched as one might imagine. Could both have been created for the benefit of international scientists? Were the henge creators from the British Isles, or could they have been a broad-based group that came from elsewhere to take advantage of the various astronomical benefits delivered by the latitudes of northwestern Europe?

At this stage, at least, we do not know. All we can say for certain is that they used units, namely metres and seconds, as well as Megalithic Yards. The evidence, such as it is, paints a picture of a people who could use this technology, but we struggle to believe that they created it. It is simply too advanced.

Having extracted as much as we can out of the structures in the British Isles for the time being, we moved on. Our attention now turned to that other supposed model of Orion's Belt far away on the sands of Giza.

The Giza Connection

In our own personal libraries we both have a book that dates back to 1994. It is the work we discussed in Chapter 1, namely *The Orion Mystery*, written by Robert Bauval and Adrian Gilbert. They describe how they came to conclude that the three pyramids of Giza were a copy of Orion's

Belt. The notion seemed quite reasonable, but neither of us was either a supporter or a detractor. If we had been asked to express a view at the time we would have been a little sceptical, but fully supportive of the need to investigate the idea further. Certainly, the argument had merit, and the objections of some opponents were less than impressive.

In early 2008, the Giza pyramids and their layout suddenly flashed up mid-screen on our radar. Once we realized that the henges at Thornborough really were created as a representation of Orion's Belt, the work of Bauval and Gilbert gained a new meaning for us.

It was not a complete surprise as we had established an apparently inexplicable link between megalithic Britain and ancient Egypt several years earlier. In our first book together, *Civilization One*, we had found that the two major units of length, the royal cubit and the *remen*, seemed to come from the pendulum-derived Megalithic Yard.

We had discovered that a circle with a circumference of one Megalithic Yard had a diameter of one royal cubit. And the *remen* was the hypotenuse of a square around that circle (*see* figure 14).

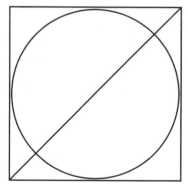

The circle has a circumference of 1 Meg Yard. The hypotenuse of a square around that circle is 1 Egyptian *remen*.

Figure 14. The relationship between the Megalithic Yard and the Egyptian *remen*

It is for this reason that the Great Pyramid of Khufu appears to have been built using the ratio we know as pi. The concept is a little difficult to explain but let us suggest that the Egyptian priests made a trundle wheel that had a circumference of one Megalithic Yard. Let us now assume that they used this to measure out 279 rotations along the ground for each side of the pyramid. Now instead of using the wheel for the sides of the pyramid, a measurement equivalent to the diameter of the wheel was used 279 times for the pyramid's height. This being the case, the finished pyramid would be bound to exhibit pi, whether the builders understood it or not.

Taking Bauval's theory together with our earlier discoveries of megalithic measures on the Giza Plateau, it seemed as though a careful re-read of *The Orion Mystery* was necessary. We were not disappointed by what we found.

One aspect we had not fully appreciated until we re-read the book was how important the river Nile was to the sky picture the Egyptians were apparently trying to create in the desert. When seen from the Earth amongst the backdrop of stars Orion's Belt lies adjacent to the Milky Way. The Milky Way is the galaxy to which our Sun belongs and the milky white smear across the night sky is created because we are looking sideways into the centre of the galaxy with its millions of stars. Only someone who has seen the sky on a really clear, moonless night, and in a place far from any lights, can truly appreciate its magnificence. Anyone sky-watching under such circumstances could be forgiven for seeing the Milky Way as being similar to a great silver river, snaking away across the sky.

A central theme of *The Orion Mystery* is the proximity of the three Giza pyramids to the River Nile. We know from inscriptions in tombs and temples, and from surviving papyrus documents, that the ancient Egyptians often referred to the Milky Way as the 'Nile in the Sky'. Was it not likely, Bauval and Gilbert asked, that this association had been built into the attempt of the Egyptians to recreate Orion's Belt on the ground? The idea seemed reasonable to us, and more so now because we realized immediately that a similar state of affairs existed at Thornborough. Looking down from the air it can be seen that the River Ure snakes past to one side of the super-henges — a not dissimilar situation to the one found at Giza with the pyramids and the river Nile. It has to be a possibility that those who laid out the three henges in North Yorkshire were also considering the adjacent river as an earthly representation of the Milky Way.

The work of Bauval and Gilbert has not been without its critics. One such criticism came from astronomer Ed Krupp of Griffith University Los Angeles. He suggested that the authors of *The Orion Mystery* were guilty of a deception in that they had 'turned the map of Egypt upside down' when demonstrating the similarity between the three major pyramids at Giza and the stars of Orion's Belt. Robert Bauval in particular strenuously and staunchly defended the position he had taken in *The Orion Mystery*. He received support for the way he had handled his evidence from astronomers such as Archie Roy, emeritus professor at Glasgow University and Dr Percy Seymour, a South African astronomer and astrophysicist.

According to Robert Bauval's theories it isn't simply the three major pyramids representing Orion's Belt that demonstrate the cosmological building efforts of the ancient Egyptians. He also sees other stars around Orion's Belt as being represented by pyramids in locations elsewhere in the Egyptian desert sands. This may well be the case but our initial interest was focused on the three main pyramids at Giza – because of their Orion's Belt associations and also on account of the megalithic measurements we had found there during the research for our book *Civilization One*.

We began to collect the most accurate measurements we could for the pyramids on the Giza Plateau. Clearly the plan of the pyramids was not as large as that of the Thornborough henges, even if the work that went into creating them was significantly greater. The direct measurement from henge A to henge C at Thornborough is 1,500 m, whereas the measurement, centre to centre, between the Great Pyramid (Khufu) and the smallest of the three pyramids (Menkaure) is about 943 m. Searching through as many records and surveys as we could, we came to the conclusion that the gap between the centre of Khufu's pyramid and the centre pyramid (Khafre) is about 479 m and the gap between the centre pyramid and the southern pyramid of Menkaure is around 463 m.

The magic of the Thornborough henges. They were built at a point that is 1/10th of the Earth's polar circumference from the North Pole. The straight-line distance between the northern henge (A) and the southern Henge (C) is 1500 metres. The distance between henges A and B is 366 MY and between B and C is 360 MY — perfectly imitating the relative positioning of the stars of Orion's Belt. The red line to the left of the picture shows the latitude difference between the centres of A and C (true north/ south), which is exactly 4 Megalithic seconds of arc (4 x 366 MY).

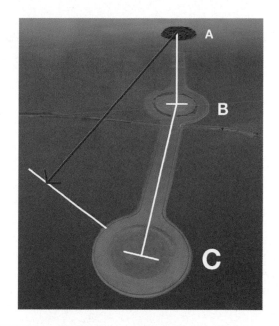

The three pyramids of the Giza Plateau. From left to right are the pyramids of Khufu, Khafri and Menkaure. The pyramids stand elevated above the modern city of Cairo which is in the background. The River Nile, lifeblood of the Egyptian civilization, can also be seen. In ancient times the Nile's waters lapped around the bottom of the Giza Plateau.

Courtesy of Guido Alberto Rossi/Photolibrary

3. The corner of Khufu's pyramid with Khafre's pyramid in the background

4. The edge of the Giza Plateau where the desert stops and Cairo now starts. At the time of Khufu the flood waters of the Nile washed these banks and it was from here that the dead kings set sail to the stars.

5. The original boat that carried King Khufu to the stars, now on display next to his pyramid.

6. The extremely ancient Sphinx faces east in front of the later pyramids of Khufu and Kha

7. and 8. ABOVE Druidic and craft symbols from carvings in King's Circus, Bath

9. RIGHT Carved acorns along rooflines in King's Circus, Bath

10. The Pentagon, Washington DC
Photograph by Master Sgt. Ken Hammond, US Air Force, DefenseLINK

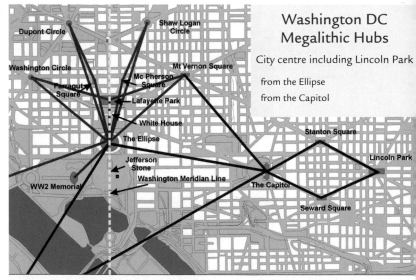

11. Washington street plan, including Lincoln Park

Washington DC

33-degree Megalithic Second Triangle

12. ABOVE Washington street map with 33-degree Megalithic Second Triangle

13. BELOW The arrow in Washington DC

Labels on upper map: The Ellipse, The Capitol, The Pentagon

Labels on lower map: Dupont Circle, Logan Circle, Washington Circle, Mt Vernon Square, Mc Pherson Square, Farragut Square, Lafayette Park, White House, The Ellipse

14. ABOVE The Capitol Building, Washington DC

15. The Statue of Liberty, New York
Courtesy of US Department of the Interior

Taking this information into account, we quite quickly discovered something that surprised us almost beyond belief. It became quite obvious that the ground plan for the three major pyramids on the Giza Plateau had not been planned in their native Egypt, but thousands of kilometres away – at the triple-henge site of Thornborough in Great Britain!

Chapter 9

·

SAILING TO THE STARS

A Meeting in Spain

Robert Bauval caused a sensation when, together with Adrian Gilbert, he wrote *The Orion Mystery* back in 1994, which claimed that the Giza pyramids were planned as a representation of the stars of Orion's Belt. It seems a reasonable enough claim, given that it is known that these stars were important to the pyramid builders, but virtually since the day it was written Egyptologists have been up in arms to dismiss it in favour of their own pet theories.

Robert may not walk like an Egyptian, but he certainly thinks like one, being born and brought up in Alexandria to parents of Belgian origin. He is a fluent Arabic speaker and has spent most of his life living and working in the Middle East and Africa as a construction engineer.

We decided that we needed to share our findings with Robert, who we knew had for some time lived in southern England. However, we soon found that he had left the country, having had the good fortune to sell his house just as the credit-crunch of 2008 hit the Western world. He was obviously missing the warmer climes of his youth in Alexandria as he had now taken an apartment on the Costa del Sol in southern Spain. By some coincidence Robert's new residence was just a 15-minute drive from a house Chris has as a holiday home, so it was a simple matter to arrange a convenient date and time for a meeting.

We left England early on a very icy January morning and arrived less than three hours later to the pleasantly warm city of Malaga. Without hold baggage we picked up our hire car without delay and headed out on our 30-km journey down the motorway signposted to Cadiz. After calling at the local supermarket for some essential supplies we were soon sitting by the swimming pool in hot sunshine planning how best to introduce Robert Bauval to our discoveries.

We arrived at Robert's home early the next day. It was a delightful apartment in a high building that gave him a fantastic panoramic view of the Mediterranean. In the first few hours we talked about many things and Chris was surprised to hear that a friend of his had visited Robert and his wife the previous evening. This was the American novelist, Katherine Neville. A few years earlier Chris had enjoyed a memorable dinner with Katherine and her husband, Professor Karl Pribram, the award-winning medical academic and neurosurgeon. The conversation had been delightfully varied, extending from the motive behind the fall of the Knights Templar to Karl's latest researches into the quantum state of the Bose-Einstein condensate elements within the human brain.

We could only hope that today's discussion was going to be as much fun – but hopefully less complicated!

Robert had invited his elder brother, John Paul, to join us. John Paul is an architect and has lived in this part of Spain for 45 years. He has been a major force in its development as a tourist location. But he is also a talented amateur mathematician, who was keen to hear more of the metrological properties underlying our findings.

Our meeting with Robert was going well. Both Robert and John Paul were excited about our discoveries, and Robert was finding powerful connections with his own recent researches. Both brothers immediately saw the logic of the 366-degree circle arising from the Earth's axial spins per solar orbit. But when we discussed the 233-732 relationship used at Thornborough to produce a circle with a circumference of 2×366 equal units, Robert raised his hand in the air, as though calling for a pause in the conversation.

'These numbers – 732 arising from double 366 with 233 and pi. We have also found these in Egypt – firstly at Saqqara by Jean-Philppe Lauer,'

Robert said, as he looked down at the plans of the British henges. He jumped up and retrieved a copy of his book, *The Egypt Code*, from his bookshelves. He flicked through the pages and pressed the book flat before passing it for us to see

The Saqqara pyramids are a few kilometres south of the Giza Plateau and some decades older. On a plan of the boundary wall Lauer had identified that the northern and southern walls of the boundary wall of the Djoser complex each had 2 × 366 panels. At first glance it appeared to be a ceremonial acknowledgement of a 'magical' number pattern rather than a practical application for astronomical purposes. But nonetheless, it was obvious that someone in Egypt knew about the importance of these values 100 years or so before the Giza trio were planned! This was getting very interesting.

After several hours of conversation we set out to walk to a fish restaurant, some 3 km along the beach, to continue our wide-ranging discussion. The sun shone with the power of a good English summer's day, and the food was as good as the conversation. We continued talking as the sun fell lower across the sea.

As we walked back to Robert's apartment, we wondered what he would make of hearing a new take on his famous Orion correlation theory. He might love it but, then again we were well aware that he might not.

A Possible New Angle on the Orion Theory

Without doubt Robert Bauval is 'master of the Giza Plateau' and one does not lightly tell him that he might be wrong. So we didn't attempt to. But we did show him an argument for considering one significant adjustment to his famous theory.

What we had found was based on our discovery that ancient cultures measured stars by timing their relative movements with pendulums. It seems that nobody, including Robert, had ever given a great deal of thought to how the pyramid builders of Giza had measured the relative position of the stars in order to map them so accurately onto the ground. It appears that most commentators have simply assumed the builders did it by looking upwards to gain a mental impression of the star group and then drawing the arrangement on a sheet of papyrus or a slate before evolving their awesome ground plan through artistic interpretation alone.

In our opinion this simply would not work, or rather it would not work to the level of accuracy we knew existed in terms of the Giza pyramids and Orion's Belt.

Our years of work on prehistoric and ancient metrology had already taught us to respect these long-gone builders as true engineers, rather than casual artists. The magnificent quality of the Thornborough and Giza layouts screams out that there was heavy-duty science behind their unerring accuracy.

Because stars as seen in the night sky are little more than 'pin pricks' of light, any two stars can be compared with any two objects on the ground at any arbitrary scale. But when three stars are compared to three terrestrial objects, unless there is a flawless fit, one has to decide which two are correct (as two always will be) so that the degree of inaccuracy for the placement of the third can be established. The standard way of comparing the three main Giza pyramids with the shape of the stars of Orion's Belt, both by Robert and his critics, is to consider Khufu's and Khafre's pyramids as being the 'correct' ones and then arguing a smallish error in the placing of Menkaure's pyramid (the southernmost and by far the smallest of the three).

We are as certain as it is possible to be that this is not a correct assumption. Because the tool employed was the pendulum, and because we know from our findings at Thornborough and elsewhere that distances on the ground were direct translations of time in the sky, we knew that the outer two pyramids (Khafre and Menkaure) had to be positioned first and then the central pyramid of Khufu fitted in last.

This is because, as described in Chapter 6, the period of time between the outer stars of Mintaka and Alnitak reaching a fixed point was measured in seconds as they rose above the horizon, which can then be translated into the same number of any units of length. The gap between the first and second, and the second and third, was gauged when the Orion's Belt trio were level with the horizon (at their maximum altitude – exactly south). However, whilst the ancient observers could accurately gauge the 'off-centredness' of the middle star in horizontal terms, there was no way they could measure its vertical deviation from the straight line between the other two stars.

This one element could only be estimated by eye alone.

We would therefore expect these perfectionist pyramid-engineers to get every aspect of the ground plan extremely accurate – apart from the amount of deviation of Khafre's pyramid to emulate the dogleg shape of the stars they were copying. The builders knew the precise point on the SW–NE 'back sight' line to place the middle pyramid, but not the 90-degree offset towards the northwest.

We would therefore expect to find some level of error to be present on the ground plan in relation to this aspect – and this aspect alone. This is exactly what we found when we made a slight twist in the logic of Robert's Orion correlation theory.

Our meeting with Robert and John Paul had been wonderfully exhilarating and stimulating. But now we were to introduce the idea that we believed needed to be aired. It does not form any part of our core thesis – but we still had to share it.

We put it to Robert that maybe there was a different way of looking at the Giza ground plan in the light of this one expected error. And, we suggested, it was a solution that fitted all of the available facts even better than anything discussed before.

We had been sitting in the bar of our hotel in Giza, some months earlier, drinking ice-cold Egyptian beer whilst looking straight up at Khafre's pyramid, when the idea began to develop. On that same day we had taken a long and close look at the reassembled pyramid boat housed near the Great Pyramid, and it seemed to us that the importance of this vessel, and of others like it, might have been underestimated by earlier Egyptologists.

Seven boat pits have been found in the whole complex of Khufu at Giza, two of which are associated with the lesser so-called Queen's Pyramids. These boat pits are very large – over 50 m long, 7 m wide and nearly 4 m deep. Whilst some of the pits have been found to be empty, two intact boats were discovered in 1954 by the young Egyptian archaeologist Kamal el-Mallakh. When one of the slabs was raised from the eastern pit, the planking of the great boat was seen – it had been dismantled and carefully flat-packed four and a half millennia before. One of these Lebanese cedar boats had its 1,224 individual parts reassembled by Ahmed Youssef Mustafa during a period of some 10 years, and is now on display in a superb boat-shaped museum next to the Great Pyramid.

In the absence of any ancient written records about these vessels, scholars have speculated about their purpose and meaning. According to the Egyptian Director of Antiquities, Zahi Hawass, the boats to the south of the pyramid are solar boats in which the soul of the king symbolically travelled through the heavens with the Sun god. Others suggest that the pit, which lies parallel to the causeway, might have contained the funerary boat used to bring the king's body to its final resting place. But that raises the question as to why the boat was not returned to other duties after completing this task, instead of being so carefully interred at Giza. It seems to us that the boats were placed in their pits for a supposed future purpose rather than because they were no longer needed.

To us, it seems that Dr Hawass is probably quite close to the mark. As Egyptian religious beliefs developed, Pharaohs were buried along with artefacts necessary for use in the afterlife, and therefore is seems reasonable to assume that these boats were packed away so expertly for later use – for the dead king's journey to the Duat, the realm of the dead that existed amongst the stars.

Slightly later records from the pyramids of Saqqara tell us the way that ancient Egyptian kings thought about the journey to the afterlife – which was all about sailing to the stars. There is no doubt whatsoever that Orion's Belt and Sirius were of special importance to the ancient Egyptians. Amongst the inscriptions found on the walls of the Saqqara pyramids is the following incantation:

> Be firm, Oh king, on the underside of the sky with the
> Beautiful Star upon the Bend of the Winding Waterway…

The Beautiful Star of Isis is Sirius (Sopdet to the ancient Egyptians), which, at its heliacal rising at the summer solstice, marked the opening of the life-bringing Nile flood. This was the flooding that brought life back to the entire land of Egypt. It is, of course, to Sirius that the three stars of Orion's Belt point.

A few weeks after the annual inundation began, the swollen Nile would be lapping against the edge of the Giza Plateau. Anyone standing next to Khufu's pyramid looking southwards, towards Sirius rising before dawn at this time of year, would see the light of the billion stars of the Milky Way reflecting on its surface so that the horizon itself melded into a continuous waterway, right from their feet and extending far up into the heavens. Could it be that the kings believed that their boats would set sail at the moment that Sirius broke above the waterway, leading the way for their voyage to the Duat? The Saqqara inscriptions seem to describe it, and the boats were ready for the journey.

The Egyptians associated their gods with constellations, or specific astronomical bodies. The constellation Orion was considered to be a manifestation of Osiris, the god of death, rebirth, and the afterlife. The Milky Way represented the sky goddess Nut who gave birth to the Sun god Ra. The horizon had great significance to the Egyptians, since it was here that the Sun would both appear and disappear on its daily journey. The Sun itself was associated with a number of deities, depending on its position within the sky. The rising Sun was associated with Horus, the divine child of Osiris and Isis. The noon Sun was Ra, god on high, and the evening Sun was Atum, the creator god who lifted Pharaohs from their tombs to the stars.

The red glow of the setting Sun was considered to be the blood of the Sun god as he 'died' and became associated with Osiris, god of death and rebirth. This led to the night being associated with death, and the dawn with rebirth and life.

It seems to us that great kings such as Khufu, Khafre and Menkaure, who saw themselves as gods in life, expected to take up their new life, after earthly death, by travelling to the stars – the realm of the gods. But how did they expect to get there? According to the records left to us, the answer is by sailing down the Nile and past the horizon into the heavens and onwards to Orion.

And in what did they expect to sail? Surely the boats, so carefully packed away next to the pyramids, provide a large and tangible clue? And the next question then has to be: How exactly did they envisage this journey happening?

The Journey to the Duat

As far as we are aware, there is no known Egyptian text that explicitly describes the anticipated structure of the world of the afterlife – the heaven amongst the stars. But the later Greek culture drew heavily on Egyptian ideas and they described the starry heavens as follows:

> The heaven is solid and made of air (mist) congealed by fire, like crystal, and encloses the fiery and air-like (contents) of the two hemispheres respectively.
>
> Aetius, II, 11, 2

> The fixed stars are attached to the crystal sphere; the planets are free.
>
> Aetius, II, 13, 2

So, the Greeks considered that the stars were attached to a crystal sphere that was fixed above and parallel to the surface of the Earth. It seems highly probable that the earlier Egyptians saw things in a similar way.

We put it to Robert Bauval that the ancient Egyptians may have built the pyramids as an earthly connection to the stars of Orion's Belt. Not as a symbolic copy of the star arrangement in honour of Osiris, but a physical star-to-pyramid correlation – a direct conduit between the realm of men and the realm of the gods. The stages of the journey might have been something like this:

1. The three pyramids were carefully constructed to fit the stars – to effectively 'plug into' them. This was achieved by taking careful measurement of the star group, using a pendulum to time the gaps between the rising stars. After this, the timed swings of the pendulum were converted into pendulum lengths on the ground. The centre of each pyramid corresponded to the point of each star.

2. Each pyramid, and therefore star, was associated with one of the three kings (father, son and grandson). The largest pyramid, nearest the Nile is Khufu's, the next Khafre's and the smallest one, Menkaure's.

3. The first star of Orion's belt to rise above the horizon is Mintaka. Khufu was the first king to 'rise' at birth and to eventually 'set' at death. The

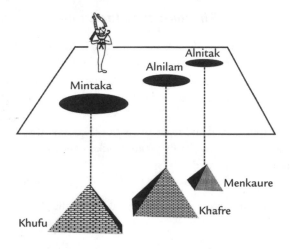

The evidence strongly suggests that the ancient Egyptian kings believed that the stars were on a plane parallel to the Earth and that they could stand in heaven and look down upon the land of mortal men. This explains why the pyramids were designed to correlate with the stars of Orion's Belt as viewed from heaven rather than from the surface of the Earth.

Figure 15. The 'crystal sphere'

second star is Alnilam and therefore corresponds to the next king, Khafre, and the third to rise is Alnitak, which makes it Menkaure's star. (This has an obvious logic – but it does reverse the sequence as described by Robert Bauval.)

4. The boats may well have brought the bodies of the deceased kings to the pyramids, but then they were dismantled and stored in the 'graves' prepared for them. The bodies of Khufu and Khafre were taken to their pyramids as they died 34 years apart. Then when Menkaure died 22 years later, the three kings were ready for their journey.

5. The 'spiritual boats', in other words the 'essence' of the boats that had been so carefully created and buried on the site, were assembled at the jetty in front of the pyramid complex in the same order as the pyramids.

The dead kings set out to the stars with Khufu sailing south down the Nile in his mystical boat, followed by Khufu and then Menkaure.

6. The journey began after dark and, as Sirius rose, the blaze of the Milky Way was perfectly reflected in the river to create a sparkling and uninterrupted waterway from Earth to heaven. Khufu's boat, representing Mintaka, was first to cross the horizon. The three boats rose one after the other into the heavenly waterway and sailed in sequence up the Milky Way towards Orion's Belt.

7. They sailed onto the plain of the stars that was parallel to the Earth but far above it; where even the mightiest of birds could not fly. Here the brilliant white stars existed on a celestial 'ground' – just like the equally brilliant white pyramids below them.

If this explanation were correct, it would mean that the relationship between the stars of Orion's Belt is different to Robert's original correlation. In this case the pyramids would be reversed and inverted in terms of the stars they represent. Instead of simply looking at Orion's Belt from an Earth perspective, the key to the problem would be to look from the heavens downwards. From the parallel realm of the gods the deceased god-kings of Egypt could gaze down on the nation they once ruled.

We think that our revision of Robert's Orion correlation theory has the benefit of fitting all of the available facts. Most particularly it largely removes the apparent inaccuracy in the layout of the pyramids in relation to the three stars – except for the anticipated tiny error in the deviation of the 'dog-leg'. We explained our idea and Robert was not slow to respond.

'This cannot be correct,' he said, waving his hand from side to side. 'You are proposing a level of accuracy in the position of the pyramids relative to each other that could not be achieved.'

We could not help but agree with his reasoning and yet the lateral error disappeared completely when our slight alteration of Robert's evidence was introduced.

'That is indeed strange,' John Paul said with a nod and raised eyebrows. Perhaps he shared our view that it was an odd argument to suggest our explanation was wrong because it fitted the known facts 'too' well.

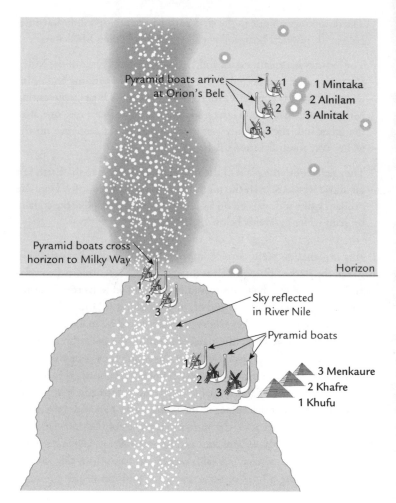

The boats of the kings were believed to sail to the afterlife in the order of the pyramids – Khufu, Khafre and Menkaure. They sailed down the Nile in order and at the horizon, where the Milky Way merged into its own reflection, the craft lifted off to sail up the 'heavenly Nile'. They crossed the sky and arrived at Orion's Belt so that Khufu became one with Mintaka (the first to rise), Khafre became Alnilam, and Menkaure was Alnitak.

Figure 16. Solar boats in the sky

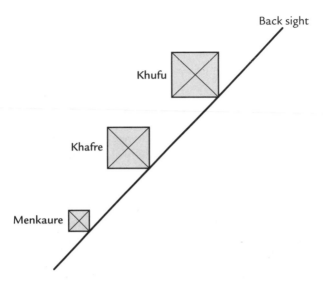

The back sight at Giza. The three pyramids are aligned at their southeastern corners. The line was aimed straight towards Heliopolis, the city of the sun, in the northeast. The point where each pyramid touches this virtual line marks the time gap between the stars of Orion's Belt, measured in seconds-pendulum beats and converted to pendulum lengths on the ground. The greater gap is between Khufu's Pyramid and Khafre's Pyramid, demonstrating how the pyramid of Khufu represents Mintaka, not Alnitak as previously suggested by Robert Bauval.

Figure 17. Pyramids and back sight

Academic Inertia

One of Robert's reasons for not wishing to pursue our suggestion was that he believed it had been aired before, for different reasons, in a very aggressive and public manner. In this case the attack had come from that icon of fair-mindedness and objectivity – the BBC.

The ability of the 'establishment' to rebuff new ideas, and particularly when that change comes from individuals deemed to be amateurs, should never be underestimated. It is right and proper that new ideas are put to the test but sometimes the process is less than objective. In 1999 the highly regarded BBC science programme, *Horizon* had set out to 'rubbish' Robert's correlation theory. The two programmes were made with Robert's cooperation, but he was unaware that they would be broadcast under the inflammatory titles 'Atlantis Revisited' and 'Atlantis Reborn'. The *Horizon* team knew that anyone associated with the term 'Atlantis' is likely to be viewed as a fantasist.

Robert Bauval and Graham Hancock were both badly treated by these *Horizon* productions and, following a formal complaint, the Broadcasting Standards Commission judged that the central part of *Horizon*'s attack on Hancock and Bauval was indeed unfair. The complaint upheld by the BSC specifically identified *Horizon*'s unfair representation of the Giza-Orion correlation theory, in which Robert Bauval's critic was given the opportunity to explain his point of view, but Robert's own evidence was largely edited out.

For what it is worth, it is our opinion that Chris Hale, the producer of the *Horizon* programmes, was not knowingly dishonest – he was just a victim of his own prejudices. He explains his point of view in a section of a publication called *Archaeological Fantasies*, edited by Garrett G Fagan.[1] Hale has some fundamental issues with an aspect of claims made by Hancock and supported by Bauval, and this led him to give a very partial review of the evidence regarding the Orion correlation theory. We discuss this collision of thinking styles in Appendix 10, which we believe has considerable implications for the broader process of identifying what constitutes legitimate approaches to reasoning.

It is human nature to protect ideas that we have adopted over many years of reasoning and very few people are willing or able to deal with new information that is not a small or incremental adjustment to embedded ideas. It matters not whether someone is a world-class professor in his or her subject or a believer in alien abductions – people seek out information that supports existing assumptions and reject anything that would demand a major overhaul of their existing world-view. This not only applies to ideas themselves but to the method of reasoning used.

And Robert Bauval is no exception, but in this case for the good reason that he believes he has dealt with the point we were making when he countered the *Horizon* attack. We fully understand that our suggested variation on the correlation theory looked similar to the one raised by Ed Krupp, director of the Griffith Observatory in Los Angeles. Interviewed for the *Horizon* programme the American astronomer had said:

> When *The Orion Mystery* came out my curiosity was naturally aroused. Anybody coming up with a good idea about ancient astronomy I want to know about it. And in going through the book there was something nagging me. In *The Orion Mystery* there's a nice double-page spread (showing two pictures of the Giza Pyramids and Orion's Belt) and anybody looking at this would say, ah! Giza pyramids, Belt of Orion, one kind of looks like the other, you know, you've got three in row, three in a row; slanted, slanted; we've got a map!

Immediately, Krupp had painted the picture of a halfwit seeing two sets of three objects in a bent row and leaping at the unwarranted assumption that there was a direct connection. This failure to mention a whole raft of reasons for the proposed connections feeds the preconceptions of the conventionalist group. Krupp continued:

> And what I was bothered by turned out to be really pretty obvious. In the back of my head I knew there was something wrong with these pictures, and what was wrong with these pictures in their presentation is that north for the constellation of Orion is here on the top of the page. North for the Giza pyramids is down here. Now they're not marked, but I knew which way north was at Giza and I knew which way north was in Orion. To make the map of the pyramids on the ground match the stars of Orion in the sky you have to turn Egypt upside down, and if you don't want to do that then you have to turn the sky upside down!

Krupp's argument was not exactly insightful. Apart from a completely arbitrary modern convention, why assume that north equals the top and south the bottom? Some people are still confused by the fact that Upper Egypt is in the south of the country and Lower Egypt is the northern half.

This description refers to the fall of the River Nile from the higher altitudes towards sea level at the delta that spews the Nile's fresh water into the Mediterranean.

What we were trying to say to Robert was quite coincidentally related to Krupp's comment but arrived at for entirely different reasons. In fact we believe our description of events negates Krupp's objection and makes the correlation theory sounder than ever.

Solar or Stellar?

In the Introduction to the aforementioned book, *Archaeological Fantasies*, the editor says:

> Whatever is theorized about the pyramids must be coherent with the way in which other aspects of Egyptian civilization are described.

This is obviously good advice – most of the time. But it would be foolhardy to insist that it is a rule that must always be applied in all cases as stated here.

It is important to keep an eye out for the completely unexpected. One eminent geologist from Cambridge University once said to Chris: 'You are assuming a closed system. What if it was not a closed system?' He had been responding to Chris's comment that the ancient global flood stories, such as Noah's Flood, cannot be true because there is not enough water to flood everywhere simultaneously. In this case, what if the Egyptian pyramid builders were directly influenced by a group from outside their own culture? If we automatically rule out candidate ideas to explain the available evidence, just because they don't seem to fit our previous expectations of the culture, it would be impossible ever to spot the arrival of a major external influence.

One of the criticisms of Robert Bauval's theories regarding the Giza pyramids is the apparent over-emphasis of stellar issues involved, when the Old Kingdom is generally considered to have been overwhelmingly a solar orientated culture. The importance of the Sun to these people is beyond question, from the god Ra to the incredibly important city of Heliopolis. It was only much later, most probably as a result of Babylonian influences, that Egyptians are known to have taken a serious interest in astronomy.

Before the primary pyramid age, and indeed for some considerable time after it, the study of stars does not appear to have been of specific importance to the ancient Egyptians. Yet the pyramids do seem to imply a great interest in the stars and this is also borne out by many of the 'spells' or 'incantations' included amongst the Pyramid Texts. And if we are right about the pendulum method used to map the stars onto the Giza Plateau, the level of observational astronomy amongst whoever planned the pyramid sites must have been considerable.

So where did this astronomical knowledge come from?

Before we deal with this question, it is worth looking at one anomaly regarding the pyramids. This anomaly concerns the ruined pyramid of Djedefre, which stands about eight miles north of Giza at a place now called Abu Rawash.

Djedefre was the successor and son of Khufu and he became king in 2528 BC, upon the death of his father. He apparently died eight years later when his brother Khafre came to the throne, who was in turn followed by his son, Menkaure. The question is, if the three pyramids of Egypt were, as is normally accepted, conceived as a single project, why was Khufu's eldest son excluded from the plan by having his pyramid constructed inland of the Nile and further north?

The name Djedefre means 'enduring like Ra' and he was the first king to use the title *Son of Ra* as part of his royal title, which is generally considered to show an indication of the growing popularity of the cult of the solar god Ra. Could it be that this king had no time for newfangled, and perhaps alien ideas about stars being as important as the Sun?

A boat pit has been found at this pyramid, but it was empty apart from fragments of over 100 statues, mostly representing Djedefre on his throne. Three more or less complete heads were found, including one now in the Louvre in Paris and another that resides in the Egyptian Antiquity Museum in Cairo. The statues appear to have been deliberately destroyed, as though to deny the king's status. It is widely thought that there were deep rifts and that Djedefre had gained the throne by murdering his older half-brother, Kauab. He then married his sister Hetepheres II, widow of his dead half-brother, to strengthen his claim to the throne, as his own Libyan mother was a 'lesser wife' with no ties to the royal family.

Perhaps because of the break with his father's family, Djedefre moved his mortuary temple and monument north to Abu Rawash, where he began to construct a large pyramid. This structure had only risen to about 20 courses when he died. The possibility of a family feud looks all the more likely because work on the pyramid was stopped immediately. Furthermore, there are no explanations as to why Kauab was not succeeded by any of his own sons, Setka, Baka or Hernet, so it may have been that they all died before, or at the same time as, their father.

It has been further widely speculated that Khafre murdered Djedefre, and then destroyed all images associated with his brief rule of just eight years. And it is possible that he also killed Djedefre's sons to remove any competition for the throne.

It is certain that all Egyptian kings had respect for Ra and we already knew that the back sight, which links the three Giza pyramids, points northeast towards Heliopolis, the city of the Sun. But Djedefre shows an even greater liking for Ra. From his pyramid at Abu Rawash, the summer solstice Sun rises out of Heliopolis – a fact that must surely have driven the king's choice of location.

Was Djedefre cut out of the plan completely? The available evidence now suggests not.

The feud theory is now under question, as the broken statues seem to have been smashed during the Roman and Christian era. Furthermore, it would also appear from fragmentary evidence around his pyramid that, after Djedefre's death, he enjoyed a lengthy cult following that was not disrupted by his successor. Why Djedefre chose to build his pyramid at Abu Rawash is still considered a mystery, but there is evidence that Djedefre definitely had a religious departure from his family. His pyramid has a number of elements that seem to revert to earlier times, while his adoption of a 'son of Ra' name indicates his religious deviations away from the stellar leanings of his father Khufu. Whether or not the sons of Khufu set about murdering each other in a fight for the kingship, there is good reason to believe that the family were all happily working together – at least during the lifetime of Khufu. Recent evidence suggests that it was Djedefre who completed his father's burial at Giza and was responsible for the provision of his funerary boats, where Djedefre's name has been found.

And we believe that there is a perfectly good explanation as to why Djedefre's pyramid is at Abu Rawash and not Giza.

No one appears to have looked closely at the relative positions of the pyramids associated with Khufu and his sons Khafre and Djedefre. Using satellite mapping we measured the distance between Djedefre's pyramid and Khufu's at Giza. The first thing that leaped out was the angle of the straight line. Drawing a line from the northwest corner of Djedefre's pyramid, through its centre and the southeast corner and onwards for just over 8 km, it intersects Khufu's pyramid at the northwest corner, continues through its centre and then hits the southeast corner. The pyramids are as perfectly aligned as Khufu's is with Khafre's.

Khufu's pyramid is aligned so that the diagonals of its sides are both perfectly aligned to the pyramids of his two sons. It looked for all the world as though Khufu was facing the setting Sun and stretching his arms out toward his sons exactly 90 degrees apart. The chances of this arrangement happening by accident are virtually nonexistent, and it must have taken great skill to get the alignment so accurate over a distance well beyond the horizon. So we conclude that even this distant pyramid was part of a complex plan created by Khufu during his lifetime. It may be that he accepted Djedefre's single-minded religious beliefs concerning Ra, the Sun, but still wanted to involve him the largely star-orientated theology that he had been developing, to ensure that he and his progeny found an eternal home in the Duat above.

When we looked at the distance between Khufu's and Djedefre's pyramids it was 8,218 m centre to centre, which was immediately interesting. We then measured the distances between the locations of each sarcophagus and found that the mummified bodies of the two kings had been placed 8,235 m apart – which, to an accuracy of 99.6 per cent, happens to be 10,000 Megalithic Yards!

Surveying the Stars for the Giza Pyramids

So, let us now return to question as to where the astronomical knowledge underpinning the planning of the pyramids came from. Our answer is that it came from the British Isles – and there are very hard-edged reasons for making this apparently outlandish claim.

The British Isles, along with some other parts of Western Europe, still has the remains of tens of thousands of structures used for tracking and measuring the movements of the Moon, planets and stars. Thornborough itself had been in use for almost a millennium before the pyramids were built. Given that both the henges of Thornborough and the three pyramids of the Giza Plateau appear to be built in the form of Orion's Belt, there are three possible explanations for the connection.

First, it could be that there is no connection at all. It is simply that two different cultures naturally focused their attention on Sirius, the brightest of all stars, and then noticed a nearly straight line of three stars rise ahead of it and point almost at it. They then attached some mystical significance to these stars and decided for some reason to build a model of them on the ground.

The second option is that there was contact between the ancient Egyptians and the people of megalithic Britain, and the Egyptians adopted the beliefs of the Northerners by merging their star-based astronomical 'magic' into their existing solar theology.

The third possibility is that the astronomical priesthood of the British megalithic culture was actively involved in the design and layout of the pyramids. Whilst all of the evidence shows that the people of Britain were far behind the Egyptians in terms of stone building and the production of bronze tools, they were clearly ahead in their astronomy and the adoption of complex multifunctional measuring systems. Critics might argue that any association between these two groups would have led to the adoption of metals in Britain at a far earlier date, but we have good reason to believe that this would have been an anathema to the megalithic priesthood. This is an argument too complicated to enter into within the scope of this book. To follow this third, 'strong' version of the British-Egyptian theory, it could be that either the megalithic priests came to Egypt or that the Egyptian kings sent their builder-priests north to investigate the 'magic' of the stars understood by a people they had learned about.

The evidence suggests it was the latter of these options that occurred.

If the pyramids were placed as we have argued – by timing the stars of Orion's belt rising and then converting the pendulum lengths used into linear units – then we can detect where and when it was done. This is because the angle of the rising of the stars changes by latitude, and when we looked at the rising of the stars of Orion's Belt at Giza in circa 2500 BC we found no correlation whatsoever with the actual layout of the pyramids in any units at all.

But then we tried Thornborough and the fit was immediate – and astonishingly accurate! Using standard astronomy software we took the timings on the autumn equinox at Thornborough on 14 October in 2500 BC and we found that the three stars rose at following times of day, using a 24-hour clock:

Mintaka 21:02:27
Alnilam 21:10:49
Alnitak 21:18:11

As we have previously said, it is the two outer stars that have to be measured at rising because the dogleg of the middle star distorts the true timing and therefore ultimately the linear distance between the stars. This means that the time taken between the rising of Mintaka and Alnitak was 15 minutes and 44 seconds – a total of 944 seconds.

The time lag between the rising of the first and last stars represented 944 swings of a seconds-pendulum that was 99.55 cm in length: 944 such lengths would measure 940 m. The gap between the centres of Khufu's and Menkaure's pyramid, as best as we can tell, is 942 m. This gives a fit of 99.8 per cent, which is as close to perfect as it is possible to get, given that we could be slightly out in our estimations of the true distance between pyramid centres, and bearing in mind that the Egyptians could have been slightly out in placing them.

Either it is a huge coincidence that both structures are copies of Orion's Belt and the measure of the stars at Thornborough in 2500 BC fit the pyramids' position on the ground, or there is a connection. It becomes obvious that further and quite extensive research into possible connections between the two cultures in question is going to be necessary. From our own point of view we remain utterly convinced that the three major pyramids on the Giza Plateau were built upon a footprint that was not created first on the desert sand by the side of the Nile, but in the green and pleasant land of North Yorkshire. Both the Thornborough henges and the Giza Pyramids were planned by engineers, and engineers cannot avoid leaving evidence of their presence. In both these cases we can see their footsteps as clearly as if they walked this way yesterday.

Chapter 10

·

REVELATION IN ROME

Hall of All the Gods

At the end of February 2009 we set off to Rome where we were due to give a talk at a conference on new developments in Egyptology. It was an early start, but we were picked up at the airport by a driver and dropped at our hotel before 10 o'clock, and 30 minutes later we were outside a building which both of us had quite separately identified as the greatest structure of the Roman period. The Pantheon, or 'place of all gods', is in the heart of this beautiful city and it leaves all others, from St Peter's to the Coliseum, trailing a long way behind for beauty, engineering and sheer visual impact.

It was built early in the 2nd century AD by Hadrian, to replace an earlier structure destroyed in AD 80. This earlier Pantheon had been lost in a great fire, believed to have been started by proto-Christian Jews seeking revenge for the killing of James, the brother of Jesus, and subsequently destroying the entire city of Jerusalem in AD 70.

Behind its façade of Corinthian pillars lies a gigantic concrete domed hall that is 43.3 m (142 ft) in diameter, and the same in height to the open circle at its highest point. The 5,000-tonne dome still holds the record for the largest unreinforced concrete dome in the world.

Without doubt Rome is a fabulous city. Despite having many structures destroyed in the 7th century it remains tremendously unspoilt, and is still a relatively small city that can be fully walked well within a day. We realize that for many visitors, especially from the New World, this must seem an ancient place. Thoughts of dramatic events from the remote past excite the mind. It was here that Julius Caesar entertained his lover, Cleopatra, the beautiful Hellenistic Pharaoh of the Egyptians. Here the emperor met his death at the hands of assassins. His ally Mark Anthony eventually travelled to Egypt where he also began a liaison with Cleo-patra. Caesar's child by Cleopatra was strangled and never saw Rome. All ancient high drama.

Whilst the city is old and associated with power and strife in equal measures, it does not seem so ancient in our scale of measure. Remember that the city did not come into existence until some 3,000 years after the Thornborough henges were first constructed. So the days of the Roman Empire are much closer in time to us today than they are to the Neolithic structures that stand across the landscape of the British Isles.

It was, of course, Julius Caesar who conducted the first Roman invasion of Britain in 55 BC, and according to the woefully under-informed purveyors of 'standard' history, they met a bunch of primitive tribesmen who painted themselves blue. They did bring quite a lot of new ideas with them, but not all of them were quite as original as the invaders believed. The straight roads were already here, and even flushable toilets have been found in 5,000-year-old settlements such as the apparent college at Skara Brae in Orkney. And even when they eventually brought their new cult of Romanized Christianity, the locals told them that they had known of this dying and resurrecting god for 1,000 years.

As we meandered around Rome's narrow streets and spacious squares, we began to discuss the challenge of fitting in the key points of our recent findings into a relatively short talk to people who would be unfamiliar with the British Neolithic period. However, when we gave our talk the next day it went down extraordinarily well, despite the difficulties of translation. Kind as they were, it was not the audience that made this trip an unexpected success – it was two fellow contributors that we had met at dinner the previous evening, both of whom had just flown in from different sides of the USA.

The Sphinx and the Flood

One of the speakers was Robert Schoch, a geologist from Boston University, who was accompanied by his delightful ballerina wife Kate. Robert is a hard-nosed academic with an open mind. He spoke eloquently and convincingly about the dating of the Great Sphinx (on the Giza Plateau) by means of water erosion. He pointed out that, whilst much of the Sphinx has either been overcut or repaired across the millennia, the original workings can be dated by the excavated pit which was cut out of bedrock around the first monument. The walls of the cut-out rock face show that the base was lowered in relatively recent times, but the main part of the digging was completed before a long and sustained massive flooding took place. Consequently, he puts the original Sphinx as being more than double the age of the pyramids that stand above and behind it on the Giza Plateau.

He explained that geological evidence of ancient comet impacts is changing, or should be changing the way we view the past. The idea of these cataclysmic events occurring with some relative frequency is now becoming widely accepted within geology, as having brought catastrophe to the world with terrifying frequency over the period that humankind has existed on the planet. Such impacts on the oceans understandably create mega-tsunamis that drive deep into continental landmass and cause monsoon rains to fall for perhaps decades.

According to Schoch, the features of the rock around the rear and sides of the Sphinx can only have been caused by massive and sustained water flow, such as would occur after a comet impact.

In 1999 Chris wrote *Uriel's Machine* with Robert Lomas, describing the geological case and the anthropological evidence that the biblical Flood had caused a major global catastrophe. Whilst Chris' argument had begun with evidence published by leading geologists, it was good to hear detailed confirmation that this did indeed occur. Although, it would be preferable to be wrong – because according to the previous intervals of such horrible events, we are more than due for another impact. Then we will know what 'climate change' can really mean. Several years ago Chris was flying from Dallas to San Francisco, and he noticed that there was a white circle in every major hollow in the desert below him, which made him look further north and think of the salt flats of Utah. If there had been a massive flood here (and a major comet fragment hit off the coast of Mexico) this area would have had a super-giant tsunami ripping across the landscape. As it lost momentum and ran back to the sea it would, logically, have left huge pools of seawater trapped in low-lying areas.

Could those circles be sea salt and could the salt flats be the residue of a seawater incursion?

Upon returning to England, Chris found that the answer was 'yes' and 'yes'. It is known that 10,000 years ago, in what is now the US state of Utah, humans fished freshwater lakes in a pleasant green landscape, and then suddenly it changed. And the salt is not any old salt, it is clearly sea salt – containing all of the various minerals (including traces of gold) that the oceans possess.

This part of North America was devastated by a comet impact, and old Native American stories tell of the survivors on high ground watching a wall of sea hurtling towards them.[1] So too was North Africa. The plains that were once full of lakes, foliage and animal life were overtaken by heat and became the Sahara Desert. Another speaker at the Rome conference, Mahmoud Marei, has conducted expeditions deep into the Sahara and found cave paintings depicting a green landscape with giraffes.

The world can and does change rapidly and, for humans, unpleasantly.

The Ancient Astrophysicists

The most startling new evidence came from a third speaker at the conference: Thomas Brophy, an astrophysicist who has worked with the NASA Voyager Project, the Laboratory for Atmospheric and Space Physics and the Japanese Space program.

In conducting our own researches we have found that the megalithic system and the so-called metric system were used in conjunction during the fourth millennium BC. However, we had concluded that it was unlikely that we were looking at a resurrection or revival, rather than a genesis, for these complex concepts. It seemed to us that there must have been some much more advanced progenitor culture somewhere in the distant past. And here, in Rome, we were hearing new ideas that could represent a major missing piece of the jigsaw we were attempting to put together.

Brophy explained how he has become involved in the investigation of a group of megalithic sites, deep in the Sahara in southern Egypt, known as Nabta: a structure we knew of but had little or no information about. This extremely remote location is a place that neither humans nor anything else much ever visit. It is on the Tropic of Cancer and is made up of a number of standing stones – some in the form of a circle. But even more interesting is what lies beneath this ancient surface feature.

Below the sands of the Sahara lies another, far older structure – in fact a structure which long predates the desertification of this huge swathe of North Africa. And its properties are, if Brophy is to be believed, utterly mind-bending. He calls it 'The Origin Map'.

As Robert Schoch put it, Brophy's work creates three distinct levels of problem to confront. The first one is not too academically controversial, the second is very challenging, and the third will have conventional archaeologists reaching for a gun. There are three basic levels of knowledge that the ancient builders at this site had, as, inferred by Brophy's findings,[2] various artefacts at Nabta indicate:

1. Maps and markers denoting objects, alignments, and events that can be observed in the sky with the unaided (naked) eye.

2. Markers indicating celestial phenomena and events that cannot be observed (apparently) with the unaided eye.

3. Detailed astronomical and cosmological information, such as the distances to stars, the speeds at which stars are moving away from the Earth, the structure of our galaxy (the Milky Way), and information on the origin of the universe, which we have either only just discovered in modern times, or possibly information (for example, that concerning planetary systems around stars) which we do not even have available to us at the moment.

Heavy claims indeed! But, apart from the convention for believing that we are the smartest dudes ever to walk the Earth, there is absolutely no reason why even the third level cannot be true. Archaeologists cannot even express an informed opinion, as this is new territory for them.

A particularly interesting aspect of Brophy's work is the interest these people had in the stars of Orion's Belt and an understanding of the three-dimensional space between the three stars. It is also interesting to note that it has recently been discovered that a region within the constellation of Orion is the nearest 'star factory' to Earth – a place where stars are being manufactured at a considerable rate.

Brophy argues that the relative distances of Mintaka, Alnitak and Alnilam, as well as their velocity away from us, is recorded in this ancient astronomical observatory. And Brophy claims to know just how old the structure beneath the Sahara actually is – because its builders dated it!

It is an incredible 18,000 years old. That is long before the end of the last Ice Age.

This was identifiable because of the precession of the equinoxes (*see* Chapter 5) the 26,000-year wobble that changes the position of stars relative to the horizon and the Sun.

It is of note that Brophy points out that the stars of Orion's Belt, as represented in the Nabta circle, are shown as it appeared on the meridian, which is an imaginary line in the sky that runs directly overhead from north to south and bisects the sky, at the summer solstice. This puts the circle (on top of the desert sands) at a date between 6400 BC and 4900 BC, and accords with the findings of the team led by Fred Wendorf that discovered Nabta. However, other parts of the circle are, according to Brophy, clearly aligned to 16,500 years BC. Robert Schock said of this:

> This is a date of such antiquity that debunkers, and hardcore conventional academics will immediately stop reading, but Brophy makes a compelling case that this is in fact what the stones represent.

Of course, given the dismissal of the findings of Alexander Thom, how much worse can it be for Thomas Brophy – an astrophysicist who would overturn the cosy standard story of the past, who would open the door to our theories having to be seriously considered?

But Brophy knows a thing or two about statistics. He has calculated the chances of all this being accidental. He says of just one set of stones:

> The probability that these stars aligned with the megaliths by random chance can be estimated according to the method developed by Schaefer (1986) ... The more conservative of the range of estimates gives random chance probability of these seven stars aligning with the megaliths according to this system of less than 2 chances in a million. That is more that a thousand times as certain as the usual 3 standard deviations required for accepting a scientific hypothesis as valid. The more liberal of the range of estimates gives a random probability of about one in ten to the thirteenth power, or about as likely as picking at random the same human being out of all people on Earth twice in a row. By even the more conservative estimate, these are by far the most certain ancient megalithic astronomical alignments of any known in the world.

Game, set and match?

We doubt it. As some academics will quietly agree, many will not like the possible outcome. Science and religion are far closer bedfellows than most people imagine.

A man who is considered something of a maverick Egyptologist – John Anthony West – has written the Afterword of Brophy's book. Here he takes a view on how Brophy can expect to be received by the chieftains of the tribe:

> In one sense Brophy's work will seem radical; revolutionary. Yet in another it can be seen as just the latest (admittedly most dramatic) contribution to a reappraisal of ancient history that has been lurching along by fits and starts for more than a century – over the raucous, concerted opposition of the entire community of archaeologists, historians, Egyptologists, anthropologists and all the other academic disciplines devoted to studying the past.
>
> So what is in store for *The Origin Map*? Given the reception accorded far less radical ideas, the reaction to Brophy's claims may be anticipated with some certainty.

There are few things in this world more predictable than the reaction of conventional minds to unconventional ideas. The reaction is always and invariably some combination of contempt, outrage, abuse and derision. As a common corollary, the level of outrage expressed is proportionate to both the quality of the supporting evidence and the magnitude of the challenge posed by the new idea – the better the evidence, the more radical the idea, the louder and shriller the response.[3]

Beautifully put, Mr West. And subsequent events have proven you correct.

As we returned from Rome we once again discussed the apparent impossibility of the Neolithic people having actually devised the wonderful system of measurements and geometry which they had self-evidently used. Could it be that the knowledge we had come across, and that had been used to build the pyramids, had originally come from Egypt anyway?

We could not know the answer – not yet and maybe we never will. But we now felt more confident than ever that we had found some very important parts of the puzzle. And if people like Thomas Brophy are prepared to publish and be damned, there is a good chance that between us we will eventually have a clear picture of the real past.

Chapter 11

·

CELTS, DRUIDS AND
FREEMASONRY

The Myth of the Celts

Despite being extremely busy with our various trips around Europe and beyond, and all the astronomical deskwork we were undertaking, there was one strand of our investigations we were conscious had been left unattended. We would never have recognized the importance of any of the British henges in the first place, had it not been for the chance encounter with the ancient British city of Bath and an extraordinary architect called John Wood.

Wood's most famous structure, the King's Circus in Bath, with its 366-MY circumference, had led us to look first at Stonehenge and then at the giant henges elsewhere in Britain. Of course it was entirely possible that the whole thing came about as a tremendous coincidence. John Wood simply copied the dimensions of the original henge at Stonehenge when he planned the King's Circus and, by so doing, without any knowledge of megalithic measures he provided the clue we needed to set us on a course of discovery. Indeed, had John Wood been just another genius of the 18th century, of which there were many in Regency Britain, we may have looked no further. However, bearing in mind his esoteric credentials and his fascination for ancient history, we could not absolutely dismiss from our minds the possibility that John Wood knew very well that the dimensions of the King's Circus were extremely important. To discover the truth we would have to know much more about Wood himself, and about the city of Bath.

John Wood, the man who planned and built some of the most important parts of Regency Bath, was born in Yorkshire in 1704, though his family heritage was from Bath, where he would return as a full-blown architect and town planner in 1727. From an early age he had shown an interest in art and architecture, and he cut his teeth on several commissions in London. As he grew and matured he met some influential people and somewhere along the line he developed what can only be described as an obsession for British history and, in particular, Druidism.

Archaeology was in its infancy, and history was rather misunderstood in Wood's 18th-century Britain. The general view of Britain's ancient past was confused and often plain wrong. Roman writings from the days of Empire had described the fierce warrior-priests of people they called Celts, referred to by Julius Caesar in particular as 'Druidi'. Gentlemen scholars of the 18th century came to suppose that any prehistoric religion or culture associated with Britain must have owed something to these strange and enigmatic characters described by the Roman invaders of long ago.

Even today most people associate the megalithic structures and henges of the British Isles and Brittany with the Celts and their Druidic priesthood. Modern Druids turn out in fanciful garb to celebrate Beltane (May Day) and other pagan celebrations, in the belief that they are touching the ancient wisdom of their ancestors. Unfortunately, the Celts (an 18th-century word adopted from the Roman *Celtae*) are a central and eastern European tribe that did not emerge until the late Iron Age – thousands of years after Thornborough or Stonehenge were built. These Austrian-Hungarian peoples moved west and north to arrive in the British Isles only relatively shortly before the Romans. Their 'new' language still lives on in parts of Ireland, Scotland, Wales, Cornwall and Brittany, though it died out in their original homelands. The Celts were definitely not the architects of any prehistoric structures in the British Isles or western France.

It is possible that Celts arriving in Britain did become aware of ancient ideas and assimilate them into their own culture memory, indeed the Druid priests may have been adopted by the Celts, along with their knowledge from indigenous peoples such as the so-called Grooved Ware people or the Beaker Folk. This seems all the more likely because the Druids are not (as far as we can find out) known in the central European Celtic areas.

The term Druid is an Indo-European construction, with a literal meaning of two parts: 'oak' and 'seeing'. It has been suggested that the 'oak' part was a reference to oak-like qualities – old, strong, established, solid; and the 'seeing' element meant understand, knowledge, and is related to the Irish word for 'magic' and the Welsh for a seer. The overall effect is that these people were the repository of a great knowledge that was associated with magic. Interestingly, the word 'magic' exists in ancient cultures from China to Persia where it is associated with the Magi – astronomer-priests that date back 5,000 years. Like the Druids, the Persian Magi wore white robes and were believed to possess great powers by virtue of their knowledge of the Sun, Moon and stars.

A recent find of many mummified bodies in the Tarim Xinjiang Uigur Autonomous Region in western China may provide a clue to how the concept of astronomical magic reached that remote country. Thanks to the salty desert sands in which these people were buried, the 4,000-year-old bodies are almost unbelievably well preserved with intact skin, flesh, hair and internal organs. They are believed to have ruled this part of China, yet they are western Europeans with red hair and even the women are over six feet tall. These ancient people are dressed in colourful robes, trousers, boots, stockings, coats and pointed 'witch' hats.

One expert, Elizabeth Barber, professor of archaeology and linguistics at Occidental College in Los Angeles, has said:

> Yet another female … wore a terrifically tall, conical hat, just like those we depict on witches riding their broomsticks at Halloween or on medieval wizards intent on magical spells. And that resemblance, strange to say, may be no accident. Our witches and wizards got their tall, pointy hats from just where we got the words magician and magic, namely, Persia. The Persian or Iranian word Magus (cognate with the English might, mighty) denoted a priest or sage, of the Zoroastrian religion in particular. Magi distinguished themselves

with tall hats; they also professed knowledge of astronomy and medicine, of how to control the winds and the weather by potent magic and how to contact the spirit world.[1]

Dr Barber suggested the origin of these ancient people by saying:

> The dominant weave (of these people) proved to be normal diagonal twill and the chief decoration was plaid, as in the woollen twill of a Scottish kilt … Many historians have assumed that the idea of plaids was relatively new to Scotland in the seventeenth century. Archaeology tells a different story.

We congratulate Professor Barber on some stunningly good work. But we cannot help but wonder how many archaeologists specializing in the British Neolithic period have stepped out of their box and caught a plane to China to view these stunning artefacts at first hand? Not too many, we suspect.

Another expert, Victor Mair, Professor of Chinese at the University of Pennsylvania, has stated that the old Chinese word for a court magician was *mag* which is phonetically from the same root as 'magi'. Furthermore, the Chinese written character for *mag* is a cross with slightly splayed ends, identical to that used by the medieval Order of the Knights Templar (a subject to which we shall return).

The world of myth and mystery that has evolved into modern yarns, such as the *Harry Potter* books and films, contains all kinds of cultural memories of a long lost science. The broomsticks upon which these people ride in the light of the Moon is often shown as an old-fashioned twig brush – but the term is 'broomstick', i.e. just a stick about as stout and long as would be used for a broom. The henge and megalithic builders undoubtedly used such sticks to make alignments and to cast shadows in order to calculate time of day, direction, and time of year. These were the primary tools of the magi, and they were still used in the Middle Ages to establish the direction of east when a church was being built.

The first break of sunlight over the landscape cast a shadow from such a stick. The place where the sun rose was considered to be the east and the shadow, running east–west, cast by the stick formed the line along which the north-facing wall of the church was built (the foundation stone always being placed in the northeast). Of course the sun does not always rise due east, sometimes it rises north of east and sometimes south of east, dependent on the time of year. Even today it is possible to work out the name of an old British church by looking at the shadow of a stick and researching the relevant saint's day. For example, a church aligned to either solstice will generally have originally been a church of St John.

One can imagine how simple people would be in awe of those with the ability to predict an eclipse, for example. These astronomer-priests would be considered witches and wizards, who probably flew across the sky to visit the Moon and the stars on their big sticks under cover of darkness. Furthermore, one can also guess that they used their perceived powers to good effect when they wanted the cooperation of the masses – a kind of 'do as I say or I'll turn you into a frog at the next full Moon.'

So, the story of the builders of the henges and megalithic structures looks as though it is far more diverse and complex than most people believe, and a linear pathway from Thornborough to the Druids of Roman times is probably a smaller part of the picture. But it is what people believe, however mistaken, that counts.

Whatever the Druids of Roman Britain were about, they must have been very well-educated people. According to Roman accounts the people they called Druids were peripatetic priests. Individuals chosen to become Druids studied in specific 'colleges' for anything up to 20 years before they could even begin to practise their arts – whatever they may have been. They were also lawgivers, and their decisions and judgements crossed all tribal boundaries. To harm a Druid meant instant death and in arbitration their word was sacrosanct. At the time of the invasion of Britain in AD 43 the Romans knew that they could never have control over the locals until they had destroyed the Druids and assumed their power. Their Legions chased the unfortunate Druids around the country until they had retreated to their last main base at Anglesey. So desperate were the Roman forces (made up largely of mercenaries from places as diverse as Iberia and Judea) that they crossed the treacherous tidal flow of the Menai Straits by swimming in their armour and with their horses.

The Romans took control of each megalithic site held by the Druids, and then resurfaced what was already a comprehensive road network for the benefit of their chariots. Many people think that the Romans brought straight roads to Britain; they did not – they merely had a large budget for a road improvement scheme.

Undoubtedly some Druids escaped and the now secretive priesthood popped up now and again throughout British history right up to the 15th century. It has been suggested that Druidic wisdom, beliefs, and even mode of dress, became preserved within a very early Celtic Christian monastic tradition known as Culdee.

So important did the Druids appear to those gazing back into the mists of time from the 18th century that it must have seemed reasonable to suppose that structures of unknown origin, such as Stonehenge in Wiltshire, had originally been temples and the most likely people to have planned and run them were the Druids – who were, after all, known to have been priests.

The City of Bath

At the time John Wood was coming to prominence, an age of romanticism was dawning across Western Europe. Landed aristocrats were beginning to open up wide vistas on their estates, sometimes peopled with deliberately placed hermits, shepherdesses, structural follies and Elysian statuary. The whole concept of the pastoral idyll was gaining ground and the white-robed Druids with their long beards, badges of honour, and golden sickles, fitted the mood of the time extremely well. Julius Caesar had described the Druids as being the most learned men of their culture – the absolute repositories of science, religion and law.

John Wood could hardly have failed to be influenced by what was happening around him, but he was a trendsetter rather than a follower. Wood had written about Stonehenge and the Stanton Drew stone circle, and he was fascinated in particular with the history of Bath, the origin of which he credited to a king by the name of Bladud. Wood was familiar with what is clearly a mythical tale about Bladud. It tells of a man who was cast out by his fellows in a remote time because he had some horrible skin disease. Together with his pigs, which were similarly afflicted, Bladud wandered far and wide until he found the hot springs of what would one day be Bath. There his pigs bathed and were soon cured of their infirmity. Bladud did likewise and was also healed. He went on to become king of the area and founded a great city on the site of the healing spa.

Almost certainly Bladud never existed, but the story was popular at the time and John Wood most certainly believed it. During the early part of his career Wood was also mixing with some very powerful, influential and fashionable people, and it is to his association with some of these individuals that we might partly credit his growing fascination with both Druidism and Freemasonry.

John Wood undertook commissions in and around Bath, and his work was highly regarded. Despite a degree of success, Wood had a dream for Bath and although he had to modify his plans a great deal, the King's Circus would be his greatest achievement. Wood's original idea had been to create three magnificent public areas, all in different locations, but each equally wonderful. The first of these would be a 'Royal Forum', the second would be a great circus for the exhibition of sports, and the third building, just as magnificent, would be for medicinal and physical exercises and would be called 'the Imperial Gymnasium'. Exactly where these three structures were intended to be is not known, though in the fullness of time we would come to have a possible clue. In reality the only one that came to full fruition was the Circus, which in the end became a circle of houses rather than a forum for sport.

No better explanation of Wood's intentions for Bath are to be found than those expressed by Paul Newman in a book on Bath published in 1986 by the Pevensey Press.[2] Newman says of Wood:

> He conceived of a city where houses were not set down in jumbles of isolated units but joined in graceful terraces, crescents and squares, all built of the lovely pale freestone producing an effect that was regular, majestic and harmonious ... Certain Bath effects seem almost eerily beautiful; no other English city can show such a rare combination of composure of design and decorative ebullience.

All of this became possible because Wood believed that the proportions of classical architecture had been divinely inspired – and no doubt he thought the same about Stonehenge and other stone circles. He revelled in order and symmetry, and with his fascination for astronomy he accepted without question the mythical/historical belief that each of Bath's seven hills represented one or other of the heavenly bodies.

True, the finished King's Circus would be far from the edifice he had originally conceived, but it would at least be the 'right size' and shape – a theoretical equilateral triangle within a circle of divine proportions. Bearing in mind all that we came to know about Wood, his interests and obsessions, it seemed and still seems highly unlikely that there was anything coincidental about the dimensions of his ultimate masterpiece. This is borne out by the fact that Queen's Square, an earlier creation of John Wood's and slightly south of the King's Circus, had identical dimensions. (A diagonal line taken from corner to corner of Queen's Square measures 96.6 m, which is the diameter of King's Circus.) In other words, Queen's Square too has undeniable megalithic credentials. Queen's Square cannot be a coincidental copy of Stonehenge simply because it is a square and not a circle. What is more, it was built 'before' King's Circus.

Another indication that John Wood knew exactly what he was doing has been brought to light in recent years. The British television presenter and architect Dan Cruickshank was not the first to point out that if one looks at the King's Circus on a map, or on aerial photographs, it is plain that when one extends a line down from the Circus to Queen's Square, what is achieved when one takes in both the Circus and the Square is a huge 'key'. More than one commentator, including Cruickshank, has suggested that the geometry and measurements of these two structures, and the road that joins them, offers 'the' key to John Wood's esoteric mind in his plans for Bath.

Exactly what association John Wood had with modern Druidism is hard to say. In a formal sense modern Druidism came into existence in 1717. The Druids may have been meeting in an unofficial way for some time, but it was on the day of the autumn equinox in 1717 (23 September) that they took their first official steps. This meeting took place at the Apple Tree Tavern in Covent Garden, London, and was attended by many of those who had famously founded the first Grand Lodge of Free-masonry at the Goose and Gridiron in St Paul's Churchyard, London, three months earlier at the time of the summer solstice – the feast of St John the Baptist.

Here we have the same people formalizing two arcane but highly influ-ential bodies that both claim to be the repositories of ancient knowledge going back many thousand of years. And they chose astronomically key dates to resurrect themselves.

As regards Freemasonry, we are confident that they do have such knowledge because Chris has spent over 30 years reconstructing the transmission of these secrets.

At the time the Druids came into official existence, which had been made possible (like Freemasonry) because of a relaxation of draconian religious laws in England and Wales, John Wood was only 13 years of age. It seems that he came to Druidism as a result of his own interest in megalithic structures such as Stonehenge. He certainly knew William Stukely, who was arguably Britain's first serious archaeologist. Stukely was a founder member of the Society of Antiquaries, a Freemason and the Grand Master of the Ancient Order of Druids, a position he held for 46 years from 1722. Throughout his life the Reverend Stukely popularized the semi-mythical historical order. Ultimately Stukely did not have very much time for John Wood, or rather Wood's own conclusions about Stonehenge. However, despite the fact that Stukely is referred to as the 'father' of archaeology, John Wood created better and more accurate plans of Stonehenge than either Stukely or any other gentleman historian of the period.

There is no documentary evidence that John Wood was either a prac-tising Druid or a Freemason, though when one looks at the evidence left by his buildings and their ornamentation there can surely be little doubt that he was deeply influenced by them and, more likely, fully involved in both.

Above the ground level of the houses around King's Circus in Bath are friezes carrying carved images. These are an odd collection but many of them are deeply Masonic in origin and would be recognized as such by any modern Freemason. Amongst the carvings are to be found compasses and squares, reaping hooks and stooks of corn, acacia plants, five-pointed stars, equilateral triangles, pyramids, beehives and a host of other Freemasonic icons.

Did John Wood really leave a 'key' within the buildings of Bath that he had so carefully created, and if so, what was the lock it was meant to open? Could Wood have known about the Megalithic Yard and about megalithic geometry, or were his use of them the result of his surveying of sites like Stonehenge?

Our minds went back to an earlier book we had co-written. This was *Solomon's Power Brokers* published in 2007. *Solomon's Power Brokers* was a book about the secrets of Freemasonry and about a mysterious but continuous transmission of knowledge that seems to have survived from truly ancient times but is still evident today. This knowledge, which seems to have been absorbed by and transmitted through Freemasonry, includes aspects of megalithic geometry, and inclines its adherents to an ancient philosophy and resurrection-based rituals that claim to be archaic in origin.

We called those who possess and transmit this specific knowledge the 'Star Families' because included amongst their beliefs and knowledge is a great deal of astronomy and a deep understanding of the role of the planet Venus and its relationships with the Sun. There are times in history when it is clear to see that the Star Families represented a hereditary line, but also other periods when the knowledge was passed on via fraternities and institutions. Freemasonry and Druidism were undoubtedly two of these.

However, we do not suggest that every Freemason or Druid, either historical or modern, is in possession of the Star Family knowledge. On the contrary, it seems to have been reserved for a very few people at any point in time and it could be that Freemasonry, modern Druidism and the like, together with older institutions such as the Cistercian monastic order and the Knights Templar, have simply offered a conduit through which this deeper and more esoteric material can be transmitted to the chosen few.

Our Star Family research seemed to lie outside the scope of the present book and we may have disregarded the importance of the City of Bath, or at least put it to one side for another time, had it not been for what came to light subsequently. It was almost by chance that we happened to spot another circle in Bath, not too far to the right of King's Circus, and when we carefully measured the distance it was immediately megalithic.

The first circle was of course King's Circus, and the second, in an easterly direction, is now Henrietta Park. This park is named after Henrietta Laura Pulteney, who was the first countess of Bath and heiress to a huge fortune, much of which was spent in and around the city of Bath. Henrietta was not born until 1766, by which time John Wood the architect had been dead for 12 years. He died in his 50th year, just before King's Circus was completed, but during his lifetime he had been very close to the Pulteney family, which was reputed to be the wealthiest family in Europe at that time.

It is not at all clear exactly what the site of Henrietta Park was originally intended to be. Its circle can be seen on an old map of central Bath that dates back to the time when the King's Circus was either being built or had just been completed. On this map all that can be seen is a perfect circle in the midst of what was obviously at the time undeveloped land. Henrietta Park was not opened to the public until much later, in fact in 1897, but development of land in this part of Bath had been significantly slowed down by, of all things, the American War of Independence. Much of the Pulteney holdings were in North America and the West Indies. Unrest, caused by the fallout between Britain and its American colonies, had a significant bearing on the family fortunes and it can be seen that for this, and other reasons, land to the east of King's Circus was not developed fully until well into the 19th century.

Our reason for paying any attention at all to the circle that eventually became Henrietta Park was that centre-to-centre it is an incredibly neat 2 Megalithic Seconds or 732 MY (607.3 m) from the King's Circus. This could be a bizarre coincidence.

We could not help but wonder if a third had been planned, or indeed built and since lost, so as to make a perfect copy of the Orion's Belt henges at Thornborough. This is an investigation that will have to continue after this book is completed.

Ancient Freemasonry

This information was another highly significant staging post in our research, not least because it was these circles that alerted us to the henges in the first place. For years we had come across 'hints' that aspects of knowledge regarding the megalithic system had survived and that some of them had been encapsulated into that most peculiar of institutions, Freemasonry. This was certainly not evidence that could confirm or deny a Freemasonic link to these megalithic values – but it certainly raised our level of suspicion. However, we would not have to wait to long to find extraordinary evidence of such knowledge being used by Freemasons at that time and since.

According to some modern Freemasons, the fraternity is nothing more than an 18th-century invention – an amalgamation of historical facts and fantasies, deliberately created to foster comradeship and to promote good citizenship amongst its members. Even those senior Freemasons who encourage this line of thought, notably the paid officers of the United Grand Lodge of England, know it is untrue.

Chris wrote his first book in 1996 after 20 years of private research into the origins of the rituals used by Freemasonry. He had expected to find that they had evolved from the rituals used by medieval stonemasons (as the standard history cautiously intimates) but he found that that was way off the truth. In fact, he found that the many old rituals of the order correctly tell a story of the transmission of information from deep antiquity.

Those who ask to become Freemasons, and are accepted (invitation is not strictly speaking permitted), are put through three stages called 'degrees' which are astronomically structured. The temple is laid out with the Worshipful Master in the east to mark the rising equinox Sun, a Senior Warden in the south to mark the Sun at its meridian and the Junior Warden in the west representing the setting Sun. The Worshipful Master has the two pillars that stood outside King Solomon's Temple, Boaz and Jachin, behind him on either side – representing the extremes of the Sun on the horizon at the solstices.

Jachin (meaning foundation) is in the northeast, marking the summer solstice, and Boaz (meaning strength) is in the southeast marking the winter solstice. In the first degree, the candidate is given certain information whilst standing in the line of the shadow cast by Jachin, and in the second degree in the shadow of Boaz. Finally, in the third degree, the candidate is made a Master Mason in a totally dark room after being symbolically 'killed' and resurrected to a new life under the light of the rising Venus at the equinox.

This is exactly the layout used at megalithic sites such as Newgrange in Ireland, where the light of Venus penetrates into the centre of the structure once every eight years – although this is just before dawn at the winter solstice.

The mode of the 'death' of the candidate for the third degree is a re-enactment of the supposed assassination of Hiram Abif, the architect of King Solomon's Temple; an event that, if true, would have taken place around 980 BC. Hiram Abif had been supplied by the Phoenician king, Hiram of Tyre, at great cost because he brought great secrets with him that Solomon desperately needed. The architect is said to have been murdered by workmen who tried unsuccessfully to extract those great secrets.

Once a Master Mason (the highest degree in mainstream 'Craft' Masonry) the individual is free to join other degrees such as those of the Ancient and Accepted Scottish Rite. The Scottish Rite is of particular significance as its 33 degrees originally told (unfortunately many have been altered) the story of the progress of an ancient knowledge from before Noah's Flood through Old Testament times to the Middle Ages and beyond. In the United States anyone who sticks around long enough can reach the 32nd degree (without participating in most of the intermediate degrees at all), but the 33rd degree is restricted to about 1 per cent of eligible Masons.

To anyone embarking on the Freemasonic road and expecting finally to understand exactly what the hotchpotch of gestures, icons, flowery passages and paraphernalia might actually mean, disappointment is the final destination. In reality what seems to matter most to Freemasons is not the ceremony (though most would admit it has some very beautiful and prosaic elements) but rather its fraternal and charitable elements.

This seemingly nonsensical series of lectures, ceremonies and the award of various degrees, beyond the three recognized ones of 'Entered

Apprentice', 'Fellowcraft' and 'Master Mason', were as much of a puzzle to Chris, when he embarked along this road many years ago, as they were to any of his fellow Masons. The difference in the case of Chris is that he decided to discover what Freemasonry was really all about – if anything.

His results are detailed in the best-selling book *The Hiram Key*,[3] written with fellow Mason, Robert Lomas. Far from being nonsense, Chris came to understand that Freemasonry had genuine historical integrity and that elements of it did indeed go back far into the mists of time. It turned out that rather than being assisted by the formalization of Free-masonry that took place in 18th-century England, the Craft was actually depleted and diminished at that time. Prior to the Grand Lodge being formed in London, Freemasonry had been a peculiarly Scottish institution and it was in its Scottish pre-18th-century intentions and cere-monies that Chris found the 'heart' of the order.

According to *The Hiram Key* the true secrets of Freemasonry were to be found within, or perhaps more probably below, a strange little 15th-century Scottish building known as Rosslyn Chapel. Our past researches, both in common and individually, have shown in a number of books just how important Rosslyn Chapel actually is to Freemasonry. Rosslyn Chapel is nothing more or less than an attempt to recreate King Solomon's Temple on British soil – although it is actually based on knowl-edge of King Herod's Temple rebuilt at the time of Christ. Although it purports to be a Christian chapel, and merely a part of something that was intended to be much bigger, it has been acknowledged by several experts that it is nothing of the sort. It stands in stark isolation – its unfin-ished western end inferring that it would eventually have been only the eastern end of a much larger church, but the ragged stonework at the western end is nothing more than a sham – perhaps a way to deceive a jealous Catholic Church about the building's real pedigree.

It is suggested that the true secrets of Freemasonry are to be found far below the chapel, buried there by William Sinclair in around AD 1440. Sinclair was the powerful Scottish aristocrat who created this amazing little masterpiece of stone carving. The *Hiram Key* shows a detailed ground plan, and deliberate architectural messages and clues that point to the secrets of Freemasonry that are believed to be carefully hidden deep beneath the structure. Up to now, those who have a responsibility for the so-called chapel have seen fit to leave its possible treasure undisturbed, but Rosslyn remains a place that attracts hundreds of thousands of visitors each year. It is a virtual shrine to Freemasonry, whose members come from all over the world to see it.

Even Dan Brown in his novel *The Da Vinci Code* saw fit to take Chris' observations about Rosslyn and weave them into a brand of fiction that is wholly outclassed by real history when it comes to intrigue and mystery.

Following on from Chris' research, Alan joined forces with John Ritchie, a historian and researcher who grew up in the village in which the chapel is to be found. They took careful measurements of the building and were granted access to its roof and to the gallery above the retrochoir. The details of their discoveries are to be found in the book *Rosslyn Revealed*.[4] Alan's expertise in historical astronomy came in handy because it was possible to reveal just how important Rosslyn Chapel was in an astronomical sense, and just how much trouble had been taken over its dimensions and its geographical position.

The Rosslyn temple, as it should more properly be called, is as significant in terms of its latitude as was Solomon's Temple, far away in Jerusalem. Both are built from identical rock – from the same seam – and both allowed for a unique view of a rare event known as the 'Shekinah', which is a coming together in the pre-dawn sky of the planets Mercury and Venus just ahead of the Sun. More details of the Shekinah and its historical significance can be found in *Solomon's Power Brokers*.[5] But what became quite obvious in the research leading up to the publication of *Rosslyn Revealed* was that Rosslyn Chapel was built with naked-eye astronomy in mind and that it could be described more reasonably as an 'observatory' than a church.

And just as Solomon carefully laid the foundation stone of his temple 1,440 years (one complete Shekinah cycle) after the Flood abated, Rosslyn was begun 1,440 years after the assumed birth of the Messiah.

There can surely no longer be any doubt that Freemasonry owes a great debt to Rosslyn Chapel. It has been suggested that it was in this location that the Craft was actually born. Secrets, both under Rosslyn

Chapel and most likely within its architecture and sumptuous carvings, had to be safeguarded from both Church and State in the extremely dangerous days of the 15th century. One way of achieving this secrecy would have been to enrol all the masons involved in the project into a secret brotherhood – an extension of the already powerful craft guild to which they would have belonged since the time of the Knights Templar. Since Rosslyn Chapel was a carefully created copy of King Herod's reincarnation of the Jerusalem Temple, it seems appropriate that the Temple and its foundation lie at the heart of Freemasonry.

From its Scottish origins Freemasonry became Anglicized, after James VI of Scotland also became James I of England. Many of its core ceremonies were altered during infighting between groups designated as 'Ancients' and 'Moderns', and some of its origin fables were changed or replaced to infer a more English ancestry. In our estimation the heart was torn out of Freemasonry when it became an essentially English institution just after the beginning of the 18th century. It therefore seemed natural to assume that any truly ancient legacy, such as knowledge of megalithic measures and the fantastic old system of which they were part, would have been lost to Freemasonry. Certainly during the many talks we have both given to Freemasons around the world we have never seen the slightest 'glimmer' or recognition in the eyes of our audience when factors such as the Megalithic Yard were mentioned – not even amongst the most elevated Masons.

However, Freemasonry describes itself as being at least as ancient as the earliest megalithic structure. But the standard reaction, quite understandably, is to assume that these very old rituals are romantic invention. We have very good reason to believe that there is substance to the claims.

When one spends years collecting and interrogating the oldest rituals of the Scottish Rite – begged from some of Scotland's earliest recorded lodges – a picture emerges that is utterly startling. At the very root of Freemasonry is the idea that before the biblical Flood, there was an advanced civilization that was adept at the sciences – from mathematics to astronomy. When the story is pieced together it tells how knowledge of this progenitor science was written down on a pedestal known as the 'Delta of Enoch'. This pedestal is described in a Masonic ritual that has not been used for over 200 years. It is described as being triangular in shape and the centre-piece for a temple built by Enoch; this at the time that Newgrange and other major megalithic sites were being constructed in the British Isles. Whilst Enoch's temple was built in the land that would become known as Canaan and eventually Israel, the Book of Enoch describes, by means of astronomical observation, how he travelled to the latitude of Newgrange and there met God.[6]

The Book of Enoch is one of the earliest texts known to mankind. It became lost from the first century AD until it was rediscovered by a Freemason in Ethiopia, in the 18th century – long after the Masonic degree had been in use.

The ritual describes how Enoch took his secrets and eventually stopped in the land of Canaan where he excavated down into the ground, creating nine apartments, one above the other with each roof arched – with the bottom one cut out of solid rock. In the crown of each arch he left an aperture closed with a square stone, and over the very top he built a small temple. All of this was before the biblical Flood, and designed to withstand the pressures of the crashing waters and protect the ancient secrets therein. The ritual states:

> None knew of the deposits of the precious treasure: and, that it might remain undiscovered, and survive the Flood, which was known to Enoch would soon overwhelm the world in one vast sea of mire, he covered the aperture, and the stone that closed it, and the great ring of iron used to raise the stone, with the granite pavement of his primitive temple.[7]

According to Masonic legend, the Flood came and did its worst, and Enoch's Delta remained safely preserved beneath the ruins of his temple for thousands of years.

The ritual eventually moves forward to the time of King Solomon, around 3,000 years ago. After David (Solomon's father) has taken the city state of Jerusalem, he decides to build a temple, but this task is finally undertaken by his son, Solomon. The new king orders his workmen to clear the ground above the city and they hear a hollow sound as they strike a rock. Upon examination they discover an underground chamber. Investigation eventually leads to the recovery of Enoch's lost secrets.

The Temple of Solomon is then built on top of the super-ancient site.

As the story told by the rituals moves on, it tells how the Temple was destroyed by the Babylonians and rebuilt, destroyed again by the Romans in AD 70 and left for 1,000 years. Then it recounts how the Knights Templar, as the descendants of the Jerusalem priesthood, arrived in 1118, after the first Crusade, and dug down in search of their lost secrets. They found them in 1128 and instantly became the richest and most influential religious order the world has ever known.

The Templars rediscovered the ancient secrets and immediately began immense changes to society. Socially, architecturally, politically, commercially and spiritually – these people radically altered the world. To understand the complexity of their task and the enormity of their success, see our book – *Solomon's Power Brokers*.

The bottom line is that Freemasonry consistently claims to be the guardian of ancient scientific knowledge – and every aspect of the ritual is based in observational astronomy. Could there be an awareness of Neolithic science?

So, the question stands – was John Wood in possession of ancient knowledge when he designed the modern city of Bath? It seemed strange to imagine, yet if the oldest rituals of Freemasonry were not complete invention, someone understood the ancient secrets of science.

We had less than a year to wait for an unexpected piece of luck that transformed the possibility of Wood's megalithic intentions from long-shot to odds-on. Quite by accident we were to discover that another, far greater city, was designed using a pure form of megalithic thinking.

Chapter 12

•

A NEW JERUSALEM

A Very Modern Henge

The team from the TV production company in LA had travelled to London for the making of a two-part documentary for the History Channel on the Founding Fathers of the United States, and Chris had agreed to be interviewed concerning the Masonic connections of this august group. The evening before, Chris consulted some of his previous books to remind himself of some points of detail – and his mind went back to a pleasant visit to Washington a few years previously when he had stayed at a small hotel in Georgetown.

Georgetown is a historic settlement that became a town in 1751 but is now absorbed into the city of Washington DC. It still has an old-world feel to it and, being on higher ground to the northwest of the city, it provides a splendid view across to the Washington Monument and beyond. Chris had walked from his hotel down to the Potomac River to look across at Rosslyn – a name that held a lot of interest for him. As he was at his computer, he opened up Google Earth to see if he could use the aerial views to spot the hotel and the route he had taken that day.

As he was about to close the program down, something caught his eye and he moved the object to centre screen. Oddly, there was a very large circle that looked extremely henge-like. Of course it could not be a henge here in the New World, but if it had been in England Chris would have been surprised if it were not. It was ridiculous really, but he opened the measuring device within the program and converted its diameter from metres to Megalithic Yards just to see what would happen. His eyes widened as he realized that it was extremely close to being 2 Megalithic Degrees across.

A little investigation proved that it was indeed a henge and within its huge circumference sits the home of the Vice President of the United States of America. It is, however, a very recent henge. Known as the 'Observatory Circle' it was constructed by the navy in 1893 and, according to the official White House website, it was created so that scientists could 'observe the sun, moon, planets and selected stars, determine and precisely measure the time, and establish astronomical data needed for accurate navigation'.[1]

What finer definition of a henge could there be?

Nothing really changes even after 5,500 years. Instead of hand-swung pendulums the US Navy astronomers will have used pendulum clocks – which are exactly the same thing except the more modern version has a labour-saving wind-up mechanism attached to it and a dial to read out the passage of time, so the users no longer have to count the beats themselves. But it is an identical process requiring identical skills and delivering identical benefits to the civilization concerned.

This discovery made us more bemused than ever. Given that a relatively modern circular earthwork is known to be used to measure time, accumulate astronomical data and aid navigation, why is the similarity displayed by Neolithic henges rejected as a valid theory? It is fully accepted that these ancient people must have been sailors, so they would have wanted this information. If the academic researchers dug up a Stone Age coffee cup and saucer, would they make a connection with hot drinks or would they assume it was some kind of religious talisman for collecting the spirits of the dead?

The Observatory Circle in Washington DC is a fine piece of evidence for an archaeological theory. Human beings have not changed physiologically or intellectually for over 100,000 years. Their curiosity, their need to know, must surely be much the same, and the techniques to achieve the required results will not, indeed cannot, change in principle.

Our next question was to try and establish whether the Naval Observatory had an apparently megalithic dimension by accident or whether it was a deliberate construction.

We began by looking at key landmarks such as the White House, the Capitol Building, the Washington Monument and the Jefferson and Lincoln Memorials. And immediately we began to see a web beneath the street design – all mapped out in Megalithic Seconds of arc.

We were completely lost for words.

The Secret of the Ellipse

What we were starting to uncover was extraordinary in the extreme – is it conceivable that Washington was designed using megalithic proportions?

We had to be cautious in jumping to any undue conclusions because 366 MY is very close to being 1,000 ft (996.25 ft) following from the ancient Minoan foot used 4,000 years ago. The Observatory Circle *could* have a deliberately engineered megalithic diameter, but measuring the Circle absolutely accurately is difficult and it may be that those designing it had intended it to have a diameter of 2,000 ft. After all, the statute foot was in common use in the United States when the Observatory Circle was completed, as it still is to this day. This was the most likely answer, although all British large-scale historical measurements in the United States tended to be measured in yards, rods, poles or furlongs rather than feet. Using yards would mean the Circle was an ungainly 666.6 units, and using rods produced 121.21 units.

We are not aware of anyone in history using 1,000 ft as a major unit but we knew that the Neolithic British peoples, and the later Minoans, used a second of arc that was 366 MY or 1,000 Minoan Feet. This was of course a 1/360th subdivision of a Megalithic Second of arc of the polar circumference of the Earth.

We needed to be highly circumspect about what we were starting to find, because chance results do crop up.

Because our books have gained a lot of interest we receive a lot of correspondence from people who have their own ideas that they wish to share. This is a wonderful thing – indeed we met because Alan contacted

Chris after *The Hiram Key* appeared. A number of people who have contacted us over the years have had some really interesting ideas, whilst others appear to be fanciful in the extreme. There is a category of people whom we call 'dot-joiners'. They take a map and draw lines between selected points to produce symbols or other supposedly meaningful shapes – but the points chosen always seem to be selected to fit the required pattern. They ignore similar points that do not fit, and they often take unrelated objects to complete the pattern. It is like a visual form of numerology where patterns are found for little or no reason.

There are people who are certain that the government of the United States represents a Masonic, and/or sometimes Jewish, plot to instigate a 'New World Order'. These people and are convinced that all manner of secret patterns are to be found when one connects particular Washington structures together. There are many books that concentrate on this preoccupation, not to mention a number of odd-ball websites. People claim to have found all manner of shapes and symbols when connecting Washington DC's various landmarks, including, most famously, a rather obvious huge pentacle.[2]

Given the frequent use of symmetry, building geometric shapes within Washington DC's ground plan is not difficult. The city plan was first laid out by the French engineer and architect Charles L'Enfant and, although his original plan was somewhat modified by Andrew Ellicot, the essence of L'Enfant's original design remains. L'Enfant allowed for wide avenues, circles and squares at major intersections, and lots of parks. Together with the gridiron pattern of the streets of Washington DC it is therefore quite easy to create a host of different geometric shapes, using only a map, a pencil and plenty of imagination.

One shape that was nearly as important as the circle to the Neolithic builders of Western Europe was the ellipse, which has a natural centre but is constructed around two foci. This is a shape that can easily be constructed on a beach, for instance. Place two sticks in the ground and create a loop of rope that is slightly longer than the gap between the sticks. Then place the loop over the sticks and, with another stick in your hand, draw in the sand with the stick inside the loop at full extension. The shape in the sand after one circuit will be an ellipse.

In the case of the Washington Ellipse, the two foci (the sticks) were 276 ft either side of the centre. However, it was the major axis (east–west) that grabbed our attention. We took the path that runs right around the edge of the Ellipse to represent its intended original extent. From the centre of this path on the west side of the Ellipse to the centre of the path on the east side of the Ellipse is exactly 366 MY, and quite definitely not 1,000 feet.

Then we turned our attention just to the southeast of the Ellipse – to the Washington Monument. This huge, white stela was designed in 1836 by Robert Mills, an architect and a Freemason. Excavation for the foundation of the Monument began in the spring of 1848 and the corner-stone was laid as part of an elaborate Fourth of July ceremony conducted by the Freemasons.

Around the base of this major monument are two intersecting circles defined by another ellipse. This ellipse, too, is 366 MY in length at its widest part.

Remembering what we had discovered in Bath, we thought it worth measuring some of the distances between specific important buildings in Washington DC, as well as to and from geometric focal points such as the meridian marker at the centre of the Ellipse. We struck gold immediately. The direct distance between the Ellipse centre and a position right under the centre of the dome of the Capitol building is 2,429 m. In Megalithic Yards this is 2927.7 MY. Working in blocks of 366 MY (1 Megalithic Second of arc of the polar circumference of the Earth), the distance between these two points is 8 × 366 MY, or 8 Megalithic Seconds of geographic arc.[3]

When we first started to use Google Earth for measuring henges and megalithic structures, we conducted a series of checks of known distances on the ground and found that the program is highly accurate. However, henges are all at ground level and there are no perspective and parallax problems. But tall buildings introduce distortion, especially when the photograph was not taken directly overhead. Looking at the Capitol Building as shown on Google Earth, we identified exterior features that were at interior ground level and projected them inwards to find the true centre under the dome. We believe that this gave us a suitably accurate point of reference. Had we simply used the top of the dome as it appears in the aerial shot, we would have been well over 100 ft out.

In this instance we were unlikely to be dealing in units of 1,000 ft. Eight units of 1,000 ft would of course have measured 8,000 ft, whereas the measurement we obtained was 7,970 ft, a full 30 ft short of 8,000 ft. But it was extremely accurate in terms of Megalithic Yards – in fact completely within the possible accuracy levels we were working with.

Was this yet another random result? This certainly did not seem to be the case because the meridian marker at the centre of the Ellipse turned out to be a very important hub for megalithic measurements across much of Washington DC.

Northeast and northwest of the Ellipse centre, beyond the White House, are two matching parks, each with circles at their centres. They are two of the main features in the original layout for Washington. The one to the northeast is McPherson Square and the one to the northwest is Farragut Square. The distance between the middle of the Ellipse and centre of each of these parks is 2,988 ft, which is 3 × 366 MY. In other words, each park is precisely 3 Megalithic Seconds of arc from the centre of the city.

Now, someone might protest that it was probably meant to be 3,000 ft (i.e. 1,000 yd) and they made a bit of an error. But why should there be any integer distance for these features? This has nothing to do with the street layout – this is a web beneath the superficial city plan. And the centre of the Ellipse has never, openly at least, ever been described as significant for anything. And why would they measure in feet?

If the Capitol and these squares are the only features of Washington that have relationships that are integer in terms of Megalithic Seconds of arc, then maybe it is just a weird coincidence.

Further to the northeast of the Ellipse is Logan Circle Park. This is another of the legacies of the original Washington ground plan. Its distance from the Ellipse was 6 × 366 MY, and therefore 6 Megalithic Seconds of polar arc.

To the northwest is a matching circle park, this one called Dupont Circle. It too is 6 × 366 MY and 6 Megalithic Seconds of polar arc,[4] but from the western foci of the Ellipse this time. The accuracy for both of these circles was not quite as good as the inner circles but it was still better than a 99.5 per cent fit.

Even a sceptic will by now have wrinkled brow. This is not a coincidence. Somebody has carefully, and secretively, planned all this!

Lower in the northwest is Washington Circle Park. The measurement from the centre of the Ellipse to the centre of this park is 5 × 366 MY or 5 Megalithic Seconds of arc. There is a corresponding park in the northeast that is named Mt Vernon Square and this is also 5 × 366 MY from the meridian stone marker at the centre of the Ellipse. In both these cases the measurements are under 5,000 ft and much closer to being the 4,980 ft expected for 5 × 366 MY. Once again there seems no practical or obvious reason for such strange measurements to exist at all.

Another important road intersection is Seward Square, about 3.3 km southeast of the Ellipse. Its centre is 11 × 366 MY from the centre of the Ellipse.

About 615 m north of the centre of the Ellipse, and also just north of the White House, is Lafayette Square, a park named after one of the most important French Freemasons who fought for the American Republic at its foundation. At the centre of the square is an oval containing a monument. The distance between this oval centre and the centre of the Ellipse in megalithic terms is 2 × 366 MY. At each of the corners of Lafayette Park are freestanding monuments. The distance around all of these monuments totals 2 × 366 MY.

There can be no doubt about it: Washington DC has been planned so that major sites are linked by a web measured in Megalithic Degrees. There is no possibility of coincidence and whilst the street plan of the city is on open view, this under-scheme is invisible to anyone who does not know it is there. And whoever created it kept it entirely secret.

The Eye of the World

The Ellipse is situated almost immediately to the south of the White House and has an interesting and somewhat mysterious background. When Charles L'Enfant designed Washington, the Ellipse was one of his first and central features. From what we have discovered it must have been designated as the focal point of the new city from the outset. The centre of the Ellipse is at:

Latitude   38° 52' 38.17002" North
Longitude   77° 02' 11.55845" West
Elevation   5.205 m (17.077 ft) above sea level

During the Civil War (1861–65) the area was known as the 'White Lot' and was used to garrison troops, leading to it becoming a complete dump. The Ellipse was finally laid out during 1877–80 by the Army Corps of Engineers under the command of Lieutenant Colonel Thomas Lincoln Casey. Casey's 1878 report indicates that levelling the land for the new Ellipse is well underway – all except for an area right at the centre that he says was not under his authority but that of the 'District Commissioners', apparently on account of an incomplete sewer below the ground.

Once the Ellipse was complete the land that now forms the National Mall (running west from the Capitol as far as the Lincoln Monument) was drained of water.

The line that runs north to south through the centre of the Ellipse also runs through the White House to the north and the Jefferson Memorial to the south. Back in the earliest days of Washington, Thomas Jefferson decided that the new United States needed its own meridian.[5] Up to this time the infant United States had used the 'prime meridian' that ran, and still runs, through Greenwich in England. As we have explained in detail in our previous book *Civilization One*, Jefferson had tried to create a new system of length, weight and capacity for his new nation, and a zero meridian through the new capital city was a natural extension of this ambition. None of his suggestions was adopted, except for his currency idea, the dollar.

Charles L'Enfant originally proposed placing a Washington DC meridian one mile east of the Capitol, though why this should have been his preferred position is not known. By the time Thomas Jefferson become President of the United States in 1801 he, or someone close to him, had decided that the Washington DC meridian should run north–south straight through the centre of the Ellipse. At the centre of the Ellipse, and slightly below the surface, is the Meridian Stone.

Where the intended meridian intersected the line that ran directly west from the centre of the Capitol, another stone was placed. This marker became known as the 'Jefferson Pier' or 'Jefferson Stone' and it remained in its original place until after the Civil War, when it was apparently accidentally discarded. The Washington meridian was never adopted and it remains only as a historical curiosity demonstrating the spirit and unbounded drive that the Founding Fathers had to distance themselves from British rule and establish their own powerful nation. In an increasingly globalized world the United States has never replaced the prime meridian that runs through Greenwich in England.

The Jefferson Pier stone was found again and reinstated on 2 December 1889. Due to errors, either when the Jefferson Pier was initially surveyed or when it was replaced, its centre is now located 2.23 ft (0.680 m) south of the Capitol's centreline. It had originally been a waterway and the Jefferson Pier had often been used as a hitching post for boats.

This stone marker, placed at ground level at the centre of the Ellipse, remains but it has never been a tourist attraction. It is quite small and carries the inscription 'U – S Meridian 1890'. Strange, we thought, that this particular tiny point is the 'true' centre of Washington DC and therefore the United States – and, in terms of political power, the eye of the modern world.

In many ways Washington is what Jerusalem once was – the hub of the world. And this almost forgotten stone in the middle of the Ellipse is the epicentre of the hub, just as the Delta of Enoch, at the heart of Jerusalem, was believed to have resided in prehistoric times.

This was an analogy that would make increasing sense.

Thomas Jefferson was a great scientist and mathematician. We had studied him carefully for our book *Civilization One*, not least of all because he created a brand-new measuring system based on the length of a seconds-pendulum rod. This system, though Jefferson himself almost certainly didn't know, turned out to be resonant with the ancient megalithic system and had much in common with it. Jefferson had an ever inquisitive mind and had known very well that apparently random imperial measurements, such as the pound, the pint and the foot used at this time, were far from being random at all. He reasoned that they must be remnants of a science from deep antiquity. He was particularly interested in geometry and it is entirely appropriate that the meridian marker is to be found at the centre of a great ellipse, because this was reportedly his favourite geometric shape.

At the time the Jefferson Stone was placed close to where the Washington Monument now stands, the new Washington DC meridian also had another marker stone about two miles away. This meridian marker was a good deal further north, in a place that is officially known as Meridian Park.

The distance from the centre of the Ellipse to the centre of Meridian Park is 10 × 366 MY.[6]

We have already seen that there was a direct megalithic relationship in terms of the distance between the Ellipse centre and the Capitol building. What we wanted to establish now was whether or not the Capitol was another important focal point for megalithic measurements in its own right. We therefore measured the distance between the centre of the Capitol and the centre of a square intersection to be found just under a kilometre to the northeast. This is Stanton Square and it appears to have been part of the original L'Enfant plan for Washington DC. The distance between the centre of Stanton Square and the centre of the Capitol is 3 × 366 MY.

Parks and intersections on the original plan of Washington DC often had mirror images created for them, and such is the case with Stanton Park. To the southeast of the Capitol is Seward Square.[7] The centre of this square and intersection is also 3 × 366 MY from the Capitol.

Further east than Stanton Park and Seward Square is Lincoln Park. The distance from both parks to the statue 114 m along Lincoln Park, is 3 × 366 MY.

It started to become clear that there are at least two major nodes that have been present since the very foundation of Washington. The first is the centre of the Ellipse, which itself is situated on the proposed Jefferson Washington DC meridian, and the second is the Capitol building itself. Between them, these two nodes enjoy megalithic relationships with a high percentage of squares and circles that form the framework of Washington DC's geographical layout. In effect, underpinning the road layout we see today is a 'spectral' plan based entirely on megalithic measurements The Capitol building is the seat of government and arguably the most important building in the country – even compared to the White House. But what, we wondered, makes the centre of the Ellipse so significant?

What we had found, almost by accident, is explosive.

Washington DC has a completely secret structural plan lying beneath its sidewalks. What is more, it demonstrates a good understanding of megalithic geometry that has, apparently, been lost to the world for some three and a half millennia. We needed to understand and look more closely at the group of men that created the city – with particular reference to their Masonic connections. For Freemasonry is the only conceivable conduit for the transmission such super-ancient information, as regards the last 600 years at least.

Chapter 13

·

THE FOUNDING FATHERS

Freemasonic Washington

It is no secret that Freemasonry played an important part in the found-ing of the United States of America. Indeed, it would have been very strange if this had not been the case. The intellectually motivated radi-cals that inspired both the French Revolution and its counterpart in the British Colonies of North America were exactly the sort of men that would be drawn to Freemasonry. From its outset, Freemasonry espoused the virtues that were shouted in both Paris and along the eastern seaboard of the Americas as the white-hot anger of people who felt themselves sorely oppressed found its expression. These virtues were liberty, frater-nity and equality.

So pivotal are these concepts to the very basis of Freemasonry that it might be suggested that the presence of Freemasonry was, in great part, what 'allowed' both the American and French Revolutions to take place at all.

At Freemasonic meetings all brothers are equal. Differences in class and station mean nothing in the lodge and all Freemasons are bound by the same rules and mutually held agreements. Together with the unam-biguous secrecy of the Craft this made Freemasonry a wonderful conduit for revolutionary ideals and even revolutionary activity in the 18th century. British and American Freemasons might be quite circumspect about their early revolutionary credentials these days, but the Grand Orient of France – the governing body of many French Freemasons, makes no bones about its involvement in both the American and then the French Revolution. Its own website, discussing a French Freemason called Lafayette who assisted in the American War of Independence, says:

> Thus Lafayette received a sword from George Washington [himself a high-ranking Freemason][1] in honour of the part played by French Freemasons in the American War of Independence.

In this way, the preparation of the ideas of liberty and equality in the Masonic lodges contributed to the great reforms of the French Revolution.[2,3]

Jacobin Clubs, formed in pre-revolutionary France for the discussion of political ideas and the planning of specific activities associated with revolution, were often merely extensions of Freemasonic lodges. This was certainly the case with regard to the highly influential 'Lodge Les Neuf Sœurs', established in Paris in 1776. This lodge was derived from a charitable organization known as the 'Société des Neuf Sœurs,' which itself had close associations with the French 'Académie des Sciences' about which we will have more to say. These French lodges offered both advice and material support to the American colonialists in their efforts to split from Britain.

The existence of Freemasonic lodges in the American colonies allowed secret discussions to take place amongst the citizens of the colonies and ultimately led to the formation of militias that fought against the British Redcoats once revolution broke out in 1775. Some of the major happenings that spurred the American War of Independence were entirely led by Freemasons. A good example of this was the famous 'Boston Tea Party' in which a group of colonialists, dressed as American Mohawks, went aboard ships belonging to the East India Company. The entire cargo of tea aboard the ships was dumped into Boston harbour as a protest regarding the East India Company's virtual monopoly on tea brought to the colonies. This event, which took place on 16 December 1773, is seen as being a major precursor to the American War of Independence. The attacks were planned at The Green Dragon Tavern in Boston, a building that had been purchased by the St Andrews Freemasonic Lodge of Boston in 1764.

The organization that destroyed the East India tea was known as the 'Sons of Liberty', but nobody has ever doubted that the majority of those involved, and certainly those organizing the event,[4] were Freemasons from St Andrews Lodge, which met regularly in a room above the Green Dragon Tavern.

It is common knowledge that George Washington, the most famous American general in the War of Independence and later the first President of the United States of America, was a Freemason. Indeed he never attempted to hide the fact. For example, he presided at the laying of the cornerstone of the US Capitol on 18 September 1793 in full Masonic regalia, which was about as public a demonstration of his allegiance to Freemasonry as would have been possible.

Although the percentage of Freemasons involved in the War of Independence, and the subsequent republic that followed, is sometimes exaggerated, there can be no doubt about the influence of those who were of a Freemasonic bent. At the signing of the American Constitution on 17 September 1787, 9 of the 39 men who signed the document were already Freemasons and 6 more became Freemasons subsequently. Thus we can see that, of the 39 signatories, almost half (15) were, or would be, Freemasons.

A slight diversion is called for at this point, specifically regarding the signing of the American Constitution and also the laying of the cornerstone of the US Capitol in Washington DC. Both dates are quite significant in terms of something we have discovered about Freemason-inspired ceremonies that had not been noticed prior to our own individual and common research. These have a bearing on our later findings regarding Washington and megalithic measurements.

Just one of the facts that made us suspect a commonality between Freemasons and those who had inspired and used the megalithic system of geometry and measurements so long ago, was a specific interest in the planet Venus. We demonstrated in *Civilization One* that Venus had provided the means of setting the size of the Megalithic Yard after around 3200 BC. It was Venus that was observed, across one Megalithic Degree of the sky (at specific times during its orbit) that had allowed the mega-lithic priests to set the length of the pendulum that in turn offered the true size of the Megalithic Yard. Although we have shown that the technique of establishing the true size of the Megalithic Yard was origi-nally reliant on the movements of a star, this would have proved to be too variable for the extreme accuracy required. It was at a period sometime around 3500 BC that Venus was first used for the purpose. Venus was also important in setting the length of the 1-metre–1-second pendulum.

The Power of the Goddess

In most cultures of the world Venus, as a deity, has been considered feminine. This is probably not too surprising. Both as a morning and an evening star Venus is a spectacular and beautiful sight, far outshining any celestial object apart from the Sun and Moon. No other planet and no star come anywhere near to the brightness of Venus and in a moonless sky it is capable of casting a shadow.

Many Freemasons would be shocked to discover that much of their Craft is based on the adoration of the planet Venus and on goddess worship, but there are many reasons for believing that this is indeed the case. Arguments favouring Freemasonry as being based upon a species of Mystery Religion in which the Great Goddess, who was once worshipped universally across Europe and Asia, are set out in Alan's book *The Virgin and the Pentacle*[5] and also in our co-authored book entitled *Solomon's Power Brokers*.[6]

Substantial evidence, not only for the importance of the 'feminine' in Freemasonry but also regarding the Craft's deep interest in astronomy and astrology, comes from studying not so much *what* Freemasons have done in the past but rather *when* they did it.

As an example, let us first look at the signing of the American Con-stitution, which we can reasonably assume would have been influenced by leading Freemasons such as George Washington and Benjamin Frank-lin. The chosen date for the ceremony was 17 September 1787 in the then capital city of Philadelphia, where Franklin was a past Grand Master of the Provincial Grand Lodge of Pennsylvania. Before this date the infant

United States had relied heavily on the Declaration of Independence that had been rather hastily drawn up and signed on 4 July 1776, without much in the way of prior planning. The United States of America did not become a true republic until it had a constitution, and this was not finally thrashed out until 1787.

The delegates from the various fledgling states of the original United States had come together in Philadelphia as early as May of 1787 and they had gathered and talked throughout much of the following three and a half months. In fact there is good reason to believe that the substance of the Constitution was decided upon quite some time before 17 September, but there were agencies involved that clearly wanted the ratification of the Constitution to take place at a very specific time on a very particular date.

We now come to the world of astrology, which deals not just with the position of planets and stars in the sky from a scientific point of view, but rather with regard to the bearing these positions might have on the Earth and its inhabitants. Astrology has been more or less totally debunked by science and astronomers in particular hate any mention of it. However, this does not matter a jot as far as historical research is concerned because although most intelligent people may not give astrology much houseroom these days, our forebears certainly did. Freemasonry is riddled with astrological lore, and at the time it came into official being it was in good company. It disturbs many astronomers to learn (which is why they rarely talk about it) that their greatest hero, Sir Isaac Newton (1642–1727), the eminent English scientist and all-round genius, spent far more of his life studying astrology than he ever did astronomy or physics!

We are both individually convinced from separate and mutual research that Freemasonry is based on astronomy and, by ancient dint, a variety of astrology. One significant source of evidence for this view came from a photocopied version of an old book that came into Chris' possession some years ago whilst on a talking tour in the USA. At the time this book, *Stellar Theology and Masonic Astronomy*[7] was not generally available and, as it was clearly astrological, Chris passed it to Alan, who has studied this subject for many years. To say this book was an eye-opener for Alan is something of an understatement. He devoured it. It was originally written in 1882 by an American Freemason, Robert Hewitt Brown, and to anyone with a good understanding of historical astronomy and astrology it demonstrates one specific fact beyond doubt: It shows that Freemasonry is not merely *influenced* by astronomy and astrology – its entire framework is built upon them.

As an interesting side issue, in the photocopied pages of *Stellar Theology and Masonic Astronomy* certain passages were extremely difficult to read. This was because the passages in question had been intentionally 'crossed out' in the original book, presumably so as to prevent those consulting the book in the Masonic library from reading these particular sections. By a great stroke of luck the process of photocopying the pages had re-instated the words below the pen strokes – at least enough to read them. Almost all the sections in question dealt with the planet Venus, the zodiac sign of Virgo and information appertaining to the Mystery Religions and Demeter. Someone, at some time in the past, obviously did not want run-of-the-mill Freemasons to access this information.

Alan began to look closely at Freemasonic events from the past in order to ascertain whether those organizing such occasions had taken note of what was happening in the sky over their heads at the time. There have been long periods of history, both ancient and more modern, in which nobody would make an important move regarding a treaty, an important dynastic marriage or in fact any other major event of state, without consulting a competent astrologer.

Alan drew up an astronomical/astrological chart for the date upon which the American Constitution was signed and, although he expected that something significant might be forthcoming, the result shocked even him.

At the time of the signing of the Constitution, the Sun, together with the planets Mercury and Venus were all in the zodiac sign of Virgo. Just as surely as Venus is the 'planet' of the goddess, Virgo is her zodiac sign. The zodiac sign called Virgo is named for 'the virgin', one of the guises of the Great Goddess of ancient religion to this very day. As a modern example there is nothing remotely coincidental about the appearance of the Virgin Mary in the New Testament of the Bible. If anyone was going to adopt the new religion in its very early days, the virgin simply *had* to be there. Why? Because she was in just about every other religion, and her presence was especially pivotal in the 'Mystery Religions' that proliferated prior to, and long after, Christianity came into being.

The Mystery Religions, of which the Mysteries of Demeter and of Isis were the most popular, were celebrated across the known world. They had much in common, one with another, and without going into detail the presence of a virgin, a young god who is sacrificed and who is then res-urrected, together with much of the detail we find in the early part of the New Testament were present in all the Mystery cults of the ancient world.

The pivotal period for the sacrifice of the god, and for the lamenta-tion of his mother the holy virgin, was the start of the autumn[8] and for a very important reason. It is at this time of year that the Sun stands in the zodiac sign of Virgo – or at least it did in ancient times. In the north-ern hemisphere the period when the Sun was in Virgo was marked by the harvest. It was at this time of year that the corn was cut, and the sacrificed god was often known as the 'corn god'. In other words the corn and the god were synonymous. Of course 'as' the corn he rose again when the next crop grew, but it was necessary for him to die in order that humanity could survive another season.

We see some of the symbols of the Mystery Religions and the sacri-ficed and risen corn god still present in Freemasonic iconography and practice. Included are the sheaf of corn, the weeping virgin, the story of Hiram Abif, who was sacrificed at the completion of Solomon's Temple, the death and rebirth that are a major part of the Third Degree ceremony and in various other symbols and rituals. In short, nobody who has a really good understanding of ancient religion and astrological symbolism could possibly fail to recognize the many aspects of the Mystery Religions that exist in Freemasonry.

How far back the corn god and the virgin go, in terms of developing religion, is not known, though something of the sort was almost certainly present at the time the henges were being created in Britain and as Egypt began to rise to importance along the river Nile. Just as surely as Greece had the sacrificed god Dionysus, Egypt had his counterpart Osiris – both of whom were expressions of religious imperatives that were almost cer-tainly already hoary with age in the period we refer to as ancient. In fact we can say with some certainty that the myth of the dying and reborn corn god, together with his mother who was paradoxically also a virgin, probably goes back to the very earliest days of farming by human beings.

In Greece this Goddess was Demeter who was herself, in the conception of many scholars, merely a counterpart of a goddess worshipped in the Island of Crete, certainly prior to the middle of the second millennium BC, far back into the Bronze Age. On the mainland of Greece Demeter was especially venerated at a place called Eleusis, not far from Athens.

Each year thousands of existing Demeter worshippers, plus a large number of new recruits, gathered in September at Athens. After ritual preparation in the sea nearby they walked in procession all the way to Eleusis. There, each celebrant met the Goddess face to face in a ceremony about which we know little or nothing. The reason the Mysteries of Demeter remain so mysterious is because worshippers were warned on pain of death not to divulge anything that took place in Eleusis. It is possible that a ritual meal of barley cakes was eaten, and also almost certain that each adherent went through some figurative death and rebirth ceremony, probably not unlike the one still present in Freemasonry. Whatever the magic was, it had a profound effect on people for many centuries and Demeter worship continued well into the Christian era.

All of this is interesting enough but would have seemed well beyond our remit when we embarked on this particular book. However, it is interesting to note that when the Constitution of the United States of America took place, it happened on 17 September 1787. The worshippers of Demeter had met each year in Athens on what is now 14 September, when certain ritual objects were brought to Athens from Eleusis. The worshippers then went to the coast for ritual bathing and, on 17 September, sacrifices were made at a temple in Athens known as the Eleusinion. The procession to Eleusis began on 19 September.

Much later, in fact in the 20th century, a whole week was set aside by United States law as being special; it is known as 'Constitution Week'. It runs from 17 September until 23 September, coinciding absolutely with the period of the Demeter ceremonies in Athens and Eleusis.

As to why all of this should be important to the creation of the American Constitution is not at all difficult to see. Until the Constitution was signed, the United States was not really a legal entity. In other words, it might be suggested that despite the Declaration of Independence and the subsequent war with Britain, the states were still a British dependency.

This tie to Britain had to die officially before the new republic could be born, and that is what the Constitution represented. No period of the year could be more significant for this undertaking. What is more, the planets Mercury and, of course, Venus, rose before the Sun on 17 September 1787 – they were 'exalted' ahead of dawn. For an astrologer this happening, with both planets in the zodiac sign of Virgo, would represent a veneration of the goddess of rebirth (Venus), in her own zodiac sign (Virgo). It was also a trumpeting of the fact to the world (Mercury also in Virgo). Venus itself is representative of death and rebirth because it constantly alternates from being a morning star to an evening star and then back again. In other words it 'dies' and is 'reborn' in each and every one of its orbits around the Sun.

The signing of the Constitution took place around the middle of the day, by which time the planets Mercury and Venus were directly overhead, which is known as the midheaven. To any astrologer, and particularly to one who was an adherent of the 'mysteries' and of Venus, there could be no more auspicious time for such an undertaking as the signing of the American Constitution.

Undoubtedly some people reading this explanation will shout 'coincidence' so, just in case they do, let us also look at another pivotal moment in the birth of the United States. This time we will address the laying of the cornerstone of the Capitol in Washington DC – the place where democracy would be discussed, where laws would be decided and where presidents would be forced to capitulate to the will of the people – an essential and even a crucial component of democracy.

The laying of the cornerstone of the Capitol took place on 18 September 1793. How and why Washington DC came into existence we will deal with presently, but it is a fact that, with great ceremony and attended by a positive bevy of Freemasons from a number of different lodges, the cornerstone was laid by George Washington on that Wednesday in 1793. Washington wore his Masonic apron, as frequently depicted in paintings of the event.

Once again the event took place during that most important week in which the rites of Demeter had been celebrated in Athens and Eleusis. Once again, on that morning, the Sun and Mercury were in the zodiac sign of Virgo, but preceding them both and almost as far away from the Sun as it can get, as a morning star, was Venus, which rose a full 170 minutes before dawn.

What better or more auspicious start could there have been for the very home of American democracy?

A New Goddess for a New Nation

Presiding over all this new activity was a concept of 'Liberty', which was much more than just a word for freedom. As the Founding Fathers must have known very well, Liberty was originally a Roman goddess named 'Libertas', a goddess much loved by freed slaves and those who had been released from imprisonment. Her symbol was the Phrygian cap, the soft conical hat worn by the revolutionaries of France, but in statues she stood in splendour, with the torch of freedom held high. Any doubt about Freemasons not being aware of the connection between Liberty and the Goddess is blown away when one takes the journey from Washington DC to New York, where the huge Statue of Liberty stands to this day – a gift to the United States of America from the Freemasons of France.

Many other Freemasonic ceremonies, at different times and in different parts of the world, carry the same astronomical and astrological symbolism as the signing of the American Constitution and the laying of the foundation stone of the Capitol. As a result, we can be certain that although this specific week in September is not generally held as being special or significant by Freemasons today, it certainly was as recently as the 18th century. But we can find no mention of the fact in newspaper reports or other descriptions of either ceremony, so it is likely that although those organizing the events knew exactly what they were doing, the public did not, and it seems likely that only 'certain' Freemasons were in on the secret.

We had seen this information as being extremely interesting and informative as far as Freemasonry and its origins were concerned, and there was a strong Venus connection between Freemasons and the ancient megalithic system. All the same, it was entirely possible that this connection was simply a coincidence. After all, many civilizations and groups have venerated Venus, yet they showed no knowledge of megalithic geometry or mathematics. The likelihood of a 'direct' connection was massively increased because we had found megalithic measurements and geometry applied to the ground plan of Washington DC.

We knew that Washington DC is replete with Masonic symbolism and planning, and even its position geographically spoke legions about the true beliefs of the Freemasons that planned it. The new capital of the United States would straddle the border of two states, these being Maryland and Virginia. Although both states had apparently been named after European royals it might easily be suggested that both names carry immense symbolism in terms of the Goddess who was venerated at the time of the signing of the Constitution and the laying of the cornerstone of the Capitol. Mary is a relatively modern name for the Goddess, in her guise as the Virgin Mary, and of course the name Virginia speaks for itself.

What is more, the district that would house the city of Washington DC was called 'Columbia'. The origins of this name are somewhat lost or obscured. The standard explanation is that it is an allusion to Christopher Columbus, the mariner and explorer erroneously supposed to have been the first European to find the New World. The name in association with the British possessions in North America came about in 1738 in a copy of the British monthly *The Gentleman's Magazine*. At that time, reporting of parliamentary business in Britain was not allowed and so writers of the day often used subterfuge in order to get across to readers what was actually taking place in Parliament. One such writer was Samuel Johnson, who regularly wrote for *The Gentleman's Magazine*.

In order to get round the national censorship, Johnson reported on the parliamentary proceedings, not of Britain, but of Lilliput, a fictitious kingdom created in *Gulliver's Travels* by the writer and satirist Jonathan Swift. It was Samuel Johnson who first coined the word 'Columbia' to describe territories of Empire in the Americas. The word first appeared in *The Gentleman's Magazine* of June 1738.[9] It has been assumed that Johnson, if indeed he was the one to coin the word 'Columbia', was merely paraphrasing the name of Christopher Columbus, though of course it has to be remembered that Columbus never actually set foot on the mainland of the United States, having never gone further west personally than the West Indies. But there is no definitive proof that it is his name from which 'Columbia' derives – re- membering also that this sailor's name in his native Genoese was actually Christoffa Corombo and in Spanish, Cristóbal Colón (he was employed by Queen Isabella of Spain).

Another explanation occurs to us, though we have never seen it suggested by anyone else. If we go back to the source of the name of Columbus we find it directly associated linguistically with the name of a Catholic saint – St Columba, who flourished in the 6th century. It is generally believed that St Columba took his name from the Latin *columba* which means 'dove'. The dove has an ancient pedigree and has, from time out of mind, been associated with various versions of the Goddess. The earliest recorded and most telling references to the dove as actually representing the Goddess come from Minoan Crete, where an 'absence' of an actual portrayal of the Goddess herself in many sanctuaries is replaced by the presence of doves. Later Hellenic goddesses retained this association with the dove, which then passed to Rome as a companion of the goddess Venus.

In view of what happened regarding Columbia we think it highly likely that the name 'Columbia' probably had deliberate feminine overtones from the very start. But whether or not this was the case, it wasn't very long before there was a definite association between Columbia and a female deity. This association had certainly been made before the District of Columbia came into existence in 1791. It wasn't alone because there are at least 13 locations in the United States named Columbia. Very quickly Columbia was closely associated with Liberty, another goddess name, originally 'Libertas', who to the Romans had a special function to perform amongst freed slaves. Americans took Columbia to their hearts and she is to be seen in many sculptures and on a wealth of popular and patriotic posters

So we have the peculiar situation of the name 'Columbia' (a name for the Goddess) being given to a district situated on the border of Virginia and Maryland – the names of which are derived from the two most fundamental and powerful aspects of the female godhead.

And if all of this is not enough we discover that the shape of the District of Columbia, as surveyed in 1791, is a diamond, with its points at the cardinal points. The diamond has always had strong associations with female divinity, since time began, being a symbolic representation of the vagina. In the case of Washington DC there is one particular location, as close as makes no difference to the very centre of this diamond, that proved to be of the most pivotal importance to our research and which is dealt with in detail in the next chapter.

Astronomical Alignments

No discussion regarding the Freemasonic credentials of Washington DC would be complete without mention of David Ovason, author of *The Secret Zodiacs of Washington DC*.[10] Ovason is an astrologer and is therefore likely to notice deliberately engineered patterns in historical architecture that any ordinary historian might miss – if such patterns can be shown to have a cosmological resonance. As we have previously suggested 'we' may not believe in astrology these days but many of our forebears certainly did and therefore to ignore the possibilities of astrology, simply because of a modern prejudice, might be said to be throwing out the baby with the bathwater. We may just as well say we don't believe in oracular prophecy these days so we will ignore the presence of Delphi or any of the other ancient sites where oracular prophecy took place.

Ovason turned his attention to the ground plan of Washington DC and many of its monuments and their decoration. He noticed a great many instances of zodiacs being created in and around Washington, and across a long period of time. After a great deal of research regarding the astronomical credentials of Washington DC, Ovason came to the same conclusion that occurred to us: those planning and building Washington DC showed a great regard for astronomy and astrology and had a special interest in the zodiac sign of Virgo and in the planet Venus. Partly thanks to the observations of David Ovason it occurred to us that the whole orientation of the city might well have been planned with this specific interest in the sign of Virgo in mind.

One of the most important areas in Washington is the National Mall. This is a long tract of green space occupied by some of Washington's most important civic buildings. It runs west from the Capitol and eventually reaches the Washington Monument about 2 km away. It then continues west to the Lincoln Memorial. The whole distance from the steps of the Capitol to the Lincoln Memorial is quoted as being 3 km.

The Washington Monument, a huge obelisk more or less due west of the Capitol, was erected between 1848 and 1884. It is the tallest building in Washington DC, being 169.294 m in height. Anyone standing on the steps of the Capitol and looking west could not fail to see the Washington Monument. Because the line between the Capitol and the Washington Monument runs east to west, the Washington Monument cannot avoid being the setting point of the Sun at two particular times of year.

At the latitude of Washington DC the Sun sets well north of west in midsummer and far south of west in midwinter. But only on two evenings each year does it set at absolutely due west – at the spring and autumn equinoxes. In the case of the autumn equinox, which occurs around 21 September each year, the Sun, as it sets in Washington, is said by astrologers to be at the 29th degree of the zodiac sign of Virgo.[11]

This means that the Capitol and the Washington Monument are 'aligned' in such a way that one of the only two times in the year that the Sun sets perfectly behind the Monument, as seen from the Capitol, occurs during that crucial period in which the Sun occupies the zodiac sign of Virgo. Of course it is also the case that on that same day (the autumn equinox) the Sun 'rises' in Virgo, an event that could be observed from the Capitol by simply turning around to face east.

It might therefore be suggested that the whole orientation of Washington DC was designed with the zodiac sign of Virgo in mind.[12]

The current form of rationalism that is at the heart of modern academia is good and valuable, although it does have some very well-informed critics as regards its almost total rejection of fuzzier human qualities. However, it would be a serious error to assume that this approach to logic is the only one, or even the best one. For example, the medieval approach to intellectual reasoning would be seen as wild and undisciplined if measured against today's yardstick. Equally, the gentlemen scholars of the 18th and early 19th century were entirely open to the intermeshing of the esoteric with the exoteric. Whatever one's view of the desirability of such a thing – it remains a fact that any historian worth their salt has to understand fully. To project pure modern rationalism into the minds of scientists such Newton or Franklin, for example, would be foolish indeed.

We have found that the Megalithic Second of arc was used to create a web for the positioning of key structures, and that the surface layout was astronomical. Now there is powerful evidence suggesting that Masonic-based astronomy was also woven into the fabric of the design for the new capital of the United States of America.

In today's world, architects and civic designers sketch ideas drawn from nowhere on their pads or their computer screens to create pleasing or exciting shapes that will win awards. For the most part they have little or no understanding of, nor interest in, the power of symbolism.[13] Since the Thornborough henges were built, through Stonehenge, the pyramids, Solomon's Temple, Rosslyn and on to the city of Washington – symbolism was a fundamental driver.

However, we were soon to find that this determination to celebrate prehistoric values had not disappeared after the time of Founding Fathers. Far from it.

Chapter 14

•

THE PROPORTIONS OF
THE GODS

A New Stonehenge

Having found that Washington was planned using Megalithic Degrees of arc to connect its major points and buildings, we decided that, for thoroughness, we should check out some of the more recent structures that grace the city. In all probability the whole original idea of the megalithic connections would have been lost over the years, so we did not expect to find anything as recent as the 20th century that would lock into the pattern; but we were very wrong.

One of the most significant structures in Washington, and the military power base of the entire United States, lies just across the Potomac in Arlington, Virginia. This is the Pentagon – the headquarters of the United States Department of Defense. Interestingly, this is one building that has created its own symbolism, becoming a term for the US military command. People these days speak of 'the Pentagon' when referring to the Department of Defense rather than when merely referring to the building itself.

Chris carefully measured the distance from the centre of the Ellipse to the centre of the Pentagon. He entered the resulting figure in metres into his calculator and stared in disbelief as he looked at the result. The centre of the Pentagon has been carefully placed 10 Megalithic degrees from the centre of the all-important Ellipse – that is 10 × 366 MY. The accuracy across such a distance was stunningly impressive.

Chris called Alan immediately on Skype and told him what he had just found.

'What?' Alan exclaimed. 'That's absolutely crazy ... downright weird.' Alan opened up Google Earth on his PC and quickly zoomed into the two points to check this most unlikely result. 'My goodness. You're right,' Alan replied. 'What about other distances from the Pentagon?' he asked.

'I've just found this fit and called you. Of course we need to check for any other potential connections,' Chris replied.

But Alan was already busy measuring the most obvious next possible connection point – The Capitol.

'Good ... grief!' Alan's voice was raised more than a few decibels. 'From the centre of the Pentagon to the dome of the Capitol building is 15 × 366 MY – a beautiful 15 Megalithic Seconds of Earth polar circumference. Exactly half as far again as the Ellipse centre.'

'I think we just lost any possible argument for coincidence – which actually would have been somehow more reassuring,' Chris replied as he checked out Alan's measurement. 'There's another interesting point here ... Just look at the angle of the line from the centre of the Pentagon as it heads for the dome of the Capitol.' Chris went on. 'The Pentagon has been placed at what looks like an arbitrary angle but the megalithic line to the Capitol perfectly bisects the side that faces the river – and that looks as though it is the main entrance.'

Alan let out a long sigh. 'They put a great deal of thought into this – whoever they were!' he said. 'No one can deny that the Pentagon was orientated towards the Capitol – 15 Megalithic Seconds away!'

We continued to look at the distance relationships of the Pentagon and, almost unbelievably, we found that the distance from the centre of the Pentagon to the centre of the base of the Washington Monument is 9 × 366 MY.

Quite clearly we are not surveyors, but it seems self-evident that to fix a location that has three such integer relationships with pre-existent structures must surely be a major challenge – no matter what the chosen units of measurement may be. This seemed to be an incredible achievement. But what troubled us was the secret intent that appeared to be present in the placing of the Pentagon.

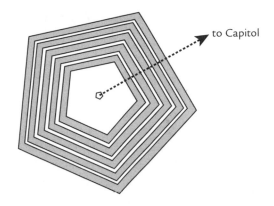

A line drawn from the centre of the Pentagon out through the centre of the Riverside entrance leads directly to the dome of the Capitol.

Figure 18. The Pentagon, Washington DC

We looked closer at this imposing building and found that it is nothing less than a perfect embodiment of a modern megalithic structure. And 'perfect' is the only word!

Looking at an aerial plan of the Pentagon, the distance between the centre of the building and any one of its five corners is 241.6 m. This means that the circumference of the circle within which the Pentagon was planned is 1,518 m. When we turn this into Megalithic Yards the result is 1,829.6 MY, which is 5 × 366 MY to an accuracy of over 99.9 per cent.

This five-sided, five-floor building is constructed within a circle that is exactly five Megalithic Seconds in circumference! That means that the arc between each of the points is precisely 366 MY long!

Stunning.

The circle within which the Pentagon was designed is a larger, and very accurate, scale model of Stonehenge and of course the all-important giant henges of North Yorkshire and Cambridgeshire in England. The Pentagon is exactly five times bigger than the henge at Stonehenge and two and a half times the size of the Thornborough henges as they appeared in 3500 BC!

A Curious Conception

It immediately became important to understand who had designed the Pentagon and then placed it in such a remarkably integrated position relative to the other hubs of Washington DC. What we discovered was very interesting.

The Pentagon was supposedly the brainchild of Henry L Stimson, Secretary of War in 1941, at a time it appeared very likely that the United States would be drawn into the Second World War. The Department of Defense had operated from a number of different buildings in and around Washington DC but, with the rapid expansion of its military might, a new and much larger building was required to centralize defence efforts. On 17 July 1941 a congressional hearing was convened to deal with the issue and Brigadier General Eugene Reybold of the War Department was given the task of reporting back within five days with a plan to solve the problem.

It was decided to place the new building across the Potomac River at a place called Arlington Farms, an agricultural research facility. The original design called for a simple rectangular footprint, but it was suggested that access roads required one corner of the rectangle to be clipped off, leaving an asymmetrical five-sided building.

The notion that the design for a superb new structure such as the Pentagon became a reality simply because an old farm was served by awkward roads does not exactly have a ring of authenticity! But it is strange how a nonsensical idea can stick when repeated enough times. How full of odd buildings the world would be if architects were required to work within constraints such as the layout of a century-old farm.

It is quite clear that none of the megalithic connections we had found would have existed if the Pentagon had actually been placed in its first suggested location at Arlington Farms. Experts are agreed that the eventual location of the Pentagon is just one factor in a curious saga. An author of a particularly thorough book on the Pentagon story[1] has expressed his great surprise regarding the degree to which the then-president of the United States, Franklin D Roosevelt, involved himself in the project. For example, says Steve Vogel, the President played the leading role in the selection of the site for the new building. The Army and the Department of War had opted for the original site, but Roosevelt became personally involved when 'someone' from the DC Commission of Fine Arts objected to the intended location at Arlington Farms, on the grounds that the building would block the main axis of L'Enfant's original plan for the city of Washington DC.

So, who was running the DC Fine Arts Commission, we wondered? It turns out it was chaired by President Roosevelt's cousin, Frederick A Delano – a man Roosevelt had personally made Chairman of the National Resources Planning Commission several years earlier.

The army officer in charge of the project, General Brehon B Somervell, insisted that the objection from Delano was not valid, but Roosevelt, who did not respond to Somervell's case by reasoned argument, overrode him. He simply pulled rank, saying, 'My dear general, I'm still commander-in-chief of the Army!'[2]

Vogel reports how the Pentagon was built upon a foundation of lies and secrecy. He claims that when the gargantuan five-sided structure was being built with miraculous speed at the start of the Second World War, the officials responsible told a series of untruths about the project, its cost and even the number of floors it would have. Vogel also describes the Pentagon as 'Roosevelt's design'.[3]

The President got his way, and at the eleventh hour the Pentagon was shifted south to its present position at a site that was a complete dump, appropriately called Hell's Bottom. The ground was broken for the Pentagon on 11 September 1941.[4] It was opened for business in January of 1943 and, considering its size, the structure was completed in an amazingly short time.

It is reported that Roosevelt planned to move the military out of the Pentagon once the war with Japan and Germany was over, on the basis that it would be far too large for peacetime needs. It was his intention that the Pentagon would ultimately become the nation's 'hall of records'. Perhaps the development of the Cold War – and the fear of a Soviet attack – put an end to such thoughts.

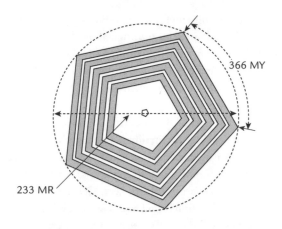

Circle diameter = 233 MR
Circle circumference = 732 MR or 5 × 366 MY = 1830 MY
MY = Megalithic Yard = 82.966 cm
MR = Megalithic Rod = 207.415 cm

Figure 19. Dimensions of the Pentagon, Washington DC

The Pentagon of the 32nd Degree

At the very heart of Freemasonry is the story of the building of a temple of knowledge at the heart of the city of God. The new initiate to the order first learns of the building of King Solomon's Temple, which is taken today by most Freemasons as a simplistic analogy regarding their own lives – build square and true, on a firm foundation – a childishly naive analogy that perhaps ought to insult the intelligence of any modern adult as a basis for membership. The reason it seems to satisfy huge numbers of members of the Craft is that they tend to ignore contemplation of the simplistic ritual and focus on the social and charitable aspects of Freemasonry. The main reason for the apparent secrecy surrounding Freemasonry is that its members dare not tell of what they do at Freemasonic gatherings for fear of derision from their family, friends and peers. In fact, the parts of rituals that are actually designated as being secret are a few unimportant passwords and signs.

However, it is important to remember that across history and certainly at the time of the Knights Templar (who began their order in the 11th century), for example, stories that transmitted important information always had two levels: an obvious one and a hidden one that was only to be understood by the 'intended' recipient.

There are 33 degrees in the very influential Ancient and Accepted Scottish Rite of Freemasonry, and many of the rituals are kept surprisingly private – even from Masons who hold the degree concerned. It has become the norm to elevate Freemasons in chunks, leaping over several degrees at a time and awarding the missing ones in name alone. One Scottish Rite Freemason once told Chris that he asked for a copy of the ritual of one of the degrees he had just been awarded but had never experienced, and was coldly informed that he could not have it.

We looked at the degrees of the Scottish Rite to see if there could be any significant connections with the imagery of a regular pentagon. And we soon found that the penultimate degree was amazingly relevant. The 32nd degree, known as the degree of 'The Sublime Prince of the Royal Secret', takes place figuratively in a military camp. The layout is said to be in the form of a series of geometric shapes. The outer form is a nine-sided figure, inside which is a seven-sided figure, then a five-sided figure or pentagon and inside this is a triangle. Finally inside the triangle is a circle, which represents infinity. However, most of the 32nd degree ceremony focuses on the military importance of a pentagon.

The candidate for the degree is asked what it is that he requires, and he is instructed to answer that he wishes to be admitted as a fellow soldier and servant in the Grand Masonic Army of Sublime Princes of the Royal Secret. He goes on to suggest that he wishes to shield the oppressed, guard the weak, protect the innocent and combat the enemies of God and humanity.

This all sounded remarkably relevant to the concept of a new head-quarters for the US military at a time when the Nazis were smashing their way across Europe. And the Japanese attack on Pearl Harbor was only months away.

Figure 20. The Scottish Rite Masonic camp with pentagon and triangle

The following explanation is given in the ritual:

> The camp of the Ancient Accepted Scottish Rite of Freemasonry is a nonagon enclosing a heptagon, within whose lines is a pentagon which encloses a triangle in the centre of which is a circle. Thus do we find the mystic numbers, 3, 5, 7 and 9, all emanating from the circle of infinity. As these numbers symbolize Divine attributes and Masonic principles, so should Masonic labour emanate from Divine love, be directed by Divine wisdom, and be exercised in Divine power for the good of mankind and the glory of God.
>
> The second emanation from infinity is denoted by the pentagon, each angle of which represents a division of the Scottish Rite Army. Take heed while their attributes are now rehearsed.

Practically the whole of the ceremonial part of the 32nd degree is taken up with the military explanations of the five corners of the pentagon after which the degree is conferred on those seeking it. Interestingly, the United States armed forces are made up of five components: the Army, Marine Corps, Navy, Coast Guard and, since 1947, the Air Force.

As the ritual of the 32nd degree develops, a rallying cry is made calling upon loyal men to fight the coming battles. There is a trumpet blast followed by a call to arms. The candidate hears cries of 'the enemy', 'Save us' and 'To the Walls'. He realizes that they are under attack and that the lives of all the men, women and children within it are in peril.

Can this strange ceremony have anything to do with Washington DC or, in particular, the creation of the Pentagon?

The degree obviously long predates the decision to build a great building to orchestrate warfare, but the men who conceived it would have been pleased to have used the symbolism of their high-level Freemasonic ritual. Naturally they could not tell anyone but their own elite, but it would have made perfect sense to those who knew. The power of symbolism can never be underestimated – and for people whose lives centre around Free-masonry this would have been a wonderful idea. It is well attested that Franklin D Roosevelt was also fascinated by, and very knowledgeable about, architecture. He designed buildings for Warm Springs, a health spa in Georgia that he bought in 1926; houses and two post offices in Dutchess County, New York, where he lived; as well as his own presidential library. It is also known that he had a taste for the past, remodelling his own home in the Georgian style. Many of Washington DC's buildings of that era, including the Jefferson Memorial, owe their neoclassical style directly to Roosevelt's preference.

Franklin D Roosevelt was also a Freemason. He was initiated at Holland Lodge No. 8, New York City on 11 October, 1911. And he was a 33rd-degree Scottish Rite Freemason. Could he have been influenced to move the Pentagon into its exact position? It seems likely that the idea of using the military symbolism of the pentagon form – as used in the ritual 32nd degree – as the inspiration for the new military HQ of the USA would have appealed to Roosevelt's instincts.

If anyone still doubts a connection between the Pentagon and the ritual of the 32nd degree of the Scottish Rite, there is one other very significant aspect of the architectural design to consider. The ritual states that there is a triangle inside the pentagon. If one draws an equilateral triangle inside the plan of the Pentagon it fits in an unexpectedly neat manner. Placing the tip of the triangle inside one of the points of the

Pentagon (as shown in the diagram used in the ritual) the base of the triangle forms the line of the inner wall of the building. That inner wall could have been placed at any level but it has, unquestionably, been designed as the base of a triangle inside a pentagon.

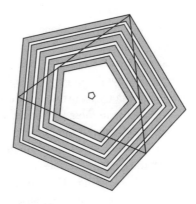

An equilateral triangle drawn from any one of the points of the Pentagon matches the building line of the inner pentagon.

Figure 21. The Pentagon with an equilateral triangle

The chances that the design of the Pentagon was not directly influenced by the rituals of the Scottish Rite appear to be extremely small. But we were to find yet more evidence that would persuade all but the most ostrich-like of individuals.

We were not short of evidence to support our claim that Megalithic Seconds were used as integer units for the planning of Washington, but there were more to be found. There is an extremely accurate megalithic connection between the Ellipse centre and one of the most important memorials on the National Mall. This is the Second World War Memorial, which is situated nearly half a kilometre west of the Washington Monument. The distance between the centre of the Ellipse and the centre of another ellipse that forms the focal point of the Memorial is a very accurate 2 × 366 MY. This was an extremely surprising result because, of course, the Memorial could not have been completed until after 1946. In fact it is very much more recent than that. The site for the Memorial was dedicated by President Clinton on Veterans' Day in 1995 and the Memorial was not finally opened to the public until 29 April 2004. We also found that the distance between the centre of the Memorial and the all-important location under the dome of the Capitol is a very accurate 9 × 366 MY, or 9 Megalithic Seconds of arc.

Megalithic planning is very much alive and well in Washington DC.

The Triangle of the 33rd Degree

As we have seen, the penultimate degree of Scottish Rite Freemasonry states that the shape inside the pentagon is a triangle – and this shape is at the heart of the final degree of Scottish Rite Freemasonry.

To recap, we had established that the distance from the centre of the Pentagon building, straight out through the front door, across the Potomac and to the Capitol, is a straight line exactly 15 Megalithic Seconds long. The distance from the Capitol to the centre of the Ellipse is 8 Megalithic Seconds, and back from the Ellipse to the Pentagon is 10 Megalithic Seconds. That creates a giant triangle across the face of Washington that has a length of 33 Megalithic Seconds (just over 6.22 miles and representing 33 × 366 MY).

Needless to say, the idea of 33 units was already familiar.

This is the journey a person could make from a humble Entered Apprentice Freemason right up to Sovereign Grand Inspector-General – if they are so chosen. In the United States of America in particular there are large numbers of 32nd-degree Freemasons – but few of them indeed ever get selected to make the final step to the 33rd degree itself.

And the key symbol used for this degree – is the triangle.

Whilst Freemasonry these days is generally very open about its activities and its structure, the 33rd degree remains somewhat shy about itself. All that is really said is that the 33rd degree is an honour that is granted solely at the discretion of the Supreme Council. We decided we should try and find out a little more about that happens at this elevated level of Free-masonry, so Chris contacted a friend who is a 33rd-degree member of the

Figure 22. Masonic symbol for the 33rd degree of Scottish Rite
Freemasonry

Scottish Rite – Southern Jurisdiction, which has its Supreme Council in
Washington DC.

The reply was astonishing:

> All 33rds receive the same ritual degree. However, only a maximum
> of 33 are 'active' 33rds at any given moment in time, in that they have
> the right to vote in the Supreme Council that controls Scottish Rite.
> The Active 33rds are called Sovereign Grand Inspectors General.
> They run the Craft throughout the state in which they live … The
> rest of us are 33 honorary with no say other than how early we get
> up in the morning …

Scottish Rite is different from all other Masonic bodies in that it
is a beneficent hierarchy. By that I mean that in all other Masonic
bodies the membership elects the Grand Master, or whatever, and
purports to control the organization. In Scottish Rite the Supreme
Commander is a full-time paid employee that dictates all activity,
most actions ratified, or at least not challenged by the Supreme
Council. The vote of the Supreme Council is final and the membership only receives the effect of their activity, but has no say or right
to challenge.

It is a dictatorship, but the beneficent argument is to provide
credibility by saying it is the most efficient Masonic organization
and can respond to needs and change instantly, whereas the Masonic

fraternity controlled by autonomous Grand Lodges in each state, without any collective national body speaking for the fraternity is terribly inefficient, and is becoming archaic.

So the Scottish Rite does not even pretend to be democratic. There is one man who makes all the decisions and expects them to be ratified without question. Where does such a person come from? Whose will do they represent? If we are right in suspecting that even President F D Roosevelt was influenced by the desires of the Scottish Rite regarding the placing and dimensions of the Pentagon – what else could have been 'guided' during the 20th century?

We are concerned; not that there are bad things necessarily happening here, but that anti-Masons (with ignorance and prejudice in equal measure) will construe this as a Masonic plot. If there was any influence on President Roosevelt back then, we certainly do not believe that there was anything negative about this activity then or at any time.

If we are right – the motive of the Scottish Rite was simply to celebrate the Craft's old knowledge and to make the United States all the stronger by adhering to the ritual of the ancients. But what exactly was the plan that they seem to have been playing out?

The Underground Chamber

The story of Enoch that is at the heart of the Scottish Rite is associated with triangles. The great triangle formed between the centres of the Pentagon, the Capitol and the Ellipse is 33 Megalithic Seconds of arc long. As there are 366 Megalithic Yards to a Megalithic degree, one could symbolically divide each degree of the Scottish Rite in 366 parts. In old times, it had been normal to attain one degree per year, which means that an initiate would progress by one Megalithic Yard for every sidereal day (one revolution of the Earth on its axis). On this basis, after 36 years of diligent study the brightest and the best would have attained the final point of distinction.

So there is a fascinating correlation between the Neolithic idea of a geodetic Megalithic Degree of latitude and a degree of the Scottish Rite.

One Megalithic Yard for every transit of a star such as Sirius across the sky. This is a perfect piece of Neolithic thinking. What else could the giant triangle on the ground be for? The importance of the Capitol and the Pentagon is obvious, but what makes the Ellipse so very special?

In considering this issue our minds turned back to the comment by Lieutenant Colonel Thomas Lincoln Casey, back in the 19th century, that he had control of the project to construct the Ellipse – except for an excavation that was taking place at the centre. This subterranean working was described as being under the authority of 'District Commissioners' – apparently concerning a sewer.

We knew that the idea of an excavation at a holy spot is of central importance in Scottish Rite Freemasonry. Chris has visited Scottish Rite temples in the USA and seen how underground chambers are routinely constructed for the purpose of conducting Enochian rituals.

Our suspicion was that this gigantic triangle (with its base connecting the structure that housed US military might with the centre of national government, and its upper point at the known excavation in the Ellipse) might be supporting something of high symbolic value; and, maybe, something much more than a symbol.

Of course, the hypothetical chamber at the centre of the Ellipse would have been planned at the same time as the Capitol, and both were developed to their present state at about the same time. But the third point of the triangle was nonexistent until Hell's Bottom was cleared for the construction of the Pentagon. Therefore, if our theory is correct, the 33-degree triangle is a mid-20th-century embellishment to a pre-existent site at the Ellipse.

That would make perfect sense to us. Every generation seeks to build upon and enhance the achievements of its forebears. The Founding Fathers had quietly built in all of the physical values of Freemasonic lore that they could – and in the early 1940s a select group of 33rd-degree Freemasons did the same when introducing a new component into the fabric of their 'New Jerusalem'.

We have already spoken about the rituals of the Ancient and Scottish Rite concerning the Delta of Enoch – which is the ancient triangle of gold that was a repository of antediluvian knowledge.

Christian scriptures include only passing references to Enoch; the Book of Enoch was very popular with the people who wrote the New Testament. While this book today is non-canonical in most Christian Churches, it is quoted in the New Testament (Letter of Jude 1:14–15) and by many of the early Church Fathers. It is the most common document found amongst the Dead Sea Scrolls at Qumran – but it became lost to the Western world by the end of the 1st century AD. It was eventually found again by James Bruce, a Scottish Freemason; Bruce had set out to find the lost book and he returned triumphant from Ethiopia in 1773. This was, of course, long after the details of the story were in use by Freemasons.

Enoch's name, in the Hebrew language, Sol Henoch, signifies 'to initiate' and 'to instruct'. One tradition states that Enoch received from God the gift of wisdom and knowledge, and that God sent him 30 volumes from heaven, filled with all the secrets of the most mysterious sciences. The Babylonians thought him to have been intimately acquainted with the nature of the stars, and they attribute to him the introduction of astronomy.

Freemasonry tells us that Enoch sought the solitude and secrecy of Mount Moriah, and it was on that spot that Enoch built a temple underground. His son, Methuselah, constructed the building; although he was not told the purpose of the structure. This temple consisted of nine brick vaults, situated perpendicularly beneath each other and communicating by apertures left in the arch of each vault. Enoch then instructed that a triangular plate of gold should be made with sides a cubit long. He enriched it with the most precious stones, and encrusted the plate upon a stone of agate of the same form. Enoch then engraved, in ineffable characters, the true name of the Deity, and, placing it on a cubic pedestal of white marble, he deposited the whole within the deepest arch. When this subterranean building was completed, he made a stone door in the ground and, attaching to it a ring of iron by which it might occasionally be raised, he then placed it over the opening of the uppermost arch, and so covered it over that the aperture could not be discovered. After the deluge, all knowledge of this temple and of the sacred treasure which it contained was lost until, in later times, it was accidentally discovered by another worthy of Freemasonry who, like Enoch, was engaged in the erection of a temple on the same spot.

According to tradition this exact location was also the place where Abraham planned to sacrifice his son around 1900 BC.[5]

The legend goes on to inform us that after Enoch had completed the subterranean temple, fearing that the principles of those arts and sciences which he had cultivated with so much assiduity would be lost in that general destruction of which he had received a prophetic vision, he erected two pillars – one of marble, to withstand the influence of fire, and the other of brass, to resist the action of water. On the pillar of brass he engraved the history of creation, the principles of the arts and sciences, and the doctrines of Speculative Freemasonry as they were practised in his times; and on the one of marble he inscribed characters in hieroglyphics, importing that near the spot where they stood a precious treasure was deposited in a subterranean vault.

The thirteenth degree of Scottish Rite Freemasonry, The Royal Arch of Enoch, uses triangles and focuses on the hiding and rediscovery of the underground chamber containing the lost knowledge of Enoch.

Figure 23. Masonic regalia from the 13th degree of Scottish Rite Freemasonry

Could the work carried on at the centre of the Ellipse during its construction have had a different purpose than the declared sewer maintenance? There can be no doubt of three facts:

1. The stone placed at the centre of the Ellipse marks the focal centre of Washington DC. A very slight mistake was made in the original positioning of the White House and this led to a further error but there

is little doubt that the place where the Meridian Stone was placed in 1890 was considered to be the very centre of the diamond that represented the District of Columbia. (*See* Appendix 9.)

2. The rituals of the Ancient Scottish Rite of Freemasonry have heavily influenced the layout of the city from its inception to very recent times. And at the heart of these rituals is the idea of a secret underground chamber containing a triangle that holds antediluvian knowledge.

3. There is, or was, a chamber beneath the stone at the centre of the Ellipse, which is at the top point of a 33-degree-long triangle that connects with the Pentagon and the Capitol.

If that chamber does still exist and contains something of great importance to Freemasonry – what could it be?

The date of the work conducted on this 'sewer' offers a potential clue.

The Ellipse was created from 1877–80 and, according to Lieutenant Colonel Thomas Lincoln Casey's report of 1878, at that time the area right at the centre was being excavated by people who were not under his control. At that time, 3,500 miles away, excavations were being conducted at Rosslyn, the so-called chapel in Scotland that was actually built as a repository for precious items recovered from beneath the Temple of Jerusalem.

An Ancient Icon for a New Jerusalem

Improvements were being made to Rosslyn at the time the Ellipse was constructed, culminating in the completion of a new baptistery and organ loft attached to the west wall in 1881. Could it be that Scottish Freemasons took something out from under Rosslyn at this time of necessary excavation and gave it to Scottish Rite Freemasons in Washington DC?

This may sound like a leap of logic, but there are many reasons why such an idea would fit all of the available evidence.

All our past evidence indicates that the desire to build a New Jerusalem took different forms at differing stages of history. As we mentioned earlier there was a strong push in the 12th century to create the New Jerusalem in Great Britain. A number of the priesthood of Jerusalem, who escaped after the destruction of the Jerusalem Temple and the slaughter of the Jewish people, fled to Europe in AD 70. A prophesy in the Book of Revelation, a work that mysteriously found its way into the New Testament, states that 1,000 years after the destruction of Jerusalem it will be sacked again and the descendants of the priests must rise up and retake the city. Exactly on cue, Jerusalem was sacked by Seljuk Turks and the families of the Jewish priests (now Christians – at least on the surface) activated the states of Europe to create the First Crusade.[6]

After the city was taken and the political climate under control, nine French knights, from the priestly families, began nine years of excavation. The Copper Scroll (one of the Dead Sea Scrolls found in Qumran in 1947) lists the documents and huge amounts of treasure hidden under the Temple by the priests who built it at the time of Christ.

This small band of excavators lived in poverty for the nine years, then suddenly in AD 1128 became the richest people in the world and founded their own military-religious order. They became the famous Knights Templar. Records within Freemasonry and elsewhere state that these treasures were brought to Kilwinning in Scotland in 1140.

In 1307, the Knights Templar were convicted of carrying out non-Christian rituals. They were declared to be heretics, and the order went underground.

We have both shown in previous books that in the 15th century a new copy of the Jerusalem Temple was built in Lowland Scotland, to house the priceless treasures.[7] This is the famed Rosslyn Chapel. It is highly likely, and now widely accepted, that whatever the Knights Templar had found in Jerusalem was committed to the earth deep below Rosslyn Chapel. Like the original Temple in Jerusalem, Rosslyn Chapel was far more than a simple building. It was nothing less than an observatory – a more modern version of what had been built at Thornborough in 3500 BC. Rosslyn Chapel was special, just as the Temple in Jerusalem had been, because at both locations the rising Sun at the midwinter and midsummer solstices split the sky in a very special way. In Jerusalem the Sun rose 30° south of east at the winter solstice and 30° north of east at the summer solstice. At Rosslyn it was 45° south of east at the winter solstice and 45°

north of east at the summer solstice. Both buildings had been deliberately constructed with this all-important fact in mind.

Imagine our surprise to discover that at the time Washington DC was planned the Sun at this latitude was rising at 30° south of east at the midwinter solstice and 30° north of east at the midsummer solstice – exactly the same as it had done at the original Jerusalem Temple! It may well be the case, bearing in mind the tremendous Freemasonic influence that was brought to bear on the creation of the United States, that this particular location was chosen for the capital at least partly, or maybe wholly, because of this fateful fact.

By the middle to late 19th century, Rosslyn Chapel had become little more than a curiosity – and it was turned into a Christian church.[8] The addition of the strange Victorian entrance at the west end, and of an organ loft, looked like moulding the building into a fairly orthodox parish church, something it was never intended to be.

Meanwhile, far to the west, the United States had wrested itself from British rule. It was everything a Freemasonically motivated state should be, a nation based on equality, liberty and fraternity. And in the eyes of Scottish Rite Freemasons this made it the epitome of the New Jerusalem. As we have previously suggested, to many Freemasons the concept of a New Jerusalem is purely figurative and allegorical; it is a construct that exists inside individual Freemasons but not necessarily something made of stone and mortar.

To the majority of Freemasons this remains true, but it is not what the 'ultimate' lessons of the Craft suggest. It has been impossible for us to get hold of a full, reliable account of the 33rd-degree ceremony and ritual – even assuming that such a thing has ever been published in a form that 'could' be obtained. However, we have been able to track down reliable accounts of some parts of the 33rd degree and we know that at one stage the Illustrious Grand Minister, one of the officers present, tells the candidate(s) in his lecture that the object of 33rd-degree Freemasons is to rebuild the '*material*' Temple of Solomon or at least to rebuild a moral temple, wherein truth and love shall dwell for its members.

There is a clear distinction here between the 'real, material' temple (something made out of stone) and the moral temple, which exists only in Freemasonic hearts. There is a plain and quite unequivocal command here to 33rd-degree Scottish Rite Freemasons to recreate the Temple as a real and quite tangible place.

At the same time the United States was lifting itself from a destructive and crippling Civil War, it was also freeing itself from the vestiges of that most pernicious scar upon its stated ideals – namely slavery. By 1865 slavery had been abolished all across the United States and the words of the Declaration of Independence at last held good. Meanwhile in Great Britain, at the same time slavery may not have been the lot of ordinary people in any legal sense, but in reality the average 'wage-slave' (including women and children) in textile mills, coal mines and a thousand other trades as the Industrial Revolution gained pace was as bad as it had been for many black slaves in the colonies.

During the 18th century and well into the 19th, thousands of people, especially from Scotland and Ireland, were forced, either physically or economically, by absentee landlords to leave their homes and to find work elsewhere. To many this effectively meant emigration. Many of these people found their way to America – the home of the free – and a good proportion of the men were undoubtedly already Freemasons. The excavation and construction work being conducted at Rosslyn Chapel in the 1870s would have presented the best possible opportunity to dig below the chapel into ground far below and to remove what had been so carefully placed there 400 years earlier.

We believe that the documents and Temple treasures were reburied under Rosslyn in a wide distribution such as was used under Herod's Temple at the time of Christ. This means that most items will be deep underground in lead sealed containers back-filled with sand. However, some objects may have been stored in the subterranean vault described in Freemasonry. This vault under the Jerusalem Temple is said to have been used by King Solomon, and it had a long tunnel leading to the King's palace – running accurately from north to south. Exactly the same chamber has been found at Rosslyn – with a tunnel running perfectly north to south for some 304 m from the so-called chapel to Rosslyn castle. We noted that this tunnel covers a distance of precisely one Megalithic Second of arc!

The centre of the Ellipse is, of course, also exactly due south of the 'King's Palace' – the White House. Could there be a tunnel? The cover story of constructing a sewer would have been a perfect excuse for any tunnelling.

We cannot know for sure if there is a chamber beneath the stone set in the middle of the Ellipse, let alone a tunnel to the White House. But we would wager a large bet that both are present and that an object or objects of considerable historic and cultural value are now residing in that chamber. It is even possible that Enoch's triangle of gold is there but, if so, it is likely to be a copy made in Jerusalem during the early centuries BC.

We truly believe that Washington was destined to be the New Jerusalem, the hub of the world that would herald in a new age – a new world order. The evidence, both direct and circumstantial, also points to an amazing treasure lying at the absolute centre of the city and the District of Columbia.

The White House was built on the 'White Lot', a piece of land deliberately left alone despite all the building going on around it. This area was thought to be the very heart, not just of Washington DC but also of the District of Columbia. Its ultimate signature as a place of megalithic proportions and importance did not become evident until the Ellipse was finished and the Meridian Stone was placed at its very centre in 1890. Things would probably have moved quicker had it not been for the exhausting Civil War.

The placing of the Meridian Stone brought to life an incredible series of deliberately planned measurements that had actually existed since Washington DC had first come into existence. The Meridian Stone became the centre of this fantastic web, though of course it isn't really a web. When seen isolated from the megalithic measurements to the south and east, the true state of affairs regarding the Ellipse becomes quite obvious. What the megalithic lines represent is nothing more or less than a huge and elaborate arrow, pointing directly at the Meridian Stone and whatever lies beneath. (*See* colour plate 13).

The arrow is a double delta, reminiscent of the delta stone of Enoch that was, and is, so important to Scottish Rite Freemasonry.

The centre of the Ellipse is a marvellous place for whatever once slept away the centuries below the Temple Mound in Jerusalem, and then in the more northerly climes of Scotland. It is part of the Presidential Park and will never be given over to development. If we are right, thousands of people walk over it every year and it is the scene of pageantry and enjoyment as the main outdoor meeting place in Washington DC.

Washington DC is the latest legatee of a continuing and constantly re-emerging way not only of viewing the world but also systematically measuring it that self-evidently began long before the pyramids.

We have traced ancient knowledge back over the last 6,000 years – back deep into the Stone Age. But if Thomas Brophy turns out to be correct about his dating of astronomic observatories in the Sahara, and they are 18,000 years old, the account retold in Freemasonic ritual – of great knowledge carried forward from before Noah's Flood – is true. It seems very possible that Washington DC is a continuation of knowledge held by an advanced culture from the extreme past. And there is still an elite group of people who fully understand this.

Let us hope they are using our heritage well.

A Time for Reappraisal

This has been the most incredible passage for us. It has taken us on a whole series of journeys and has introduced us to some amazing people, all of whom are dedicated to uncovering the truth of our common past.

It would have been impossible to imagine on that sunny day – which now seems so long ago – when we stood at the centre of the largest and most impressive structure from Britain's prehistory, how far our research would bring us. Our introduction to the giant henges brought us to an almost immediate realization that everything we had suggested about the incredible megalithic measuring system was not only real, but unequivocally demonstrated to be real by the very dimensions of these massive structures so carefully placed on the landscape. Even more important was the fact that specific comments we had previously made about what we might 'expect' our ancient ancestors to have done with the megalithic system were also born out at both Thornborough and at Dorchester-on-Thames.

These quite remarkable people knew the size and shape of the Earth. They carried out detailed experiments to qualify and to prove what they knew, and they managed to create a system of measurements based entirely on an intimate knowledge of the Earth, its dimensions and its orbit around the Sun. And Jim Russell has made a great contribution to our understanding of just how this could have been achieved.

And this was no cul-de-sac of history, as archaeology currently believes. We now know that a full 1,000 years after the great henges of Britain were constructed, the culture that planned and built them was being prevailed upon to take its knowledge far from the shores of the British Isles. The knowledge that designed and built the astronomical observatories of Britain would be used to lay down the footprint of the Great Pyramid and its companions. The same ideas and protocols were present. But the fact that the plan for the pyramids was almost certainly laid down at Thornborough bears testimony to the fact that the henge array was known, respected and perhaps even revered across a great area of our planet.

Our journeys during our research for this book, together with some of the experts we met on the way, had led us to realize that even the amazing achievements of the henge builders was not the start of the story. The existence of standing stones in Egypt, together with the evidence regarding the Sphinx and its true age, prove beyond doubt that the emergence of civilizations and almost certainly super-civilizations, took place long, long before orthodox history has ever considered. What happened to these lost people, with their amazing knowledge of the Earth and even the universe, remains a puzzle, though the vulnerability of the Earth to comet and meteorite strikes probably offers the best clue we have.

We had been led to our recognition of the importance of the British henges by the most incredible coincidence – the discovery of an 18th-century building with megalithic proportions in a pretty English city. Our research into the King's Circus in Bath, though we had never sought it, brought us face to face once again with Freemasonry, a subject we have dealt with in the past. And when it became obvious that there were other megalithic connections in Bath apart from the King's Circus, we felt duty-bound to see if these ancient measurements had been used in other

18th-century structures. It was at this point that things began to become truly incredible.

The custom-built city of Washington DC, far to the west of Britain across the Atlantic Ocean, turned out to be a veritable repository of megalithic knowledge. Not merely specific buildings but the entire plan of the city had been based upon the Megalithic Yard and megalithic geometry. Once again we came head to head with Freemasonry, and with an ancient story that began in prehistoric Jerusalem.

Nor was Washington DC's reliance on megalithic measurement and geometry restricted to the city's foundation. It was self-evidently understood and used as recently as our own century. But the most intriguing spot in Washington DC lay at the very centre of the District of Columbia, in the middle of an elliptical park with megalithic proportions. This obviously sacred spot had been planned well over 200 years ago because its creators had left a huge and unmistakable arrow on the landscape, specifically pointing to this very place.

Washington DC is an 'astronomically planned' city. It is an intended repository for 'something' that almost certainly slept for centuries beneath the equally astronomically planned chapel of Rosslyn in Scotland. Whatever this treasure may be it originally came from the Temple of Jerusalem, yet another structure that was planned according to the stars. Are we looking at something so old it was once held by the patriarch Enoch? This possibility seems unlikely but it may well have originated in the early centuries BC – or even to the time of King Solomon.

What a story, what an adventure. For the remainder of our lives when we look up at the star-spangled sky and see the three stars of Orion's Belt pointing relentlessly down to Sirius, we will know that from the lonely uplands of Stone Age Britain to the first steps of a much more recent people desperate for freedom and self-determination, we are in good company. And whoever you are, you people in Washington DC and probably elsewhere on our planet who already know these secrets and hold them sacred to this day, we can only admire a conviction, a resilience and a firm commitment that has endured for such an incredibly long period of time.

But one thought is inescapable. It is now time to fully re-examine the history of mankind and look again at old ideas of the past that are so obviously and lamentably inadequate. Archaeology must find a way to put aside its 19th- and 20th-century assumptions and move forward to a new paradigm of social and scientific evolution that respects the gargantuan achievements of our forebears.

We all have so much to relearn.

Appendix 1

•

THE PLANNING OF THE THORNBOROUGH HENGE COMPLEX

In order to establish how, when and where the Thornborough Henge complex had been planned we ran many simulations predominantly using Cyber Sky 4, an astronomical computer programme that, experience had taught us, gave reliable and stable results, even when working back in time several thousand years.

We suspected that there was a common factor involved between the length of a pendulum used to establish the correct footprint for the henge complex and the finished size of the structure as it would appear on the ground. In our estimation, getting a really accurate match between the stars of Orion's Belt and the henges on the ground would have been impossible using only naked-eye estimation. Meanwhile, we knew that the match was almost absolutely perfect. No magnification or instrumentation was available to these early astronomers and the only weapon at their disposal, in order to get the accuracy they required, was their ability to measure the passage of time by using a pendulum set against rising stars.

We tried to recreate the right circumstances from the area of Thornborough itself. We knew that included in the central henge was a cursus. A cursus is a long often straight track that was originally defined by henges and banks on both sides, that predated the henges. Although we did not have a date for this cursus it was a fair bet that the location was of interest to our ancestors for some time before the henges were completed.

No model we could run would give us the necessary pendulum/footprint relationship we were seeking, though the results were very close. In the end we discovered that the experiments necessary to plan the footprint of the Thornborough complex must have been carried out not at Thornborough itself but at its sister henge further south at Dorchester-on-Thames in Cambridgeshire, England.

This is how we believe it was undertaken:

The height of the bank tops of the Dorchester-on-Thames henge, when seen from the centre of the henge, must have given a minimum view of the sky beyond at a height of around 3° above the natural horizon. Dorchester-on-Thames occupies a latitude of 51° 38' 50" N and a longitude of 001° 09' 21" W. We estimated our experiment to have been carried out on, or close to, the winter solstice in 3500 BC (December 18). In this model the first star of Orion's Belt would have appeared above the eastern bank top at 18 21 02 hours. This star is Mintaka. The third star to appear, which is Alnitak, appeared at 18 36 56 hours. The elapsed time between the two was 15 minutes and 54 seconds of time (954 seconds).

A Megalithic half-yard pendulum, when used at this latitude, completes one beat in 0.655 seconds. During a period of 954 seconds the pendulum could have completed 1,454 beats. Each pendulum length is ? MY so to make the linear length up to 1 MY the number of beats is halved, giving a total of 727 MY. The position of the centre star, when translated to the ground, had to be calculated in a different way (*see* Appendix 2), but once this had been ascertained it would have been discovered that the ratio of the gap between the northernmost henge (Mintaka) and the middle henge (Alnilam) to the gap between the middle henge (Alnilam) and the southern henge (Alnitak) would have been 366:360.

366 + 360 = 726, which is stunningly close to the 727 pendulum beats we established for the difference in rising time between Mintaka and Alnilam. Thus we can see that, following the rule of pendulum beats to linear measurements, the full range of henges should have been Mintaka to Alnitak 366 MY and Alnitak to Alnilam 360 MY. To follow this procedure strictly would have meant that smaller henges would have been necessary so, in our opinion, a decision was made to increase each

proposed Megalithic Yard to a Megalithic Rod – making the whole structure 2.5 times bigger than it would have been using the Megalithic Yard.

However, the ratios remain exactly the same, which is why the stars in the sky are such a good fit when superimposed onto the Thornborough Henge group.

The true distance between the northernmost henge and the central henge centres is 366 MR, whilst the distance between the central henge and the southernmost henge is 360 MR.

We therefore suggest that what we have described above is by far and away the most likely explanation for the size of the Thornborough Henge array and explains its almost perfect match to the stars of Orion's Belt.

Appendix 2

·

PLACING THE MIDDLE HENGE

In Appendix 1 we showed how the overall footprint of the Thornborough henges was planned using a half Megalithic Yard pendulum at Dorchester-on-Thames henge in around 3500 BC. However, we soon became aware that this experiment would not have worked for accurately placing the middle henge so that the finished configuration accurately matched the stars of Orion's Belt. This is because of the angle at which the three stars rise. Trying to place the centre henge in this way would have put it too close to the southern henge, and the fit between the henges and the stars would not have been correct.

However, there was an ingenious way in which the position of the middle henge (though not the dogleg in the system) could have been established, this time using the metre pendulum with which we know these ancient astronomers were also familiar.

This experiment was most likely carried out at Thornborough and, again, around 3500 BC. Instead of timing the stars as they rise, they are timed when they are at their flattest when seen from the centre of the henge – in other words, when they are parallel to the horizon. So, whilst the first of the three stars, Mintaka, rose above the horizon at Thornborough at 124° (which is 34° south of east), this experiment was not carried out until Mintaka had achieved an azimuth of 204° (which is 114° south of east).

A simple device that could be used for this experiment is shown below. The stars are tracked as they appear from behind the upright stake. Using a 1-metre-1-second pendulum, the first star, Mintaka, would appear on 18 December 3500 BC at 23 52 51 hours. The second star, Alnilam, would appear at 23 58 57 hours and the third star, Alnitak, would appear at 00 04 57 hours. The gap between Mintaka and Alnilam is therefore 366 seconds and the gap between Alnilam and Alnitak is 360 seconds. This of course would give 366 pendulum beats of a 1-metre-1-second pendulum between the first and second stars, and 360 pendulum beats of a 1-metre-1-second pendulum between the second and third stars.

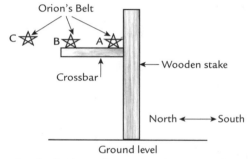

When stars A and B lie flat on the crossbar the compass bearing will be 204 degrees. The only pendulum that will then give 366 beats whilst stars A and B disappear behind the upright stake will be the second's pendulum length (1 Metre). This will also give 360 beats between stars B and C.

Figure 24. Wooden stake with crossbar

These measured gaps between the stars of Orion's Belt (in relation to the perceived naked-eye distances in the sky) are far more accurate than could be obtained using the pendulum method explained in Appendix 1. This is the same method we describe in the book that was used to achieve the same result when the pyramids were planned in 2500 BC. *The only difference is that the experiment to place the centre pyramid was not carried out at Thornborough but in Egypt itself.*

Appendix 3

·

FIXING THE DOGLEG

Anyone with even reasonable eyesight who looks for long enough at Orion's Belt will be able to see that, although the three stars are more or less in line, there is a perceptible dogleg in the alignment. In other words, if a line is drawn through the centre of Mintaka to connect with the centre of Alnilam, Alnitak will be out of line. Similarly if Mintaka and Alnitak are joined by a common line Alnilam will be out of line.

We have spent countless hours looking at computer projections of the shape and position of the stars both today and back across a vast span of time. Using the knowledge we had already amassed, plus a great deal of experimentation, we have been able to back-engineer the most likely methods used by our ancient ancestors to work out all sorts of astronomical problems. Appendix 1 and Appendix 2 demonstrate how the correct positions for the Thornborough henges were worked out in terms of their distances, one from another. But these explanations do not answer the puzzle of how our ancestors managed to cope with the offset dogleg in the three-star system.

Here we have to put up our hands and admit that we do not have a hard-and-fast answer. There appears to be no way, without recourse to modern accurate measuring equipment, to establish exactly how much out of line the three stars are. We would of course be fascinated to hear anyone else's opinion on this point and it is entirely possible that some method was employed which has not occurred to us.

When the three stars of Orion's Belt are parallel to the horizon, as described in Appendix 2, the difference in altitude between Mintaka and Alnitak is inconsequential. Both the stars have an altitude of around 12° 55'. At this time Alnilam, the middle star, has an altitude of 12° 51'. This means that the difference in altitude of the middle star and its two companions is a tiny 4 minutes of arc. Now bear in mind that a whole degree of arc of the sky is equal to the width of a human thumbnail when the hand is held at arm's length, and we begin to see what these people were up against. And yet when we superimpose the three stars of Orion's Belt onto the Thornborough henges, the fit is as good as perfect.

Common sense dictates that there was some method for establishing the dogleg when creating both the henge array and the pyramid footprint on the ground but, very annoyingly, we cannot discover what it was.

There is a possible clue at Thornborough. Across the middle henge and running from roughly northeast to southwest is a cursus. A cursus, as we explained earlier in this book, is a long, often straight line on the landscape marked originally by ditches and banks on both sides of it. There are dozens of cursus monuments across the length and breadth of Britain and there must originally have been many more than the ones recognized today.

What cursus were used for is still not known for certain, though the fact that the one at Thornborough runs at right angles to the alignment of the henge array might offer some sort of clue for this one. It seems to have been aligned to the setting point of Orion's Belt, and is thought to be earlier than the henges (but how much earlier is not known). This particular cursus may have been used, over a period of time prior to the eventual layout of the Thornborough henges, to assess how much further northeast the central henge needed to be located, relative to its companions, and in order to make the best possible match with Orion's Belt.

It seems significant in some way that this cursus should be placed across the central henge and that it should also have an alignment that, to the southwest, marks the setting point of Orion's Belt. For the moment this is the only real clue we have. It remains the case that the positioning of the central henge relative to its companions is so accurate, in terms of the shape of the 'real' Orion's Belt, that placing the central henge using nothing but guesswork seems less than likely. Our ancient ancestors have surprised us on so many occasions with their skill and determination that we would not be even slightly surprised to discover that there was indeed a method for placing the central henge on the landscape accurately.

The Pyramids

Of course the same problem also exists regarding the pyramid footprint and the placement of the middle pyramid. Yet, it stands to reason that if the Stone Age astronomers of Britain had solved the problem, their Bronze Age counterparts could simply repeat the exercise 1,000 years later in Egypt.

Appendix 4

•

USING THE MEGALITHIC PENDULUM

About Pendulums

A pendulum is one of the simplest devices imaginable. In its most basic form it is nothing more than a plumb line – a weight suspended on a piece of twine or hair. If allowed to hang, the weight will pull its string into a perfectly vertical position. Certainly the megalithic people could never have constructed any of the major sites to be found all over Britain, Ireland and Brittany without the use of this device. It is therefore reasonable to suggest that if they possessed a plumb line, then they also possessed a pendulum.

Although the device had been around for a long time, it was the 16th-century genius Galileo who seems to have been the first person to look seriously at the attributes of pendulums (or at least the first of whom we have a record). He is reported to have been bored in church one day when his attention was caught by a large incense burner, suspended from high above by a chain or a rope, gently swinging back and forth and forming a natural pendulum. Galileo realized that the swings of the pendulum were equal in terms of time, and he counted them against the beat of his own pulse.

Only two factors are of importance in the case of a simple pendulum. These are the length of the string and the gravitation of the Earth, which constantly exerts a force that will eventually bring the pendulum back to a vertical and resting position. The height of the swing of a pendulum is, to all intents and purposes, irrelevant because its time period from one extremity to the other will always be the same. In other words, if the pendulum is excited more vigorously it will swing higher but its time period will remain the same.

It was recognition of this constant nature of a pendulum that made it the basis of the clock. In modern timepieces the pendulum has been superseded, but for many centuries it ensured the smooth running of clocks all over the world. It can still be found in high-quality clocks. Clock pendulums were eventually fitted with some devices to prevent them from swinging too high, and others to regulate the nature of their arc of swing, but they are still, essentially, only animated plumb lines.

The Megalithic Yard

The Megalithic Yard was discovered by Alexander Thom as part of the composition of megalithic sites from the northernmost part of Scotland, right down to Brittany in the South. The main problem with its use, and the reason archaeologists still doubt its veracity, lies in the fact that it remained absolutely accurate across thousands of square miles and many centuries. This would appear to be impossible in the case of a culture that was, at least in its early stages, devoid of metals to make a reliable 'standard' against which others could be set. Alexander Thom himself could think of no reliable way of passing on the Megalithic Yard without some variation being inevitable across time.

We reasoned that it would be possible to turn 'time' into 'distance' by way of the turning Earth. The speed of the Earth on its axis is the only accurate measure available from nature that can be constantly repeated with the same results. Of course we cannot see the Earth turning, but we can see its effects as the Sun, Moon and stars appear to rise from below the horizon in the east, to pass over our heads and then to set in the west. In fact, although the Moon and planets do have independent movement, the Sun and the stars are not really moving at all (actually they are moving slightly, but we need not concern ourselves with this for our present purposes).

The apparent motion of the stars is caused by the Earth turning on its axis and it is this fact that offers us an accurate clock which, with a little ingenuity, we can turn into a replicable linear unit of measurement. In the case of the Megalithic Yard we eventually discovered that the pendulum upon which it is based was set not by viewing any star but the planet Venus. Venus is, like the Earth, orbiting the Sun. As a result, when seen from the Earth, it has a complex series of movements against the backdrop of the stars. Sometimes Venus rises before the Sun, at which times it is called a morning star, and at other times it rises after the Sun and is then known as an evening star. This is purely a line of site situation, caused by the fact that both Venus and the Earth are orbiting the Sun. When Venus crosses the face of the Sun to become an evening star, it is moving 'against' the direction followed by the backdrop of stars. It is within this observable fact that setting the megalithic pendulum becomes possible.

In order to create the Megalithic Yard, one has to follow the simple rules below:

Venus must be observable as an evening star, setting after the Sun and during that period at which it is moving at its fastest counter to the backdrop of stars.

The sky is divided into 366 parts. This can be achieved by trial and error, as explained in *Uriel's Machine*[1] and also in *Civilization One*,[2] but it is also achievable through a neat little mathematical trick, as demonstrated below.

1. Stand in an unobstructed position on a wide-open piece of ground with a good view of the western horizon.

2. Place a stick in the ground (stick A) and stand facing west with one of your heels touching the stick.

3. Now take 233 steps, heel to toe, towards the west. Upon completing the 233 steps, place a second stick in the ground (stick B) in front of your toe.

4. Turn to the north and place your heel against stick B. Now take four heel-to-toe steps to the north and then place a third stick (stick C) in the ground in front of your toe.

5. The distance between sticks B and C, when viewed from A, will now be 1/366th of the horizon.

This method relies on the fact that any circle with a diameter of 233 units will have a circumference of 732 (2 x 366) units. It was entirely theoretical on our part, but our research for this book has introduced us to a number of henges and other structures in which this theory has clearly been recognized and used.

It is now necessary to make a braced wooden frame, of the type shown below, which is as wide as the gap between B and C. This must be set on poles in such a way that it gains significant height and can be altered in its angle.

The purpose of this exercise is so that the angle of the braced wooden frame can be identical to that of the planet Venus as it falls towards its setting position.

Standing at A it is now necessary to observe Venus, passing through the gap in the braced frame, whilst swinging a pendulum and noting the number of swings achieved as Venus passes through the gap. A pendu-

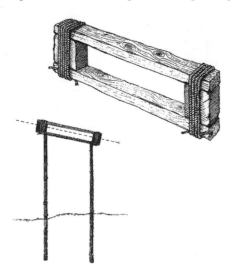

Figure 25. Braced wooden frame for tracking planets or stars

lum that swings 366 times during this occurrence must be half of a Megalithic Yard in length (41.48 cm). A cord of this length represents the full Megalithic Yard of 82.966 cm in length.

In this way the Megalithic Yard can be reproduced on any site where observation of Venus at the right part of its cycle can be achieved. We are grateful to Archie Roy, Emeritus Professor of Astronomy at Glasgow University, for suggesting the idea of the angled braced frame.

Although pendulums differ slightly with latitude and altitude, because gravity also alters slightly, we have shown that the Megalithic Yard achieved using this method will remain within the tolerances discovered by Alexander Thom from Orkney in the north to Brittany in the south – in other words across the whole area containing monuments surveyed by Alexander Thom.

The One-Second-One-Metre Pendulum

We now know that two different lengths of pendulum were available to our megalithic ancestors. These were the half Megalithic Yard pendulum, described above, and another that measured very close to one modern metre, which had a beat of extremely close to 1 modern second of time. We also now know that they were used in a number of different ways to solve different problems.

It was possible to time the rising of groups of stars using a pendulum. This was certainly the case with Orion's Belt – required for the building of both the Thornborough henges and the three major Giza pyramids. It was also possible to time stars across a given point, as was the case when it came to establishing the true position of the middle star of Orion's Belt (Alnilam) in relation to its companions.

Pendulums and Linear Distance on the Ground

Both in the case of the building of the Thornborough henges and the footprint for the Giza pyramids there is a direct relationship between the result obtained using a pendulum (whilst observing the rise of Orion's Belt) and the linear distances used on the ground.

What appears to have happened is that the length of the pendulum string, multiplied by the number of swings observed during the rising of Orion's Belt, was used in the construction of the monuments. In the case of the Thornborough henges the results were enlarged, so for example 366 Megalithic Yards became 366 Megalithic Rods, though in the case of the pyramid footprint the exact pendulum string results were used (though this was a metre pendulum). We can probably speculate that the pendulum length was considered to be divinely inspired and that the linear units used were therefore considered to be 'holy'.

Appendix 5

•

THE MINOAN FOOT
AND THE STANDARD FOOT

About the Minoans

Back in 1997 Alan researched and wrote a book about the Minoans, Europe's first super-civilization.[1] The Minoans inhabited the island of Crete in the eastern Mediterranean, and the civilization was at its height from around 2000 BC to 1500 BC.

In all sorts of ways the Minoans reveal themselves to have been very much a part of the megalithic culture that flourished in Britain, parts of France and in several of the larger Mediterranean islands. The Minoans, however, reached a very high degree of civilization in terms of their trade links, domestic architecture, farming and metalwork – they even had a form of writing (which is still not understood).

In the 1960s a Canadian archaeologist, J Walter Graham, carried out an intensive study of the remaining grand buildings of Minoan Crete, known as palaces. As a result of these studies it was possible for him to ascertain that the Minoans had used a fixed system of linear measurements. These were based upon a unit that Graham called the Minoan Foot – and he did so with good reason. Graham could achieve great accuracy in his reconstruction of the Minoan Foot because he had many foundations and even existing walls available for measurement. He concluded that the Minoan Foot had been 30.36 cm in length. Meanwhile the statute foot, still used in Britain and the United States, is 30.48 cm in length. The difference between the Minoan Foot and the statute foot is therefore about 1mm.

This would be a fairly surprising correspondence on its own, but one fact that revealed itself early on in our research is that there is a direct relationship between the Minoan Foot and the Megalithic Yard, even though this isn't immediately apparent. The reason it doesn't stand out is that the relationship is based on geometry, and what is more geometry of the 366° version.

A distance of 1 Megalithic Second of arc of the Earth's polar circumference is equal to 366 Megalithic Yards (303.65 metres). If we divide the Minoan Foot into this distance the result is 1,000. In other words the Minoan Foot is simply a decimalized version of the Megalithic Yard, in that it uses the same number of degrees for the Earth.

The fact that the Minoans had so much else in common with their British counterparts strongly hints at a cultural relationship and it is suggested by a few outsiders in ancient history studies, with a great deal of evidence to back up the suggestion, that the Minoans may have visited Britain on a regular basis. The Minoans were great sailors and traders, but two of the commodities their island home lacked were the metals copper and tin, which are necessary in order to create bronze. The Minoans could obtain copper from the mainland around the Mediterranean but tin was a different matter altogether. No matter where their tin came from they had to travel a significant distance to obtain it. One place where it existed in abundance was in the southwest of England and, although it cannot be absolutely proven, it is highly likely that the Minoans visited England to obtain tin.

No matter what the trade connections between Crete and England may or may not have been, there is no doubt about the relationship in terms of geometry. The relationship of 366 Megalithic Yards and 1,000 Minoan Feet is so close and so significant that it cannot be a random chance event. It is therefore evident that use of 366° geometry was not exclusive to Britain.

Of course critics are sure to say that, in the case of the measurement known as the foot there is no puzzle as to how it originated because the name tells its own story. It is based upon the length of a body part, an adult male foot. True as this may be in some regards it merely obscures others. Not all human feet are the same length, but the Minoan Foot, as rediscovered by J Walter Graham, never varied. What is more, his findings were validated totally when a new Minoan palace was unearthed 'after' he published his conclusions. This new site at Zakros conformed absolutely to his expectations of the Minoan Foot.

Neither has the modern statute foot got anything to do with the length of anyone's body parts. Examples of the unit are kept safe under lock and key, made from extremely durable and carefully wrought metals that hardly deviate with temperature and which do not corrode. So, whilst not arguing with the origin of the name 'foot' to describe such a unit, any relationship that does exist is peripheral to the truth of the situation.

Even some experts still suggest that the British standard foot was derived from its Roman counterpart. This is definitely not the case because the Roman foot was also standardized, and in modern terms it measured 29.6 cm, which is almost a full centimetre shorter than the British (and now the American) foot. A centimetre might not seem much but compared to the fineness of touch of the megalithic system it might as well be a mile! It can be clearly seen that the British foot is extremely close to the Minoan Foot. Since the Minoans flourished centuries before the Romans were anything more than goat herders, 'they' could hardly have been influenced by the marching feet of the legions.

What may well have developed from the Roman method of measurement is the British inch, at least as a concept. The Romans did have 12 inches to a Roman foot, though the inch in British terms seems to have little or no relationship with megalithic measurements or the 366° system of geometry. The word 'inch' comes from the Latin *uncia* and simply meant something that was 1/12th of something else.

Alexander Thom coined the name 'Megalithic Inch' for a unit that was 1/40th of a Megalithic Yard, but he was simply copying terminology regarding a unit that very roughly corresponded to a modern inch. In reality the statute inch and the Megalithic Inch are quite different in length.

What we can draw from all of this is that the modern foot is as close as makes no difference to a unit that was in existence at least as early as around 1800 BC and probably long before that. It is a metric version of a geometrical slice of the Earth's polar circumference when using 366° geometry.

Appendix 6

•

ESTIMATING THE CIRCUMFERENCE OF THE EARTH

James Russell BSc C. Eng. M. I. E. I.

There is growing evidence that an elite group of Neolithic peoples may have known the circumference of the Earth, and derived units of measurement based on this knowledge.

Thanks to meticulous research by the late Professor Thom, and statistical analysis, it is now believed that the results of a unified measurement system, a Megalithic Yard, possibly based on the circumference of the Earth, can be seen in Neolithic monuments located throughout northern Europe.

After reading *Civilization One* written by Christopher Knight and Alan Butler, I began communicating with Chris Knight regarding my proposal of methods to answer an unresolved question in the book, of how Neolithic man could have measured the circumference of the Earth using only materials available in the Neolithic period. The concept raises the question: Why would megalithic man even think the Earth might be spherical? Standing on a cliff top with a panoramic view, and looking out to sea, one gets the impression of the curvature of the surface of the sea, and hence that the Earth is spherical. There is also evidence in the Neolithic stone circles that people recognized changes in star positions dependent upon latitude. Observations of stars in the north appearing higher in the sky as they travelled north, and southern stars rising higher in the sky as they travelled south, would have reinforced the idea.

I have suggested two methods to estimate the Earth's circumference, a horizontal method and a vertical method. The horizontal method should be much more accurate than the vertical method as the sighting distances can be further apart, but the horizontal method can only be carried out with clear skies at dawn at equinox, whereas the vertical method can be done on any suitable day in the year. Both methods work with either the stars or the Sun to calculate the Earth's circumference at the observation latitude. Measurements of Polaris' position are needed to determine the latitude correction and calculate the Earth's equatorial circumference. Since August 2008 my intention has been to prove both methods by experiment. Due to bad weather there has been no opportunity to prove the horizontal method, but progress has been good with the vertical method. The methods use different first stages, and a common second stage.

METHOD ONE 'THE HORIZONTAL METHOD'

1. Sight through dark glass the perimeter of the Sun at sunrise, at equinox, or a star due east, across two pairs of crossheads A and B. The crossheads should be about 30 m apart and the pairs need to be placed about 30 miles apart east–west, set horizontal, or both at the same inclination. The time interval between the sunrise at A and the sunrise at B can then be used to calculate the Earth's circumference at the latitude of the measurements.

2. Correct for latitude by sighting onto Polaris, past the top of a vertical sight-rail to calculate the Earth's equatorial circumference.

Setting up each crosshead 'pair' requires an approximately 30-m-long trench, lying east–west, full of standing water, with the crossheads a measured distance above the water (*see* figure 26). Identical multiple eyepiece crossheads at different heights would enable several sets of readings from one sunrise. With this equipment, and the vertical sight-rail (described in figure 27 and figure 28) to correct for latitude, only five experimental measurements are needed:

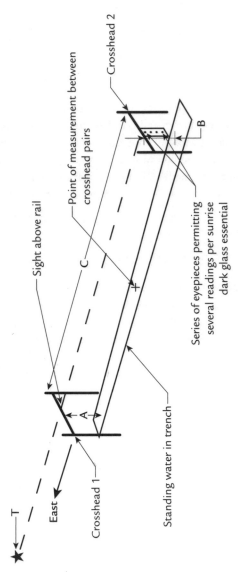

Dimensions A, B, (about 1.5 m to water level) and C (about 30 metres) to be exactly the same both crosshead sets. Two pairs required 20–40 miles apart.

Figure 26. Horizontal method apparatus: one set of two shown

1. The distance between crosshead pair A and crosshead pair B

2. The number of pendulum swings (pendulum length to be constant throughout) between sunrise or star rise at crosshead pair A and crosshead pair B

3. The number of pendulum swings between sunrise or star rise at crosshead pair A and crosshead pair A the next day (24 hours)

4. The inclined distance from a viewpoint to the intersection of a sightline onto Polaris and a vertical sight-rail set by plumb line (*see* figure 28).

5. The horizontal distance from the viewpoint to the vertical sight-rail (*see* figure 28).

To achieve accurate timings between the crosshead events 30 miles apart, the time delay in sightings could have been measured by masking signal fires, timing a signal between the two crossheads and back, then halving the time to compensate for the signal delay.

The horizontal method is open to theoretical verification using Chris' star program (which gives the location of any named star in the past or the future, given a date and time). Jim chose 21 March 2009, and two towns on the same line of latitude, 54.883° north, Carlisle and Stranraer, to test the method.

Chris' result from the program:

1. Sunrise at Carlisle was predicted to be at 06h 18m 47s

2. Sunrise at Stranraer was predicted to be at 06h 26m 47s

3. Sunrise at Carlisle the next day was predicted to be 06h 18m 46s.

Calculation

Time lapse sunrise Carlisle to sunrise Stranraer = 8 minutes
Scaling off a map, Carlisle and Stranraer are 79.8 miles apart
Therefore sunrise travels 79.8 miles in 8 minutes
Time lapse sunrise Carlisle 21 March to sunrise Carlisle 22
March = 23h 59m 59s

In 23h 59m 59s hours (1,439 minutes), until sunrise the next day, it would travel:

79.8miles × 1,439min / 8min = 14,364 miles

(the circumference of the Earth along the 54.883° north line of latitude).

The ratio of the circumference at 54.883° north to the equatorial circumference can be obtained by observing Polaris against the top of a vertical object from a viewpoint (*see* figure 28).

Then, by:

1. Making a horizontal measurement **H** from the viewpoint (figure 28) to the vertical object, and

2. Measuring the inclined length **I** from the viewpoint to the point of intersection of the line of sight of Polaris and vertical line,

3. Dividing measurement **H** by measurement **I** (modern mathematicians would recognize this as the cosine of the latitude angle).

The 54.883° circumference divided by cosine 54.883° then gives an equatorial circumference of:

14364 / 0.575 = 24,980 miles
(Any error comes from the inaccuracy of scaling a map).

This simulation using modern technology confirms that the method is viable and that, weather permitting, on carefully chosen sites, using only materials available to megalithic man, it could have been used by the ancients to approximate the Earth's circumference.

METHOD TWO 'THE VERTICAL METHOD'

Instead of method one, using sunrise, we could use either the Sun due south at midday, or a star due south at night. The ancients were familiar with the concept of a sundial. Basically this method uses the principle of two very accurate sundials by day, or 'stardials' by night.

If we have two points east–west of each other and we know the time between midday occurrences, and the total length of the day, and the distances between the points, we can calculate the Earth circumference at this latitude. Small sight-rail errors produce large errors in results. The Sun's heat significantly distorted my metal sight-rail during the day. More accurate results were obtained from the stars at night.

To prove the concept I have constructed two small-scale 10-m-high vertical sight-rails. One uses an old timber electricity pole fixed in my garden and mounted on foundation piles for rigidity. The mobile sight-rail pole is a 10-m long 168-mm in diameter hollow metal tube with the plumb line down the centre to shelter the suspension cord from the wind. It is mounted on adjustable screw feet to plumb the rail using only the plumb line for guidance. Both poles have adjustable sight-rails fixed to the side of the pole facing east. With good technique in experiments I found that an error of less than 0.1mm (4/1,000 of an inch) in these 'proof of concept' vertical 10 m sight-rails can be achieved. A much longer plumb line or a series of plumb lines above each other could plumb a much taller, and hence more accurate, straightedge. Neolithic man would have had trees up to 50 m tall to modify into vertical sight-rails. The sight rail does not have to be continuous down the pole, but must be accurate where the point of contact with the lines of sight occurs.

Four timber trestles, 1.5 m high by 1.5 m wide, were made, one placed to the south of each vertical rail and one to the north (*see* figure 28). To set a true north–south line using only Polaris, I looked north from each southern trestle to sight Polaris as it disappeared behind the vertical sight-rail near the top, when my eye was moved from east to west. A mark (figure 28, C) was placed on the horizontal trestle at the point where Polaris disappeared. Twelve hours later another sighting was taken and marked (figure 27, D). True south lies halfway between these marks. This point is now referred to as the south eyepiece; I replaced the mark with a slice of wood with a 2-mm in diameter hole. The most accurate results are achieved when Polaris is at the 3 o'clock and 9 o'clock positions. By placing a pinhole source of light at the southern eyepiece, and viewing from the northern trestle, past the vertical sight-rail, I was able to establish a northern eyepiece. From the northern eyepiece the edge of the sight-rail was a true north–south plane running through the centre of the Earth. The Sun or a star could be timed as it passed behind each sight-rail.

Sighting Polaris twice in the first part of the vertical method is for perfectionists; good results can still be obtained using one sighting to Polaris at both sight-rails, provided they are taken at the same time.

The time delay between the sightings at the two locations can be used as in the previous example.

Earth circumference at apparatus latitude
= distance between sight rails x time for one earth revolution

$$\overline{\text{Time between sightings}}$$

Latitude correction is done as in the previous example.

To confirm the accuracy of the continuous sight-rail, at night I sighted south as the constellation Orion passed behind the rail, and timed the passing of each star. The times between each star disappearance and published star charts confirmed accuracy; demonstrating that a simple vertical sight-rail could have been used to create very accurate star charts in Neolithic times.

Setting east–west lines can be done by setting a right angle from the north–south lines.

I cheated and used GPS, but distance measurement between two selected points, however far apart, would only require a unit of measurement and counting the number of times the unit is placed end to end. Prior to establishing a standard 'Megalithic Yard', any unit could have been used, the longest stick capable of being carried, perhaps by several men, would do. The final value of a 'Megalithic Yard' would be expressed as a fraction of the original stick-length. It is inconceivable that people capable of hauling 20-tonne stones for 20 miles and placing them 20 feet up on top of other stones could not have accurately measured 40 miles.

The apparatus I have constructed as proof of concept is relatively small scale; in Neolithic times the apparatus could have been many times larger and hence more accurate. In the experiment there is a trade-off between measurement of time and measurement of distance. The longer the distance and the higher the vertical rail, the more accuracy can be obtained from time measurements. For example, at 50 degrees north, if 10-m high

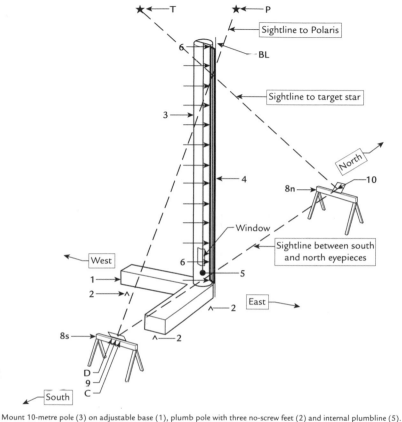

Mount 10-metre pole (3) on adjustable base (1), plumb pole with three no-screw feet (2) and internal plumbline (5).
Straighten sight-rail (4) to a temporary builder's line (BL) by adjusting 13 no bolts (6) fixed to side of sight-rail.
From south tressle (8s), sight Pole Star (P) in line with top of east side of sight-rail (4), mark point (C).
12 hours later (or 6 months later at the same time) resight Pole Star (P), mark point (D).
Drill 2 mm diameter hole midway C-D 9 'south eyepiece' (true south of the east side of the sight-rail).
Place light in south eyepiece (9), view from, and adjust north eyepiece (10) in line with east side of sight-rail.
Sight line from north eyepiece (10), (2 mm diameter) past east side of sight-rail (4) will be in true north/south plane.
Time target star (T) between two sets of sight-rails 20–40 miles apart, calculate earth circumference at latitude.

Figure 27. Vertical apparatus. Two required for experiment, located 20 to 40 miles apart, due east/west of each other on any line of latitude.

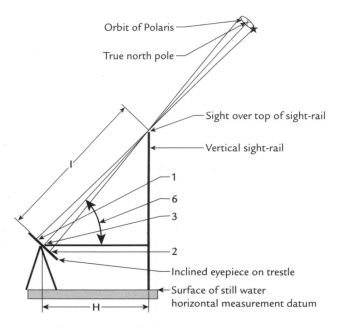

Orbit of Polaris

True north pole

Sight over top of sight-rail

Vertical sight-rail

1

6

3

2

Inclined eyepiece on trestle

Surface of still water
horizontal measurement datum

H

I

1 Mark of lowest sighting of Polaris.
2 Mark of highest sighting of Polaris (up to 6 months between sightings).
6 Angle same as location latitude.
Measure H, measure I. Use H and I in latitude correction.

Figure 28. Apparatus to establish latitude

sight-rails are 45 miles apart and the time error is one second, then the circumference error is (0.416%) or 104.6 miles.

Neolithic peoples would have had to put up with much less light pollution than occurs today. Apart from direct effects of stray light on the natural adjustments of the eyes, light from towns many miles away over the horizon can illuminate the base of clouds, and turn a poor observing night into an impossible night. Stars we have difficulty observing with the naked eye would have been much clearer 4,000 years ago. Observation of reflections of starlight on the surface of water, too dim to use today, may have enabled reflected light to be used to create longer light paths and hence produce more accuracy.

On 21 March 2009, as proof of concept I took the 'away' mobile vertical sight-rail 30 miles from home on a lorry, set up in 30 minutes, took the readings in 3 minutes and brought the sight-rail back to the yard the same evening. The result of this short experiment was a value for Earth circumference of 25,802 miles. The error in this result was due to the effect of the wind on the unprotected plumb line on the wooden pole. Perfect weather (good visibility and no wind whatsoever) is critical to the experiments. With minor equipment modifications, I am confident this small-scale vertical apparatus will consistently produce circumference values ±200 miles. Larger vertical equipment or the horizontal method would better ±50 miles. Considering that six months ago no one had even proposed a Neolithic method of determining Earth circumference, this experiment must be considered a remarkable success.

My equipment is 'proof of concept' and small scale. There are ways to improve the accuracy even on this scale. I consider I have demonstrated that Neolithic astronomers could have experimentally determined the diameter of the Earth, and could have produced more accurate results, using full-scale equipment, than I have. For either method there is no need for a henge or any megaliths. A long east–west fairly flat strip of land or foreshore (easy to measure) and a set of signal fires would have been all that was required. A Neolithic vertical sight-rail would have been made of timber and would have rotted away in a few years, the only evidence of the use of either method would be the results.

Appendix 7

•

THE MEGALITHIC SYSTEM EXPLAINED

In a solar year the Sun rises 365 times but, during the same time, a star will have risen 366 times. It sounds odd but it's true. Each day according to the rising of a star (a sidereal day), is 23 hours 56 minutes 4 seconds in length, whereas a mean solar day is 24 hours in length. That leaves a discrepancy of 236 seconds, which over a year amounts to another 24 hours. It is part of the clockwork mechanism of our solar system that there are different sorts of years, dependent on what one is observing. Our megalithic and pre-megalithic ancestors in Britain focused on the number of times a star rose in a year, and the result was 366 times.

Having made this realization what they did next is the most surprising aspect of our studies. They created an integrated measuring system based upon a year of 366 days. Just as surely as they recognized that the circle of the year was naturally split into 366 units, they then split the horizon into 366 units, which we would know as degrees of arc. They then split the units again, first into minutes of arc – they considered that there were 60 minutes of arc to 1 degree of arc.

But this was not enough for them so they split the units again. Each minute of arc was split into 6 smaller units, which we would know as seconds of arc. (Note the difference between this form of geometry and the one we use now. In 360° geometry there are 60 seconds of arc to 1 minute of arc but in the megalithic system there are only 6.)

Somehow they worked out that if they split the degree, minute and second of arc in this way, they would arrive at a stunning result because each Megalithic Second of arc of the polar Earth measured *exactly* 366 Megalithic Yards on the ground.

The actual size of the Megalithic Yard could be judged by the careful use of a pendulum of exactly half this length (*see* Appendix 4). At first this was used in conjunction with the Sun but later a more sophisticated method was established using the planet Venus during certain parts of its orbit.

What is absolutely incredible about the Megalithic Yard as a unit of length is not just that it is geodetic (fits into the polar circumference of the Earth in a logical and obviously intended way), but it does the same job on the Moon and the Sun. One Megalithic Second of arc on the Moon measures exactly 100 Megalithic Yards. On the Sun the same Megalithic Second of arc is 40,000 Megalithic Yards.

Getting the sheer genius of this system across to our readers has been the hardest part of our quest because it really is incredible but it can seem complicated. Once the penny drops, the whole system is virtually miraculous, making our modern approach to measurement systems look primitive – logic is reversed. In this system a second of arc of the sky can be seen as the same thing as a second of time of the Earth turning on its axis. In other words 1 Megalithic Second of the Earth turning on its axis also represents a physical segment of the sky, albeit an extremely small one because it is 1/366th of 1/360th of the sky. The same second is also a finite measurement of part of the Earth's circumference. Time and geometry and distance all merge into the same symmetrical whole, and astronomical calculations become much easier.

Meanwhile, with the system we use today we have degrees, minutes and seconds of arc of the sky and of the circumference of our planet. We also have minutes and seconds of time but these don't match the turning sky at all. This fact must have cost thousands of human lives as the first mariners to engage in transatlantic voyages tried desperately to reconcile minutes and seconds of time with minutes and seconds of geometrical arc and came up with the wrong answer. We eventually discovered that, in addition to measuring time and linear distance, the megalithic system had also been based on the mass of the Earth. How could this possibly be? It's absurd, and yet it is self-evidently true. The unit of mass in question is virtually the same as the unit presently known as the imperial pound. The mass of the Earth is 5.9742×10^{24} kg. In pounds this figure is $1.31708565 \times 10^{25}$ lb. With just a very slight change in the definition of the pound this figure becomes 1.317600×10^{25} lb and then something amazing happens. Imagine we segment the earth like an orange. A segment 1 Msec of arc across would have a mass of exactly 1×10^{20} lb. That's 100,000,000,000,000,000,000 pounds!

This means that the imperial pound and the pound that was a part of the megalithic system are virtually identical. The Megalithic Pound had a value of 99.96% of the modern pound! The difference is 0.4 of a gram. That this level of accuracy has been maintained across such a vast period of time is little short of incredible.

In order to turn the Megalithic Yard into a system for measuring volume and mass we need to resort to the Megalithic Inch. Alexander Thom found this unit when he carefully studied carvings that had been scratched into a number of standing stones. He established that there had been 40 Megalithic Inches to 1 Megalithic Yard. A cube with sides of 1/10th of a Megalithic Yard (4 Megalithic Inches) holds the same as a modern pint of water. If the water is poured out and the same cube is filled with any cereal grain, such as wheat, barley or even un-hulled rice, the weight of the cereal grain will be 1 imperial pound.

So what do we have?

The megalithic system is a system of geometry and measurement that is based upon a 366-day year, together with the physical size and mass of the Earth. It measures time, distance, mass and volume using the same figures throughout, and aspects of it are as relevant to the Moon and Sun as they are here on Earth. Without wishing to detract from our stunning scientific accomplishments as a species, anyone would surely have to admit that the megalithic system is better in a number of ways than any method of measurement used today. This is because it is 'integrated' and because a common terminology is used throughout. The metric system in use today may be extremely accurate, and it too was originally based on the circumference of the Earth, but it certainly does not take Earth mass into account and neither is it used for the measurement of time. Unbelievable as it may seem, thanks to our friend and colleague Edmund Sixsmith, we now believe that the Megalithic system also dealt with the measurement of temperature. If we create a temperature scale in which the freezing point of water is 0° Megalithic and the boiling point of water is 366° Megalithic something quite magical happens. Absolute zero, the lowest temperature achievable (usually considered to be −273.15 °C) becomes an absolutely round and quite accurate – 1,000° Megalithic.

Since there is little chance that our megalithic ancestors were interested in measuring temperatures, let alone in possession of the technology to do so, the megalithic temperature system stands as proof that, as ingenious and useable as aspects of the Megalithic system were to our ancient ancestors, they did not create it. Rather they must have 'inherited' it from a previous technological culture that is now lost to us.

Appendix 8

•

THE PENTAGON AND THE 32ND DEGREE OF SCOTTISH RITE FREEMASONRY

We were already very familiar with the significance of five-sided figures long before we began to look at Washington DC. We have described pentagons before as being 'inside-out pentacles' or five-pointed stars. Joining the corners of a pentagon together, as shown below, creates a pentacle.

The pentacle is the most common historical representation of the planet Venus. We have explained why this is probably the case in our previous books. Briefly, it is because five Venus cycles as seen from the Earth have almost exactly the same number of days as eight Earth years. This seemingly 'magical' coincidence therefore imbued both five-sided and eight-sided figures with a special significance in the minds of ancient star-watchers.

Five-sided figures are also extremely important to the United States. The five-pointed star can be seen repeated on the Great Seal of the United States, on the national flag and on United States currency. To Freemasons it also has a special significance. It is known as the 'Blazing Star' and from around 1735 it was detailed as being part of the furniture of the Freemasonic Lodge. It was to be found at the centre of the mosaic pavement in a Masonic temple, though it often appears above ground level, in the east, and invariably carries the letter 'G' at its centre.

As to what Freemasons consider the Blazing Star actually represents there is no apparent consensus. Many Freemasons, especially historical ones such as Robert Hewitt Brown, recognized the Blazing Star as being

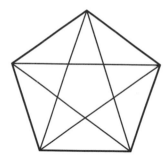

Figure 29. Pentacle drawn within the corners of a pentagon

representative of the Sun – though this is a strange way to depict the Sun, which is almost invariably shown in other contexts as an orb. Other Freemasons suggest that the Blazing Star may be Egyptian and represent the star Sirius that we mentioned so frequently in earlier chapters. For our own part we remain content that the Blazing Star represents the planet Venus. Its presence in Freemasonry is one of the clues for the Mystery Religion origins of the Craft – even if the average Freemason these days has no idea regarding this fact. It is suggested the 'G', often to be found at the centre of the star, stands for the word 'God' but of course 'Goddess' is also spelled with a capital G.

Obviously a star-shaped building for the headquarters of the United States Department of Defense would not have been very useful and would have offered very little space for its intended purpose. So even if the five-pointed star had enjoyed some symbolic meaning in the minds of those who planned the new building, a pentagon was a much more useful and practical shape.

As we have seen, the Pentagon building connects to both the Ellipse centre and the Capitol in megalithic units of 366 MY, and since the Ellipse and the Capitol share a similar relationship with each other a triangle of megalithic proportions can be drawn that joins all three sites. The sum total of the distance involved between the three is close to 10,020 m, which in megalithic terms is 33 × 366 MY. For reasons other than the simple measurements involved surely nobody would try to suggest that the existence of this triangle, with all its symbolism for Washington DC and the United States, is merely a figment of our overactive imaginations?

The corners of this triangle define Washington DC's geographic heart (the Ellipse), its democratic heart (the Capitol) and its military heart (the Pentagon). What is more, the existence of the triangle, with its 33 × 366 MY proportions, offers all the proof we need that the relationship between the three is deliberate and that Freemasons were involved.

In Freemasonic terms there is certainly significance to the number 33. As with all Freemasons, Scottish Rite Freemasons have to go through the normal three degrees that lead them to becoming a full member of the Craft. (A degree in this sense is a particular ceremony and its associated ritual that allows a Freemason to gradually climb the Masonic ladder.) Different groups of Freemasons do things in slightly different ways but the Scottish Rite, which can certainly claim to be descended from the oldest existent branch of Freemasonry, has degrees or levels well beyond the obligatory three degrees. In fact there are 32 degrees in Scottish Freemasonry that can be achieved through the Scottish Rite Freemason's own efforts and advancement, and a further degree that can be offered to any 32nd-degree Freemason who, it is judged, has given exceptional service to the Craft. This therefore makes a total of 33 degrees, which is as high as anyone can climb in Scottish Rite Freemasonry.[1]

Franklin D Roosevelt, 32nd President of the United States, was the man who steered the United States skilfully through the hell of the Second World War. This same man helped to rescue the United States from the horrors of the Great Depression and set the nation back to work. It was Franklin Roosevelt who personally ordered the change of location of the Pentagon at the last minute, ensuring it would be built in a location that would create the megalithic triangle that is 33 × 366 MY in length. Roosevelt was a Scottish Rite Freemason who had attained 32 degrees and who, for his work in the Craft, was awarded 33rd-degree status!

During the research for this book we looked at the ceremonies and rituals associated with the 32nd and 33rd degree. In the case of the latter there is not much to report because as we have pointed out the degree is 'offered' rather than 'earned' (though it is suggested that there is a more secret 33rd-degree ritual that has never been published). However, the

32nd-degree Scottish Rite ceremony is so significant we could hardly believe our eyes.

The 32nd degree is known as the degree of 'The Sublime Prince of the Royal Secret'. It is composed of three separate parts. These are the Opening Ceremony, the Ceremonial Section and the Allegory.

This particular ceremony is very elaborate, as befits someone who has climbed as high on the Freemasonic ladder as it is possible to go under one's own effort. A great deal of play-acting takes place and the various characters all have fictional names.

It is suggested that the 32nd degree relates to the fight for Jerusalem at the time of the Crusades, though no specific location is mentioned in the ritual itself.

The ceremony takes place in what appears to be a fictitious military camp that, according to what we learn later, represents a nine-sided figure, inside which is a seven-sided figure. Inside the seven-sided figure is a five-sided figure or pentagon, and inside this is a triangle. Finally, inside the triangle is a circle, which represents infinity. Most of the 32nd-degree ceremony relates specifically to the pentagon.

Freemasons who already hold the 32nd degree play the part of specific characters in the ceremony. After a typically Freemasonic preamble in which various figures such as the Commander in Chief, the Captain of the Guard and the Master of Ceremonies take part, a character by the name of Constans enters. This is the individual that represents the would-be 32nd-degree Freemasons who are present.

Constans is asked what he requires and he replies that he wishes to be admitted as a fellow soldier and servant in the Grand Masonic Army of Sublime Princes of the Royal Secret. He goes on to suggest that he wishes to shield the oppressed, guard the weak, protect the innocent and combat the enemies of God and humanity.

After a few more lines of dialogue the person playing the part of the Engineer and Seneschal rises. This is what he says:

> The camp of the Ancient Accepted Scottish Rite of Freemasonry is
> a nonagon enclosing a heptagon, within whose lines is a pentagon
> which encloses a triangle in the centre of which is a circle. Thus do

we find the mystic numbers, 3, 5, 7 and 9, all emanating from the circle of infinity. As these numbers symbolize Divine attributes and Masonic principles, so should Masonic labour emanate from Divine love, be directed by Divine wisdom, and be exercised in Divine power for the good of mankind and the glory of God.

The second emanation from infinity is denoted by the pentagon, each angle of which represents a division of the Scottish Rite Army. Take heed while their attributes are now rehearsed.

In turn, five separate and distinct characters now explain what the five corners of the pentagon represent. Each corner is symbolic of a different lodge, council or chapter. The first corner is the Symbolic Lodge and the second is the Lodge of Perfection. The third angle of the pentacle represents the Council of the Princes of Jerusalem and the fourth is the Chapter of the Knights Rose Croix. The final angle is that of the Kadosh. (The word Kadosh is taken from a Hebrew word that means 'Holy', and the degrees of Freemasonry termed as the Kadosh contain a great deal of mystical material.)

Practically the whole of the ceremonial part of the 32nd degree is taken up with the explanations of the five corners of the pentagon, after which the degree is inferred on those seeking it. Beyond this the Allegory takes place. All those who have received the 32nd degree are seated and the play begins.

Constans reappears, and we are told that he seeks knighthood and that he is to stay alone by the altar in a cathedral throughout a whole night prior to his investiture. His armour and weapons are given to him and placed on the altar. All the actors present now leave the stage and for a short time Constans remains alone. After a while a character named Florio enters. He is the first of the tempters who will try to persuade Constans to leave his vigil. Florio urges Constans to come to a dance and to meet his sweetheart.

Constans refuses and Florio eventually retires. The next tempter is a man called Urban. He offers Constans power and influence in the world – the chance to have everything he desires in a material sense. Once again Constans refuses and is eventually left alone.

The next tempter is Rufus, a peasant who tells Constans that his castle has been attacked by a traitor knight. He urges Constans to come directly. Once again Constans refuses.

The final tempter is a monk called Ignatius. He urges Constans to leave his vigil and to seek a contemplative life. Constans falters for a while but he wants to know what will become of the service he has promised to humanity. Ignatius points out that service to God and a monastic life might be preferable but even at this stage Constans remembers his promises to the world and his brothers and so refuses to leave his vigil.

For a moment Constans is left alone again but soon he hears the blast of a trumpet and the call to arms. He hears cries of 'The enemy', 'Save us' and 'To the Walls'. He realizes that the city is under attack and that the lives of all the men, women and children within it are in peril. He then learns from the voices off stage that the leader of the army is slain and that defeat is imminent.

Constans wrestles with his conscience because he has promised on his honour to keep his vigil, no matter what happens. Despite this he is in little doubt and so shouting 'How can I stay while children may be murdered and women ravished?' he eventually arms himself and rushes off.

Darkness prevails for half a minute or so and then the various commanders and the bishop reappear on the stage. It is obvious from their conversation that although their leader was severely wounded, the battle was saved by the arrival of a new commander, who turned the tide of fighting and helped to defeat the attackers. Nobody knows who this saviour was but it suddenly occurs to those present that Constans is no longer at the altar.

It is assumed he has run away like a coward and scorn is being heaped upon him when four men enter. They carry a bier upon which is the body of Constans. Everyone now realizes that it was he who saved the day by abandoning his vigil and taking part in the fight.

The Prince Commander utters the final words of the Allegory:

Constans our Deliverer. How vain is human wisdom! How blind is human judgment! In our hasty anger we said, 'Never shall Constans be created by us a Sublime Prince of the Royal Secret'. His martyr victory has made of our unjust judgment his eternal glory. It was not for mortal man to create Constans a prince. He was a prince, dubbed and created by the King of Kings whose son he is. It was not for mortal man to reveal to Constans the Royal Secret. It was enshrined in his own unconquerable soul, incarnate in that Love which was his divine inheritance. When he forsook his vigil here, Constans was true to the highest meaning and deepest spirit of his vow. He obeyed the dictates of his conscience and, in loyal response to his country's call, rushed to its defence.

Can this strange ceremony have anything to do with Washington DC or, in particular the creation of the Pentagon? Indeed it can, but to fully understand what the connection is we must first look at what was taking place in the United States when the Pentagon was planned and built.

Partly because of the horrors of the First World War, but also on account of its geographical isolation, there were many Americans who wanted nothing whatsoever to do with the war that had begun in Europe in 1940. When France fell in May 1940 Britain was, for some time, facing the threat of Nazi Germany alone. The natural instincts of President Franklin Roosevelt were to help America's old ally, Britain, but the weight of public opinion was against him. Nevertheless Roosevelt found ways in which to be of assistance to Britain, by offering armaments and food.

The building of the Pentagon began in September of 1941 but the United States did not come into the Second World War officially until December of the same year, after the attack made on Pearl Harbour by the Japanese. This means that at the time the Pentagon was planned and building had started, the United States, though helping Britain in all sorts of ways, was still not officially involved in the war. It was, in a figurative sense, like Constans at the altar of the cathedral, maintaining its own vigil.

The moment building work started on the Pentagon the triangle formed between it, the Ellipse and the Capitol was created and in a symbolic sense this was extremely important. As we have already noted the 33rd degree of Scottish Rite Freemasonry is not an 'earned' degree. Rather it is offered to those 32nd-degree Freemasons who are thought especially worthy of it. Whilst the geometric figure associated with the 32nd degree is a pentacle, the one especially associated with the 33rd degree is a triangle! As we suggested earlier, the triangle formed between the Ellipse, the Capitol and the Pentagon connects Washington DC's geographic heart (the Ellipse), its democratic heart (the Capitol) and its military heart (the Pentagon). What is more, this triangle could not exist until the Pentagon was begun, just as surely as the 33rd degree of Scottish Rite Freemasonry cannot be achieved until the 32nd is held first.

Such is the connection between the symbols and ceremonies of the 32nd and 33rd degree and the planning and positioning of the Pentagon that there simply has to be a direct connection. For years the United States kept its own vigil, as did Constans in the 32nd-degree ceremony. It did not respond to events that were unfolding in Europe during the 1930s, and even when Western Europe was plunged into war the United States did not become directly involved. Meanwhile President Roosevelt struggled with his own conscience, not least of all his Freemasonic conscience. Many of the men closest to the President in Government were also Freemasons but, Freemasonic or not, it must have become evident by 1941, to all but the most diehard isolationists, that the United States would not be able to avoid being drawn into the conflict eventually.

Just like Constans in the 32nd-degree ceremony they could eventually no longer stand in contemplative isolation, and by the careful positioning and building of the Pentagon in a figurative sense the whole of Washington DC, and ultimately the United States of America, passed from the 32nd to the 33rd degree. The name of the 33rd degree is 'Sovereign Grand Inspector General'. This is an administrative degree and just as surely as the 33rd-degree Freemason becomes the arbiter and leader of his Craft, so with its participation in the Second World War the United States became the arbiter and leader of the world. Now, in the year 2009 and after the fall of the Soviet Union, the United States is the only genuine superpower remaining.

Appendix 9

·

THE CENTRE OF THE DISTRICT OF COLUMBIA

The United States Constitution was adopted on 17 September 1787 and the need for a Federal capital for the infant United States was already a consideration at that time. Article 1, Section 8, Clause 17 specifically mentions this fact. It specifies that an area not to exceed 10 miles square should be established and that it will come under the authority of Congress. A little later, on 16 July 1790 the new President, George Washington, was authorized to find an appropriate site for the new capital and on 1 December 1800, Washington officially became the capital city of the United States of America.

George Washington took the Constitution at its word and instructed a square to be surveyed, partly in Virginia and partly in Maryland, across the Potomac River. In reality, if compass bearings are born in mind, what resulted from the survey was not a square but a diamond. Each side of the diamond was 10 miles in length and a series of 40 boundary stones were set along the hypothetical lines delineating what would henceforth be the District of Columbia. The city of Washington DC began to grow close to the centre of the diamond.

There is little doubt in our minds that a slight mistake in surveying the city itself took place right at the beginning of the procedure because we are certain that the location we have itemized, at the very centre of the Ellipse, south of the White House, was considered to be the absolute centre of the District of Columbia. A line that would connect the top and bottom points of the diamond would have a longitude of 77° 02' 26" west, whilst a line connecting the eastern and western points of the diamond would have latitude of 38° 53' 35" north.

The meeting point of two such lines is slightly west of the Ellipse and also slightly south. Therefore the 'true' centre of the District of Columbia is actually around 345 m southwest of the centre of the Ellipse.

The centre of the Ellipse has a longitude of 77° 02' 11" west and latitude of 38° 53' 38" north. This amounts to a discrepancy of 15" of arc from the true centre of the District of Columbia in terms of longitude, and 3" in terms of latitude. Bearing in mind the laborious way surveying was undertaken in the 18th century these results are probably quite close to being considered accurate, but the slight mistakes that are present are related to the chosen location of the White House rather than with anything to do with the original surveying of the District of Columbia.

When Thomas Jefferson fixed the Washington meridian line during his presidency he was living in the White House. He personally marked a line that ran from north to south right through the middle of the White House. But why did he do this? Earlier suggestions for a Washington DC meridian had been one mile to the east of the Capitol, and later a line through the Capitol itself. We cannot prove the fact but it is our contention that Thomas Jefferson chose the north–south line through the White House because he considered that such a line would intersect with the top and bottom corners of the diamond that was the District of Columbia. As it turned out he was slightly wrong, but that was because the White House had not been built in exactly the correct position relative to the very centre of the District of Columbia. The centre of the White House was 322 m too far to the east and 100 m too far north.

There may have been practical reasons for this state of affairs, for example the state of the ground on the chosen site. We cannot know, but the most likely explanation is a mistake in plotting the 'exact' position for the White House so that the magical spot that is now the centre of the Ellipse would also be the centre of the District of Columbia. This task would not have been easy and it is telling that the mistake is three times as bad in terms of longitude as it is in terms of latitude. At the time the

White House was built, plotting longitude was still a fairly difficult procedure. It was only in 1761 that John Harrison, an English clock maker,
had managed to produce a chronometer accurate enough to be used
to establish longitude at sea, but if the White House had indeed been
intended to straddle the north–south line between the northern and
southern points of the District of Columbia, even John Harrison's time-
piece would have been of little use in setting its position.

Measuring distance over undulating ground was difficult. The true
centre of the diamond in an east–west direction could have been found
through laboriously surveying the distance from the eastern corner, but
is more likely to have been undertaken in the same way our megalithic
ancestors undertook it, by use of the stars. In fact the problems any
would-be surveyor would have had were extremely similar to the problems that faced the people who built the Thornborough henges and
Stonehenge. The centre of the diamond in a north–south sense would
have been easier to find and could have been judged by the height in the
sky of the North Star at the southern corner of the diamond, the northern corner of the diamond, and then in the middle.

In the case of the 18th century, the slightest inaccuracy in the calibra-
tion of telescopes used for the purpose could easily have led to a 300-m
discrepancy in terms of the longitude of the White House. Assuming
there was a mistake right at the start it is likely to have been made by
Pierre-Charles L'Enfant, who produced the original plans upon which
Washington DC was based.

The piece of land immediately to the south of the White House was
left vacant and because it was surrounded by a white picket fence it
became known as the 'White Lot'. It seems likely to us that this piece of
land was recognized (incorrectly as it turns out) as being the very centre
of the District of Columbia. The Ellipse was not laid out until the 1870s
and 1880s and the stone marking the Washington meridian was not
placed at its centre until 1890. Part of the reason for the delay was clearly
the American Civil War, during which time most manpower was mobi-
lized and the land in question was given over to military use.

This then is our suggestion: The very spot where the Meridian Stone
was placed in 1890 was originally considered to be the exact centre of the

diamond that is the District of Columbia. Thomas Jefferson seems to have thought this was the case in terms of longitude, and the position of the stone is only about 100 m out in latitude. Thomas Jefferson was fooled because the White House had been built in slightly the wrong place.

Although not strictly correct, the position of the Meridian Stone in the centre of the Ellipse is also the centre of the District of Columbia to an accuracy of 99.85 per cent east–west and 99.5 per cent north–south.

It is also interesting to note that although the diamond that forms the boundaries of the original District of Columbia was surveyed and measured in miles, a line taken across the diamond between north and south, or east and west, has megalithic proportions, being equal to 75 × 366 MY in length.

Appendix 10

•

THINKING STYLES AND ACADEMIC OBJECTIVITY

In this book we have been critical of the way that archaeology is run. In an age of highly defined specialisms there is a widespread intolerance for ideas that originate outside of 'official' university-based frameworks. We found archaeology unwilling to evaluate the findings contained in this and our previous book *Civilization One*. Nevertheless we welcome criticism or debate.

Many academics are unaware that there are different sorts of thinking styles. They assume process-driven thinking is the only valid way to approach ideas. There is also a general assumption that if a new theory collides with a preferred paradigm it must be wrong. The way people think has been studied very closely in recent years. Awareness that there are different approaches to thinking and deduction can lead to better judgements.

Ned Herrmann was an internationally-recognized expert on creative thinking who developed a comprehensive four-part Whole Brain Model: this is now used by major corporations everywhere. It divides the brain into four quadrants. This produces a metaphor leading to a very insightful application in the Herrmann Brain Dominance Instrument (HBDI). The brain is divided left to right, with the structured thinking left-brained and free-flowing thinking right-brained. These produce quadrants that can be simplified as follows:

A   Top left – Analytical, formula based, factual, focused, technical
B   Bottom left – Procedural, practical, process, routine, conservative
C   Bottom right – Feeling, people-centric, sensory, caring, spiritual
D   Top right – Synthesiser, big picture, rule-breaking, innovative

This non-judgemental model shows preferred thinking styles in working environments proved across a million people. Most people have ability in all quadrants but retain a dominant sector. Individuals with a marked strength in any quadrant may doubt people in another – particularly opposite quadrants. It is also hardly surprising that some fields of activity attract individuals with the same working style. Accountants and academics are often strong in the A – top left category whilst entrepreneurs, explorers and artists are in the D – top right quadrant.

Our thinking styles predominate in the D category; synthesising the big-picture: lateral thinking is central to our work. We also score well in the A category because we have to verify and quantify ideas. Really good academics will also be strong in both areas but many have a very low tolerance for big-picture thinking. If archaeologists learned that evidence comes in different forms, they might perform better. The term 'pseudoscience' is used as a term of abuse by those wishing to protect preconceived ideas. Alexander Thom spent 50 years undertaking detailed examinations of Megalithic sites – only to be have some lightweights apply the 'pseudoscience' label to him.

If you are not toeing the conventional line you are a pseudoscientist. This is academic mudslinging that rejects those who hold a reasoned counter-view. We expect some people to label our evidence as pseudo-science – but it is not. We might be wrong on a number of points (time will tell) but there is nothing in this book that is not reasoned argument based on checkable facts.

Science is surely the best thing ever invented. It is a pity that so few people in academia actually use the real principles of science. Maybe guys, there is a better understanding of the past to be uncovered. But you will never know if you keep your eyes squeezed shut.

ENDNOTES

Chapter 2

1 Seen in the northern hemisphere and because of the nature of the Earth's orbit, there are a number of stars that do not rise in the east and set in the west as do most stars. Rather, they are always in view, though of course daylight blocks them out when the Sun is above the horizon.

2 Osiris was one of the most popular of Egyptian gods, and also one of the most loved and revered. His story is one of suffering and sacrifice but eventually of triumph. His worship spanned virtually the whole period of ancient Egyptian history.

3 The Pyramid Texts are a series of prayers and incantations carved into the interior passages of several early pyramids to be found at Saqqara Egypt.

4 'The Origin of the Egyptian Calendar': Neugebauer O, *Journal of Near Eastern Studies*, Vol. 1, 1942

5 'Ancient Egyptian Astronomy': Parker R A, *Philosophical transactions of the Royal Society of London*, 1974

6 *The Hiram Key*: Knight C & Lomas R, Century, 1996

7 *Myth and Symbol in Ancient Egypt*: Rundle Clark R T, Thames and Hudson, 1978

8 *The Book of Hiram*: Knight C & Lomas R, Century, 2000

Chapter 3

1 *The Palaces of Crete*: Graham, J W, Princeton University Press, London, 1962

2 *Civilization One*: Knight C & Butler A, Watkins, 2004

Chapter 6

1 This method will not work for placing the middle star accurately as a henge on the ground because of the angle at which the stars rise above the bank top. Only the next method could offer an accurate position for the middle henge.

2 Stecchini Livio C: www.metrum.org/measures/index.htm

3 The modern metre was originally intended to be based on a pendulum that beats at the rate of once per second. *See* Appendix 5 for a timeline of this unit's development.

4 *Civilization One*: Knight C & Butler A, Watkins, 2004

Chapter 7

1 *Astronomy in Prehistoric Britain and Ireland*: Ruggles C, Yale University Press, 1999

2 *Henge Monuments of the British Isles*: Harding J, Tempus, 2003

3 'Henges and Water – Towards an Elemental Understanding of Monumentality and Landscape in Late Neolithic Britain': Richards C, *Journal of Material Culture*, Vol.1, No.3, 1996

4 *Uriel's Machine*: Knight C & Lomas R, Century, 1999

Chapter 8

1 Jim Russell's experiments and results can be viewed in Appendix 6 (page 230).

Chapter 9

1 *Archaeological Fantasies: How Pseudoarchaeology Misrepresents the Past and Misleads the Public*: Fagan G G, Routledge, 2006

Chapter 10

1 *Uriel's Machine*: Knight C & Lomas R, Century, 1999

2 *The Origin Map: Discovery of a Prehistoric, Megalithic, Astrophysical Map and Sculpture of the Universe*: Brophy T, Writers Press Club, 2002

3 Afterword – *The Origin Map*: West J A, The Writers Club, 2002

Chapter 11

1 *The Mummies of Urumchi*: Barber, E W, Macmillan,1999

2 *Bath*: Newman P, Pevensey Press, Cambridge, 1986

3 *The Hiram Key*: Knight C & Lomas R, Century, London, 1996

4 *Rosslyn Revealed*: Butler A & Ritchie J, O Books, 2006

5 *Solomon's Power Brokers*: Knight C & Butler A, Watkins, 2007

6 *The Book of Hiram*: Knight C & Lomas R, Century, 2003

7 *The Book of Hiram*: Knight C & Lomas R, Century, 2003

Chapter 12

1 http://www.whitehouse.gov/about/vp_residence/

2 A pentacle is a five-pointed star that was commonly used in Christianity in the medieval period, though these days it has attracted demonic or even satanic overtones – based on prejudice and a complete ignorance of symbology. The five-pointed star has long been used as a symbol for the planet Venus, as it represents the Venus cycle. It is a symbol of knowledge and light, connected to Lucifer (Venus as the morning star), the angel of light who has erroneously become associated with evil.

3 See Appendix 7 on megalithic geometry

4 6 × 366 Megalithic Yards is what we named a Megalithic minute of arc of the Earth's polar circumference. We first suggested the existence of such a unit well over a decade ago based on a study of British and Minoan megalithic structures.

5 A line of longitude from which all other locations could be measured, east and west.

6 This measurement seems extremely likely, but since the original Meridian Stone in Meridian Park has been lost we cannot validate the accuracy of the true distance.

7 Which also has a megalithic relationship with the centre of the Ellipse.

Chapter 13

1 Our brackets

2 Web page of the Grand Orient of France: http://www.godf.org/foreign/uk/histoire_uk_02.html

3 Those who now shout loudest and negatively about Freemasonic influence in the foundation of the United States should perhaps be more circumspect because, had it not been for Freemasonry, it is doubtful that the American colonies would ever have broken away from British control.

4 Two of the chief protagonists were Joseph Warren and Paul Revere, both leading Freemasons.

5 *The Virgin and the Pentacle*: Butler A, O Books, 2005

ENDNOTES

6 *Solomon's Power Brokers*: Knight C & Butler A, Watkins, 2007

7 *Stellar Theology and Masonic Astronomy*: Brown R H, D Appleton and Co, New York, 1882 – now available in paperback from The Truth Seeker Co, 1997 ISBN 58509-203-7.

8 In the Christian Church Easter, the time of the Crucifixion, occurs in the spring. In the Mystery religions autumn was the preferred time for the sacrifice of the god. At that time, spring represented new birth and so would have been more appropriate in some ways for Christmas. However, Christmas was already needed as the birth of the expected messiah was as the Shekinah returned – which all knew was at the winter solstice (25 December) in 7 BC. The accelerated death and rebirth period of just three days was much more useful to the Romans, especially as they used some very fancy footwork to shift the blame for the messiah's execution from their governor of Judea to Jesus' own people.

9 *The Gentleman's Magazine* Volume 8, June 1738, p. 285

10 *The Secret Zodiacs of Washington DC*: Ovason D, Century, 1999

11 There is a difference between astrological positions and astronomical ones. The zodiac signs in astrology are 'fixed' in time and are theoretical rather than actual. These days, for example, on 21 September the Sun is 'actually' much closer to the start of the constellation of Virgo than its end. This peculiarity arises because the study of astrology is very ancient and whilst stellar positions have moved on due to the precession of the equinoxes, astrology has not. In the 19th century, when the Washington Monument was completed, astronomers would have said that the autumn equinox took place at the very start of the constellation of Virgo.

12 Though of course the spring equinox is equally relevant in terms of naked-eye astronomy and Washington DC's orientation.

13 The modern approach to civic architecture could be compared to the current fashion for scribbling tattoos across both male and female flesh, often as a crude and ignorant pastiche of supposed Celtic design. Arguably it is impressive imagery but it is devoid of any inner communicative value. Tattoos have been used to speak of a person's social status and origin for more than 5,000 years, as indicated by Otzi, the Neolithic man whose well-preserved body was found in Alpine ice. Modern tattoos are by comparison no more than doodles.

Chapter 14

1 *The Pentagon – A History*: Vogel S, Random House, 2008

2 *The Pentagon – A History*: Vogel S, Random House, 2008

3 *The Pentagon – A History*: Vogel S, Random House, 2008

4 By a strange twist of fate this was exactly 60 years to the day before a hijacked passenger aircraft was flown into the western aspect of the building on 11 September 2001.

5 Abraham is intimately connected with the idea of kingship through his meeting with Melchizedek. Later, all Jewish kings for hundreds of years from the time of Solomon sacrificed their children to the god Moloch in order to cement their right to rule. After the Babylonian captivity all such practices were banned and it is likely that the story of Abraham was adjusted to suit.

6 *Solomon's Power Brokers*: Knight C & Butler A, Watkins, 2008

7 *The Hiram Key*: Knight C & Lomas R, Random House, 1996

8 There still are still people in Scotland who continue to claim that Rosslyn was intended to be a Christian chapel. They ignore all of the evidence and statements of several leading experts to the contrary – that it was clearly designed as a Jewish building depicting the New Jerusalem. Some also continue to publish the fatuous argument that the building was the Lady Chapel of an intended, but never constructed, collegiate church. These claims are breathtaking in their denial of fundamental evidence that shows this theory to be utterly impossible.

Appendix 4

1 *Uriel's Machine*: Knight C & Lomas R, Transworld Books, London

2 *Civilization One*: Knight C & Butler A, Watkins, London, 2004

Appendix 5

1 *The Bronze Age Computer Disc*: Butler A, Foulsham, 1997

Appendix 8

1 In reality these days many of the degrees of Scottish Rite Freemasonry beyond the three initial degrees are offered to Freemasons in 'blocks' and so the ceremonies are not always undertaken.

INDEX